4th Grade Technology Curriculum: Teacher Manual

FOURTH GRADE TECHNOLOGY

A COMPREHENSIVE CURRICULUM

Part Five of Nine of the SL Technology Curriculum

2024

*Part Five of Structured Learning's nine-volume Technology Curriculum
Visit the companion website at Ask a Tech teacher for more resources and online assistance with this textbook.*

ALL MATERIAL IN THIS BOOK IS PROTECTED BY THE INTELLECTUAL PROPERTY LAWS OF THE USA.

No part of this work can be reproduced or used in any form or by any means—graphic, electronic, or mechanical, including photocopying, recording, taping, Web distribution or information storage and retrieval systems—without the prior written permission of the publisher

*For permission to use material from this text or product, contact us by email at:
info@structuredlearning.net*

ISBN 978-1-942101-26-0

Printed in the United States of America

Structured Learning LLC. © All Rights Reserved

Introduction

The educational paradigm has changed—again. Technology has become granular to learning, included in educational standards from Kindergarten onward, like these from Common Core:

- Expect students to demonstrate sufficient command of **keyboarding** to type a minimum of two pages [three by sixth grade] in a single sitting
- Expect students to **evaluate different media** [print or digital]
- Expect students to **gather info** from print/digital sources
- Expect students to integrate and evaluate **information presented in diverse media** and formats
- Expect students to **interpret information** presented visually, orally, or quantitatively [such as interactive Web pages]
- Expect students to make **strategic use of digital media**
- Expect students to use **glossaries or dictionaries** ...
- Expect students to use information from **illustrations and words in print or digital** text
- Expect students to use a **variety of media** to communicate
- Expect students to **use text features and search tools** (e.g., keywords, sidebars, **hyperlinks**) to locate information

But how is this taught?

With the **Structured Learning Technology Curriculum**. Aligned with Common Core State Standards* and National Educational Technology Standards, and using a time-proven method honed in classrooms, students learn the technology that promotes literacy, critical thinking, problem-solving, and decision-making by using it. It's project-based. The purpose is not to teach step-by-step tech skills (like adding borders, formatting a document, creating a blog). There are many fine books for that. What this curriculum does is guide you in providing the **right information at the right time**.

Just as most children can't learn to read at two, or write at four, they shouldn't be required to place hands on home row in kindergarten or use the internet before they understand the risks and responsibilities. The Structured Learning curriculum makes sure students get what they need at the right age. The end result is a phenomenal amount of learning in a short period of time.

If there are skills you don't know, visit our Help blog or visit the online companion resources at Ask a Tech Teacher.

* * *

"New technologies have broadened and expanded the role that speaking and listening play in acquiring and sharing knowledge and have tightened their link to other forms of communication. Digital texts confront students with the potential for continually updated content and dynamically changing combinations of words, graphics, images, hyperlinks, and embedded video and audio."
--CCSS

* * *

"Use of technology differentiates for student learning styles by providing an alternative method of achieving conceptual understanding, procedural skill and fluency, and applying this knowledge to authentic circumstances."
--CCSS

4th Grade Technology Curriculum: Teacher Manual

What's in the SL Technology Curriculum?

The SL Curriculum is project-based and collaborative, with wide-ranging opportunities for students to show their knowledge in the manner that fits their communication and learning style. Each grade level in the curriculum includes five topics that should be woven into 'most' 21st-century lesson plans:

- *keyboarding—more than typing*
- *publishing-sharing—to promote collaborative learning*
- *digital citizenship—critical with influx of web-based work*
- *problem solving—encourage critical thinking*
- *vocabulary—decode unknown words in any subject quickly with technology*

In most curricula, you find full lessons devoted to keyboarding, digital citizenship, and problem solving. Here's a quick overview of what is included at the fundamental level:

- *A list of assessments, posters, images*
- *Articles that address tech pedagogy*
- *Certificate of Completion for students*
- *Curriculum map of skills taught*
- *Monthly homework (3rd-8th only)*
- *Scope and Sequence of skills taught*
- *Step-by-step weekly lessons*

Each weekly lesson includes:

- *assessment strategies*
- *essential question and big idea*
- *class warmup and exit ticket*
- *Common Core and ISTE Standards*
- *differentiation*
- *educational applications*
- *examples, rubrics, images, printables*
- *materials required and suggested links*
- *pedagogic articles (if any)*
- *problem solving for lesson*
- *skills—new and scaffolded*
- *steps to accomplish goals*
- *teacher prep and time required to complete*
- *vocabulary used*

Programs Used

General	K-8	2-8
Email	*Drawing program*	*Word processing, spreadsheet, presentation*
Google Earth	*Keyboarding tool*	*Desktop publisher*
Web tools	*Image editor*	

Programs used in this curriculum focus on skills that serve the fullness of a student's educational career. Free alternatives are noted where available:

What's New in the Sixth Edition?

A good tech curriculum is aligned with best practices in technology and education. That means it must be updated every few years. Consider the changes in education since 2013:

- *Windows updated its platform—twice.*
- *IPads have been joined by Chromebooks as a common classroom digital device.*
- *There is greater reliance in the classroom on internet-based tools than software. This underscores the importance of teaching digital citizenship to even the youngest learners.*
- *Student work is often collaborative and shared.*
- *Student work is done anywhere, not just the classroom and home, meaning it must be synced and available across multiple platforms, multiple devices.*
- *Keyboarding skills are often critical, especially to summative year-end testing.*
- *Technology in the classroom is the norm, but teacher training isn't.*
- *Education is focused on college and career with tech an organic, transformative tool.*
- *Teachers have moved from 'sage on the stage' to 'guide on the side'.*
- *Students have been raised on digital devices. They want to use them as learning tools.*
- *Using technology is no longer what 'geeky' students do. It's what all students want to do.*
- *Printing is being replaced with sharing and publishing.*
- *More teachers are willing to try technology when used authentically.*

In response, here are changes you'll find in this edition:

- The lesson audience is now as likely to be the **grade-level teacher as the tech teacher**.
- The importance of **higher order thinking**—analysis, evaluation and synthesis—is called out.
- The importance of **'habits of mind'**—critical to college and career goals—is included.
- It's easy to recognize which **skills are scaffolded** from earlier lessons and which are new.
- Students **understand the process**, not just replicate a skill.
- **Collaboration and sharing** is often required.
- **Differentiation** is encouraged. Teachers learn strategies to meet students where they learn.
- Each lesson includes a **warm-up and exit ticket**, to assess and reinforce student learning.
- A **Table of Images** and a **Table of Assessments** are included for easy reference.
- Updated **Scope and Sequence** includes more references to Common Core.
- **Curriculum Maps** shows which month topics are covered as well as which grade.
- Each grade-level curriculum includes **student workbooks** (sold separately).

Who Needs This Book

You are the Tech Specialist, Coordinator for Instructional Technology, IT Coordinator, Technology Facilitator or Director, Curriculum Specialist, or tech teacher—tasked with finding the right project for a classroom. You have a limited budget, less software, and the drive to do it right no matter roadblocks.

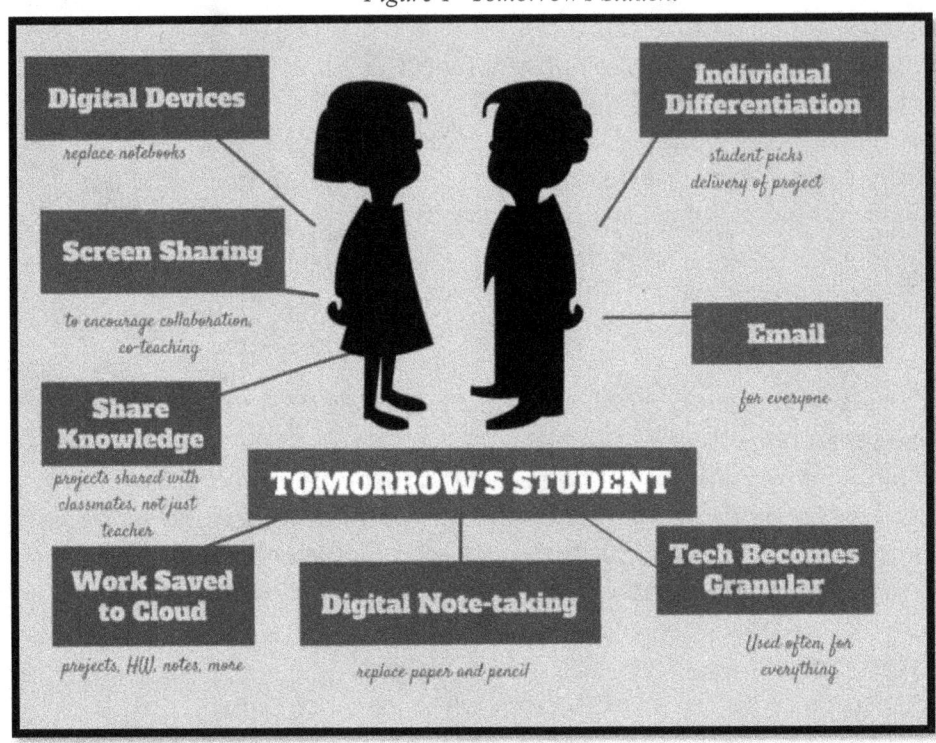

Figure 1--Tomorrow's Student

Or you are the classroom teacher, a tech enthusiast with a goal this year—and this time you mean it—to integrate the wonders of technology into lessons. You've seen it work. Others in your PLN are doing it. And significantly, you want to comply with Common Core State Standards, ISTE, your state requirements, and/or IB guidelines that weave technology into the fabric of inquiry.

You are a homeschooler. Even though you're not comfortable with technology, you know your children must be. You are committed to providing the tools s/he needs to succeed. Just as important: Your child WANTS to learn with these tools!

How do you reach your goal? With this curriculum. Teaching children to strategically and safely use technology is a vital part of being a functional member of society—and should be part of every school's curriculum. If not you (the teacher), who will do this? To build Tomorrow's Student (*Figure 1*) requires integration of technology and learning. We show you how.

How to Use This Book

Figure 2a shows what's at the beginning of each lesson. *Figure 2b* shows what you'll find at the end:

Figure 2a—Beginning of each lesson; Figure 2b—end of each lesson

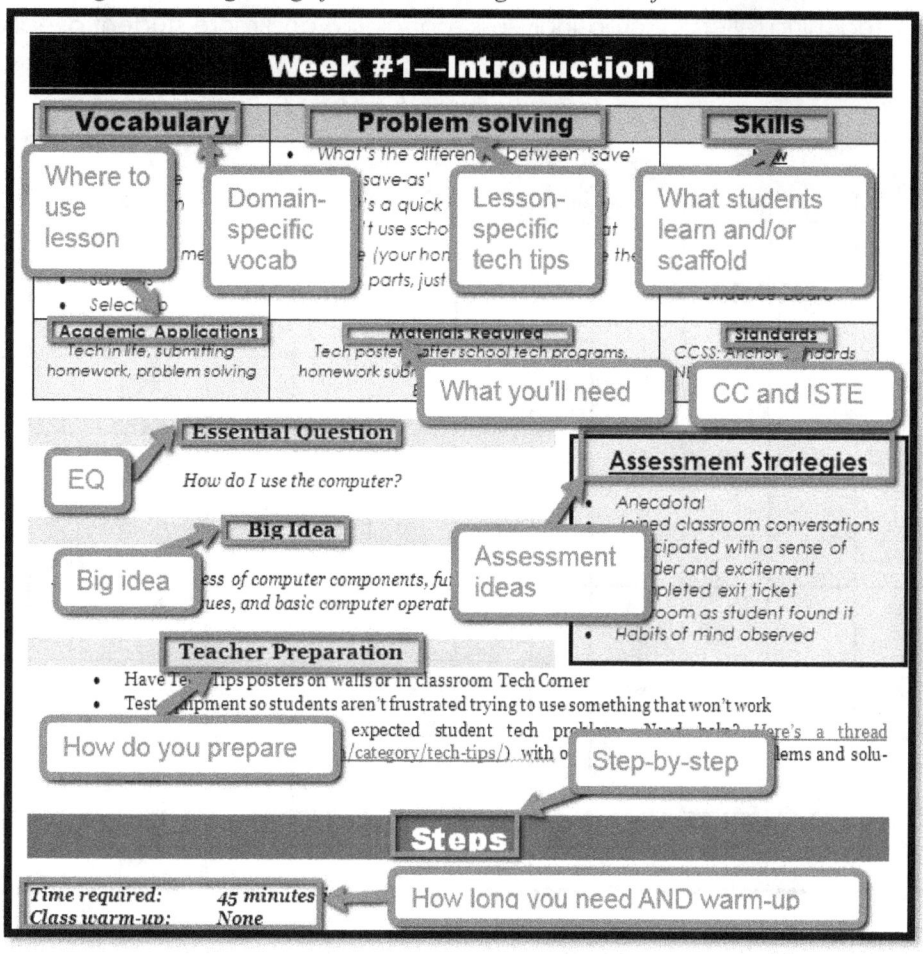

- Academic Applications
- Assessment Strategies
- Big Idea
- Class Warm-up
- Essential Question
- Material Required
- Problem solving
- Skills
- Standards
- Steps
- Teacher Prep
- Time Required
- Vocabulary

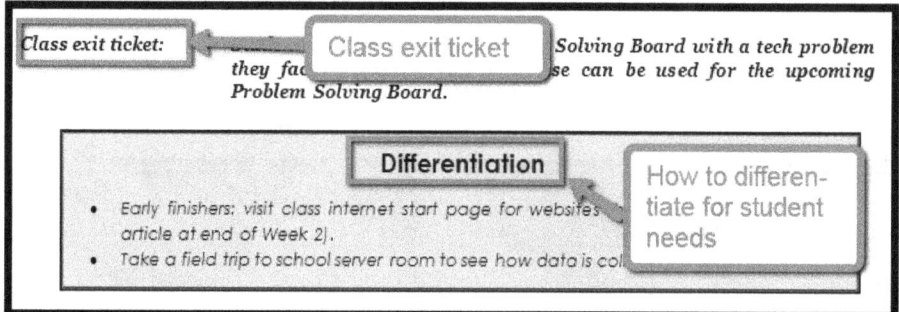

- Class exit ticket
- Class differentiation strategies

4th Grade Technology Curriculum: Teacher Manual

The curriculum map below (*Figure 3*) tells you what's covered in which grade. Where units are taught multiple years, teaching reflects increasingly less scaffolding and more student direction.

Figure 3—Curriculum Map—K-8

	Mouse Skills	Vocabulary - Hardware	Problem-solving	Platform	Keyboard	WP	Presen-tation	DTP	Spread-sheet	Google Earth	Search/ Research	Graphics/	Co-ding	WWW	Games	Dig Cit
K	☺	☺	☺	☺	☺					☺		☺	☺	☺		☺
1	☺	☺	☺	☺	☺			☺	☺	☺		☺	☺	☺		☺
2		☺	☺	☺	☺	☺	☺	☺	☺	☺		☺	☺	☺		☺
3		☺	☺	☺	☺	☺	☺	☺	☺	☺	☺	☺	☺	☺		☺
4		☺	☺		☺	☺	☺	☺	☺	☺	☺	☺	☺	☺		☺
5		☺	☺		☺	☺		☺	☺	☺	☺	☺	☺	☺		☺
6		☺	☺	☺	☺	☺	☺	☺	☺	☺	☺	☺	☺	☺		☺
7		☺	☺	☺	☺	☺			☺	☺	☺	☺	☺	☺	☺	☺
8		☺	☺	☺	☺	☺			☺	☺	☺	☺	☺	☺	☺	☺

If you're the grade-level teacher, here's how to use the map:

- Expect students to transfer knowledge of earlier-learned skills to this new school year.
- Review the topics and skills, but don't expect to teach.
- If there are skills listed as covered prior years, confirm that was done. If they weren't (for whatever reason), when you reach lessons that require the skills, plan extra time.

Figure 4 is a month-by-month curriculum map for this grade level. In the student workbook, students complete this themselves or as a group when they finish each lesson.

Figure 4—Curriculum Map—4th grade, month-to-month

	Sept *Wk1-4*	**Oct** *Wk5-8*	**Nov** *Wk9-12*	**Dec** *Wk13-16*	**Jan** *Wk17-20*	**Feb** *Wk21-24*	**March** *Wk25-28*	**April** *Wk29-32*
Blogs		x						
Class mgmt tools	x							
Coding/Programming		x						
Collaboration				x			x	

Communication	x	x		x	x	x		x
Computer etiquette	x							
Critical thinking	x		x	x	x			x
DTP				x	x	x		
Digital Citizenship	x	x	x	x	x	x		
Google Earth		x				x		
Graphics					x	x		x
Internet		x	x				x	
Internet privacy		x						
Keyboarding	x	x	x	x	x	x	x	x
Presentations							x	x
Problem solving	x	x	x	x	x	x	x	x
Publishing/sharing				x		x		x
Research		x	x	x			x	
Spreadsheets						x		
Visual learning					x	x		
Vocabulary	x	x	x	x	x	x	x	x
Webtools		x	x	x	x			
Word Processing	x		x	x	x			

Some topics are covered every month. The strategy: spiral and scaffold learning until it's habit.

Here are hints to assist using this curriculum:

Figure 1--Student workbook

- Invest in student digital workbooks (sold separately), a perfect student-centric companion to your teacher guide. Here are suggestions on how to use the workbooks:

    o *Full-color projects are at student fingertips complete with examples and directions (licensing may vary depending upon the plan your school selected).*
    o *With nominal direction, students learn tech skills.*
    o *Workbooks can be shared through a reader where you and students add your own notes, how-tos.*
    o *Students can work at their own pace.*
    o *If you want to use workbooks in your class, buy a multi-user license (room, school, district) to install eworkbooks on multiple devices (even at home with some licenses).*

- Teach lessons in the order presented in the book (grades K-5). Lessons introduce, reinforce, and circle back on skills and concepts. Resist the urge to mix up lessons even if your perfect time for a particular project comes earlier/later than placement in the book. **One exception: Coding**. Unpack this lesson when it works best for you.

- Personalize the skills taught in each lesson to your needs with 'Academic Applications'. These are suggestions for blending learning into your existing curriculum.
- Each lesson starts with a warm-up to get students back into tech and give you time to finish up a previous class. This is especially useful to the tech teacher and the LMS.
- Each class includes an Exit Ticket to wrap up learning.
- 'Teacher Preparation' often includes chatting with the grade-level team. Why?

    o *tie tech into their inquiry*
    o *offer websites that address their topics*

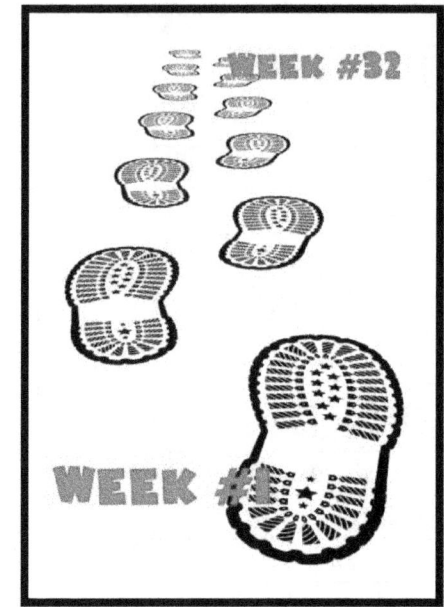

- Check off completed items on the line preceding the activity so you know what to get back to when you have time. If you have the ebook, use iAnnotate, Goodreader, Notable (Google for websites), or another annotation tool that works for your devices.
- We understand when kids and technology collide, sometimes the class is too excited about the learning to move on. Two solutions:

    o *Leave line in front of uncompleted activity blank and return to it when you have time. You'll notice after using this curriculum a few years that students finish material faster.*
    o *Take an extra week. Most school years run 35-40 weeks. This book includes 32 lessons. This provides flexibility for holidays, snow days, field trips.*

- Consider expecting students to back up their work—as a life habit. This can be onto a flash drive, by emailing the document to themselves, or saving to a secondary location on their digital device.
- Don't skip the 'Problem Solving' section. If the problems don't come up in class, bring them up! These are important scaffolding for student ability to think critically and troubleshoot issues when you won't be there to help.
- Always use lesson vocabulary. Students gain authentic understanding of word use by your example. A complete glossary of lesson vocabulary can be found in the free online resources (link mentioned earlier in book). Here, you'll find several hundred easy-to-understand definitions of domain-specific tech words.
- Some lessons provide options. For example, Lesson 7 has multiple choices to teach coding. Review the entire lesson prior to teaching and choose the option most suited to your students. All will accomplish the tech goals.
- Is class shorter than 45 minutes? Highlight what's most important to your goals and leave the rest for 'later'.

Figure 6—Glossary of tech ed vocabulary

K-5 Tech Curriculum Vocabulary

Check here for the curriculum vocabulary. Here are some good websites for geeky words:

- NetLingo
- TechTerms

Here are most/all of the words from the curriculum, collected weekly as we cover them:

- 3D–three dimensions
- address bar–where web address appears
- alignment–how data is lined up on the page
- ALT–key used in combination with other keys for macros
- Alt+F4–universal 'close' command
- Alt+Tab–toggle between two open windows
- anchor point–point in a drawing where a clone starts
- anecdotal–subjective observational stories
- animated GIF–very short movie–2 seconds
- animation–movement
- app–a program used on iPads, browsers, and more
- arrow keys–on the keyboard; move up-down or side-to-side
- ASCII art–drawing using keyboard keys
- assessment–how to judge student progress
- attachment–data connected to an email (or similar)
- auto-advance–automatically move forward with, say, PowerPoint
- auto-format–automatically formatting
- automaticity–how automatic a process is
- Autoshape–a auto-generated shape, like a cross or an arrow
- autosum–a tool that automatically adds a column
- back button (back arrow)–moves back in time one webpage
- background–image behind data on a page
- backspace–delete one character either with 'delete' or 'backspace'
- back up–a second copy of a file

- Expect students to be risk takers. Don't rush to solve their problems. Ask them to think how it was done in the past. Focus on problems listed in the lesson, but embrace all that come your way.
- Expect students to direct their own learning. You are a 'guide on the side'. You are a facilitator, not lecturer. Learning is accomplished by both success and failure. Don't expect to have free time while students work. Move among them to provide feedback and assistance, and make anecdotal observations on their keyboarding, problem-solving, and vocabulary decoding skills.
- Encourage student-directed differentiation, opportunities for them to present their knowledge in ways suited to their abilities. If the Big Idea and Essential Question can be accommodated in other ways, embrace those.
- If you have the digital book, zoom in on posters, rubrics, lessons to enlarge as needed.
- Use as much technology as possible in your class—authentically and agilely. Encourage students to do the same whether it's a smartphone timing a quiz, a video of activities posted to the class website, or an audio file with student input. If you treat tech as a tool in daily activities, so will students.
- Remind students they've learned and understand skills. Check them off in the Scope and Sequence additional times as you circle back on them.

- Lessons expect students to develop 'habits of mind'. You can read more about Art Costa and Bena Kallick's discussion of these principles in *Figure 7*, and in the article at the end of Lesson #1. In a sentence: Habits of Mind ask students to engage in their learning, not simply recite or memorize.

Figure 7—Habits of Mind

- If you need resources on specific topics, visit Ask a Tech Teacher's resource pages.

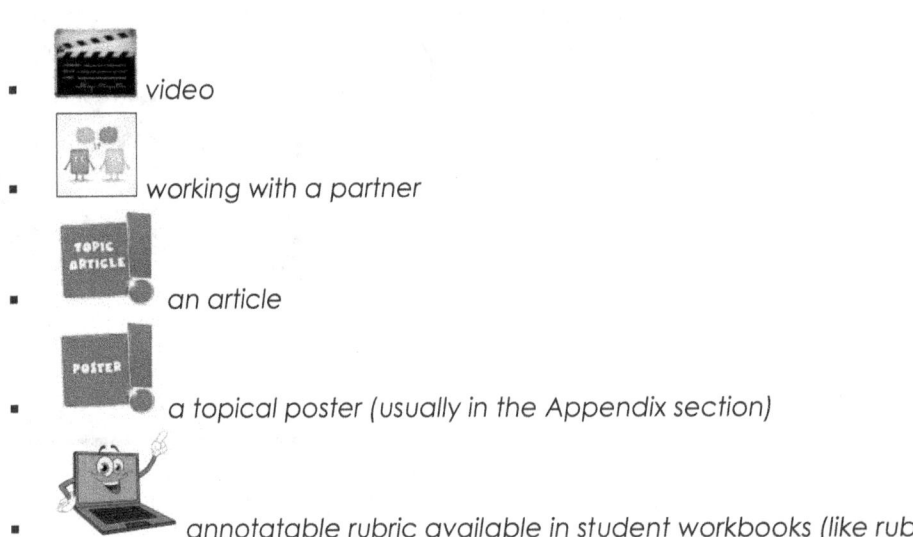

- video
- working with a partner
- an article
- a topical poster (usually in the Appendix section)
- annotatable rubric available in student workbooks (like rubrics)

- If you need resources on specific topics, visit Ask a Tech Teacher's resource pages.
- Every effort has been made to accommodate Chromebooks, PCs, Macs, iPads, and other digital devices. You will often see examples in multiple platforms. If the activity is impossible in a particular digital device (i.e., iPads don't have mouses; software doesn't run in Chromebooks), focus on the **Big Idea and Essential Question**—the skill taught and its application to inquiry. Adapt instructions to the tool you use as you work through the steps.

Figure 8—Compatible digital devices

A desktop PC, iMac, laptop, MacBook, Chromebook, iPad, or smartphone

- Throughout the year, circle back on lessons. It takes five times seeing a skill to get it—

    o First: They barely hear you
    o Second: They try it
    o Third: They remember it
    o Fourth: They use it outside of class
    o Fifth: They tell a friend

- **Need more help?** Go to Ask a Tech Teacher or email askatechteacher@gmail.com.

Typical Lesson

Each lesson requires about 45 minutes a week, either in one sitting or spread throughout the week, and can be unpacked:

- *In the grade-level classroom*
- *In the school's tech lab*

Both are covered in each lesson. In general terms, here's how to run a lesson in **the tech lab**:

- Post a **simple written schedule** on the class screen:

    o *Warm up*
    o *Main activity*
    o *Exit ticket*

Students start with a visual guideline. Add it to your class blog for students not present. Expect students to start the warm-up when they arrive to class.

Figure 2--Five times for buy-in

It takes 5 times to get buy-in:

you hope it'll go away
you try it
you remember it
you use it ouside of class
you teach a friend

©AskaTechTeacher

- **Warm up about 10 minutes,** often with typing practice. Some days, youngers work on alphabet sites.
- Three students complete **Board presentations** (grades 3-8).
- If it's the end of a grading period, use **Scope and Sequence to review** skills accomplished.
- If starting a **new project, review it** and take questions. If you're in the middle of one, students use the balance of class to work towards completion. Monitor activities, answer questions, help as needed.
- Share websites that **tie into inquiry** for students who complete the current project. Students know websites on this page can be used during free time.
- **Class exit ticket** might include lining up in arrays, answering a poll posted on the class screen, or simply leaving stations as students found them.

Here's how to run the lesson in **the grade-level classroom**:

- Take the lesson pieces mentioned above and scatter them throughout the week. For example:
    - **3-10 minutes for the class warm-up**—at the start the week
    - **10-15 minutes keyboarding practice**—any day
    - **10-15 minutes Board presentations**—any day
    - **15-35 minutes for the project**—any day
    - **2-3 minutes for the class exit ticket**—to reinforce learning

- Check off each activity as accomplished so you know what remains each week.
- In every class, **use tech wherever possible.** Be the model for what you're asking of them.

Here are useful pieces to extend this curriculum:

- *Student workbooks —allow students to be self-paced and self-directed*
- *Digital Citizenship curriculum from Structured Learning—a good addition if this is a focus of your school*
- *Keyboarding Curriculum from Structured Learning— if this is a focus of your school*

Figure 10a—Start page using Protopage; 10b—LiveBinders; 10c—Symbaloo

 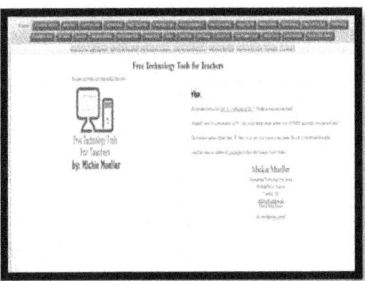 

Copyrights

You have a single-user license. That means you may reproduce copies of material in this textbook for classroom use only. Reproduction of the entire book is strictly prohibited. No part of this publication may be transmitted, stored, or recorded in any form without written permission from the publisher.

About the Authors

Ask a Tech Teacher *is a group of technology teachers who run an award-winning resource blog. Here they provide free materials, advice, lesson plans, pedagogical conversation, website reviews, and more to all who drop by. The free newsletters and articles help thousands of teachers, homeschoolers, and those serious about finding the best way to maneuver the minefields of technology in education.*

*Throughout this text, we refer to Common Core State Standards. We refer to a license granted for "...a limited, non-exclusive, royalty-free license to copy, publish, distribute, and display the Common Core State Standards for purposes that support the Common Core State Standards Initiative. These uses may involve the Common Core State Standards as a whole or selected excerpts or portions.

CCSS: *© Copyright 2010. National Governors Association Center for Best Practices and Council of Chief State School Officers. All rights reserved.*

Table of Contents

Introduction

Curriculum Maps

Technology Scope and Sequence K-5

Table of Images

Table of Assessments

Table of Articles

Lessons

1. Introduction
2. Keyboarding
3. Digital Tools in the Classroom
4. Problem solving
5. Outline in Word Processing
6. Digital Citizenship
7. Google Earth
8. Coding
9. Internet Research I
10. Internet Research II
11. Halloween Greetings
12. Word Processing Tables I
13. Word Processing Tables II
14. Word Processing Editing
15. Holiday Flier, Cover Page, Greeting
16. Timeline Trifold I
17. Timeline Trifold II
18. Graphic Organizers
19. Web-based Vocab Study
20. Storybook in DTP I
21. Storybook in DTP II
22. Storybook in DTP III
23. Storybook in DTP IV
24. Analyze Data and Excel Games
25. Internet Research III
26. Slideshow I
27. Slideshow II
28. Slideshow III
29. Slideshow IV
30. Presentations I
31. Presentations II
32. End-of-Year Challenge

Appendices

1. Certificate of Completion
2. Homework

4th Grade Technology Curriculum: Teacher Manual

Articles Included

Article 1—21st Century Lesson Plan..42
Article 2—Habits of Mind vs. CC vs. IB..45
Article 3—Which class internet start page is best?..46
Article 4—5 Authentic assessment tools..48
Article 5—5 Ways to make classroom keyboarding fun..57
Article 6—How to teach students to solve problems...80
Article 7—What happens when technology fails?..82
Article 8—Ways Twitter improves education..95
Article 9—Will texting destroy writing skills?...97
Article 10—9 Things my blog taught me...98
Article 11—Want to code on an iPad? 3 apps...110
Article 12—7 MS Word Tricks..128
Article 13—9 Google Docs tricks..129
Article 14—4 Sure-fire Ways to teach vocabulary...169
Article 15—3 Grammar Apps..171

Linked

- <u>6 Stand-alone Lesson Plans for Sub</u>
- *11 Ways to Wrap Up the School Year*
- *20 Techie Problems Students Can Fix*
- *22 Ways Any Teacher Can use Tech*
- *5 Surefire Ways to Teach Vocabulary*
- *Faceoff: Digital Devices*
- *Handwriting vs. Keyboarding*
- *How Do You Grade Tech?*

- *How do I teach a program I don't know*
- *I Can Solve That Problem…*
- *Want to Code on an IPad? 3 Apps*
- *10 Tips for Teachers who Struggle w/ Tech)*
- *What Happens When Tech Fails?*
- *What's the Class of the Future Look Like?*
- *Why Keyboarding Should NOT be Dead*

Posters

Table of Images

Figure 1--Tomorrow's Student 7
Figure 2a—Beginning of each lesson; Figure 2b—end of each lesson 8
Figure 3—Curriculum Map—K-8 9
Figure 4—Curriculum Map—4th grade, month-to-month 10
Figure 5--Student workbook 11
Figure 6—Glossary of tech ed vocabulary 12
Figure 7—Habits of Mind 13
Figure 8—Compatible digital devices 14
Figure 9--Five times for buy-in 15
Figure 10a—Start page using Protopage; 10b—LiveBinders; 10c—Symbaloo 16
Figure 11—Digital Student 33
Figure 12—Classroom rules 34
Figure 13a—Evidence board; 13b—badge 35
Figure 14a—Parts of computer; 14b—Parts of iPad 35
Figure 15—Hardware-related problems and solutions 36
Figure 16—Mouse hold 36
Figure 17—UN and PWs 37
Figure 18a—Computer position; 18b—posture 51
Figure 19—Hand position 51
Figure 20a—Keyboarding hints; 20b—keyboarding curriculum map 52
Figure 21—Important keys 52
Figure 22—Keyboard assessment I 53
Figure 23—Keyboard assessment II 53
Figure 24—Why learn to keyboard 54
Figure 25—Internet safety 65
Figure 26—How to log in 65
Figure 27—Track UN and PW 66
Figure 28—Email etiquette 67
Figures 29a-b—Email programs 68
Figure 30a--Notability; 30b--Adobe Acrobat; 30c--iAnnotate 69
Figure 31a-c—Class calendars 70
Figure 32—Class internet start page 71
Figure 33—Problem-solving board 74
Figure 34—Board info required 75
Figure 35—Common computer problems 76
Figure 36—Common shortkeys 76
Figure 37a—iPad shortkeys; 37b—Chromebook shortkeys 77
Figure 38—How to solve a problem 78
Figure 39—Problem-solving quotes 79
Figure 40—Important Keys quiz 86
Figure 41a—Outline in Word; 41b—in Google Docs; 41c—in Workflowy 87
Figure 42—Outline tools 88
Figure 43—How to save your file 88
Figure 44—Blank keyboard 91
Figure 45—DigCit topics 92
Figure 46—Digcit topic pyramid 92

4th Grade Technology Curriculum: Teacher Manual

Figure 47a—Google Earth project in K; 47b—1st; 47c—2nd; 47d—3rd 101
Figure 48—Google Earth lats and longs 101
Figure 49a-b—Programming 105
Figures 50a-d—Coding in K through 3rd grade 106
Figure 51—Popular unusual shortkeys 106
Figure 52—Create a shortkey 107
Figure 53—Parts of a website 113
Figure 54—Steps for internet research 114
Figure 55a—Group research in Padlet; 55b—Google forms; 55c—Google Spreadsheets 115
Figure 56—Rules of digital neighborhood 117
Figure 57--Website evaluation 118
Figure 58—Sample website questions 119
Figure 59a—WP project in 2nd; 59b—2nd; 59c—3rd; 59d—3rd 123
Figure 60—Images in word processing 125
Figure 61a—Word processing in Word; 61b—in Google Docs 125
Figure 62—Highlighting in word processing 126
Figure 63a—Table in 2nd grade; 63b—3rd grade; 63c—3rd grade 131
Figure 64a—Organize data in table; 64b—in columns 131
Figure 65a-b—Tables in Spreadsheets 131
Figure 66a-b—How to build a table 132
Figure 67—I can't find my file 134
Figure 68—How to turn on SafeSearch 135
Figure 69—How to use clipboard 136
Figure 70—Speak Like a Geek required info 139
Figure 71a—Sign ups with Google Apps; 71b—Padlet; 71c—Calendar 139
Figure 72—Highlighting writing conventions 141
Figure 73—Confusing sentence 142
Figure 74—Compare/contrast tools A 144
Figure 75—Compare/contrast B 145
Figure 76a—Fliers from 1st grade; 76b—2nd grade; 76c—3rd grade 145
Figure 77a—DTP flier projects in Publisher; 77b—Canva 146
Figure 78—My Life Events timeline table 147
Figure 79a—Cover in various digital tools 148
Figure 80a—Greeting cards in 1st grade; 80b—2nd grade; 80c—3rd grade 148
Figure 81a-d—Greeting card templates 149
Figure 82--How to fold card 149
Figure 83a—Timeline trifold front; 83b—inside 152
Figure 84a—Trifold using Word; 84b-c—Google Apps 153
Figure 85—How to create outside of trifold 153
Figure 86--Print border 154
Figure 87—Timeline trifold rubric 154
Figure 88—Keyboarding technique checklist 156
Figure 89--Timeline page of trifold 157
Figure 90a—Timeline in Excel and 90b—Google Spreadsheets 157
Figure 91a—Online timeline tools 158
Figure 92—How to create timeline 158
Figure 93a-c—Graphic organizers in 1st, 2nd, 3rd grade 162
Figure 94—Graphic organizer 162
Figure 95a-b—Table vs. graphic organizer 163
Figure 96—Online graphic organizer templates 163
Figure 97a—Graphic organizer for science; 97b—history 164

Figure 98—Padlet for exit ticket 165
Figure 99a-b—Hands covered for keyboarding 167
Figure 100a-c—Word clouds with digital resources 167
Figure 101—Word clouds in Google Docs 168
Figure 102--Common Core Tiered Vocabulary 169
Figure 103a-b—Highlighted stories 174
Figure 104a-b—Sample covers in drawing programs 175
Figure 105a-c—Sample pages from digital storybook 176
Figure 106—Sample GE locations 178
Figure 107—Info for GE Board 178
Figure 108—GE Board grading 179
Figure 109—Border and footer 179
Figure 110a—Story page without image; 110b—with image 180
Figure 111—Good grammar in storytelling 183
Figure 112a-d—Storybook interior pages 184
Figure 113a-c—The End page in storybook 184
Figure 114a-d—Sample storybook pages 187
Figure 115a-b—About the author 187
Figure 116—Storybook assessment 188
Figure 117a-d—Spreadsheet projects in Kindergarten-3rd grade 190
Figure 118--Spreadsheet skills for project 191
Figure 119—Invention Convention spreadsheet 191
Figure 120—Chart 192
Figure 121—How to find mark-up 192
Figure 122—Production price 193
Figure 123—Detail in cell 193
Figure 124—Retail sales price 194
Figure 125--Game spreadsheet 194
Figure 126a-b—Previous slideshow projects 196
Figure 127a-b—Storyboard for Inventors 196
Figure 128—Internet safety 197
Figure 129a—Presentation tools: PowerPoint; 129b—Google Slides; 129c—Kizoa 201
Figure 130—Presentation tool vs. word processing 201
Figure 131a—Cover slide; 131b—interior slide 201
Figure 132a-b—Cover slides in PowerPoint; 132c—Slides 202
Figure 133a—Slide 2 sample in PowerPoint; 133b—Slides; 133c—Haiku 202
Figure 134a—Slide 3 sample in PowerPoint; 134b—Slides; 134c—Haiku 202
Figure 135a-b—Slide 4-6 samples 203
Figure 136a-b—Slide 7 samples 203
Figure 137a-b—Slide 8 samples 203
Figure 138a-b—Slide 9 samples 204
Figure 139a-b—Hand position 210
Figure 140a—Keyboard speedsters; 140b—Fastest class; 140c—keyboard certificate 213
Figure 141a-d—Custom slideshow backgrounds 213
Figure 142—How to create custom background 214
Figure 143a-b—Variety of slide backgrounds in PowerPoint, Haiku 214
Figure 144a—Slideshow in PowerPoint; 144b—in Google Slides; 144c—Slideshare 217

Table of Assessments

Assessment 1—Hardware Quiz 39
Assessment 2—Parts of Smartphone 40
Assessment 3—iPad assessment 41
Assessment 4--Chromebook 42
Assessment 5—Keyboarding quiz 55
Assessment 6—Important Keys 56
Assessment 7—Blank Keyboard quiz 57
Assessment 8—Blank Chromebook keyboard 58
Assessment 9—Problem solving board rubric 75
Assessment 10--Google Earth Practice 102
Assessment 11—Research Skills worksheet 121
Assessment 12—Word processing rubric 124
Assessment 13—Speak Like a Geek presentation rubric 140
Assessment 14—Timeline trifold rubric 160
Assessment 15—Google Earth Board grading 181
Assessment 16—Storybook assessment 185
Assessment 17—Inventor storyboard 198
Assessment 18—Slideshow presentation rubric 205
Assessment 19—Slideshow presentation rubric 206
Assessment 20—End-of-year challenge 220

K-5 TECHNOLOGY SCOPE AND SEQUENCE©

Aligned with ISTE (International Society for Technology in Education) and Common Core State Standards
Check each skill off with I (Introduced), W (Working on), or M (Mastered)
Organized by ISTE Standards 1-7

I	Empowered Learner	K	1	2	3	4	5
	Students leverage technology to take an active role in choosing, achieving and demonstrating competency in their learning goals, informed by the learning sciences.						
	Use technology strategically and capably (CCSS C&CR profile)		I	W	M	M	M	M
	Are familiar with the strengths and limitations of various technological tools and mediums and can select and use those best suited to communication goals (CCSS C&CR Profile)	I	W	M	M	M	M
	Strategize personal learning						
	Understand how inquiry contributes to creative and empowered learning	I	W	M	M	M	M
	Understand how technology contributes to classroom and personal learning	I	W	M	M	M	M
	Understand how higher order thinking skills are buttressed by technology	I	W	M	M	M	M
	Select between available options, choosing one best suited to learning	I	W	M	M	M	M
	Compare-contrast available tools, determining which is best suited to need	I	W	M	M	M	M
	Know what digital tools are available and how to use them for class and home (i.e., digital calendars, blogs, websites, and annotation tools)	I	W	M	M	M	M
	Know how to read digital books both online and through readers	I	W	M	M	M	M
	Be responsive to varied needs of task-audience-purpose	I	W	M	M	M	M
	Interact, collaborate, publish with peers employing a variety of digital media			I	W	M	M
	Develop cultural understanding by engaging with learners of other cultures			I	W	M	M
	Share a summative collection of work in a way that suits communication style	I	W	M	M	M	M
	Seek feedback to demonstrate learning				I		
	Add comments to class blogs, forums, discussion boards, webtools	I	W	M	M	M	M
	Work in groups collaboratively and productively	I	W	M	M	M	M
	Transfer knowledge						
	Scaffold learning year-to-year and lesson-to-lesson	I	W	M	M	M	M
	Transfer understanding of one digital tool or device to others	I	W	M	M	M	M
	Understand tools, toolbars, symbols, and how that knowledge transfers to many digital tools	I	W	M	M	M	M
	Use familiar tech tools (like Google Earth's ruler) to solve real-world problems	I	W	M	M	M	M
	Hardware						
	Know parts of digital devices used at school and home	I	W	M	M	M	M
	Know parts of keyboard	I	W	M	M	M	M
	Understand difference between power buttons on monitor and tower	I	W	M	M	M	M
	Can troubleshoot hardware	I	W	M	M	M	M
	Operating Systems (PC, Mac, Chromebook, iPads)						
	Understand concept of Desktop or Home	I	W	M	M	M	M
	Know how to run a slideshow using the native tool in a particular platform	I	W	M	M	M	M
	Know how to log-on	I	W	M	M	M	M

©AskaTechTeacher

4th Grade Technology Curriculum: Teacher Manual

	Know how to Open/Close programs	I	W	M	M	M	M
	Understand concepts of taskbar, start button, icons, drop-down menus	I	W	M	M	M	M
	Know how to find files, add more, and save to network file folder and/or cloud	I	W	M	M	M	M
	Know how to drag-drop (or copy-paste) within a doc and between folders					I	W
	Know how to use tool tips (hover over icon) and right-click menus				I	W	M
	Know how to access different drives					I	W
	Can troubleshoot operating systems	I	W	M	M	M	M
	Know how to use software installed on PCs and/or Macs	I	W	M	M	M	M
	Online Tech for Classroom Management						
	Understand school technology			I	W	M	M
	Understand dropbox for homework				I	W	M
	Understand online tools like blogs, digital portfolios						I
	Understand Cloud for transferring school work to home						I
	Understand how to use class digital tools (digital devices, annotation, blogs, internet start page)	I	W	M	M	M	M
	Know how to use a website--back button, links, scroll bars, home, website	I	W	M	M	M	M
	Understand the layout of a website and where to click	I	W	M	M	M	M
	Know how to annotate a PDF or online document			I	W	M	M
	Know how to share out classwork (including homework)				I	W	M
	Know how to use online vocabulary decoding tools quickly and efficiently	I	W	M	M	M	M
	Understand internet basics (toolbar, tabbed browsing, home button)	I	W	M	M	M	M
	Know how to safely play online videos from a variety of sources	I	W	M	M	M	M
	Know how to legally copy-paste from internet for a project				I	W	M
	Know how to log onto webtool accounts			I	W	M	M
	Mouse Skills						
	Know how to click, hold, drag, double-click	I	W	M	M	M	M
	Know how to hover	I	W	M	M	M	M
	Introduce right mouse button			I	W	M	M
	Keyboarding						
	Know how to practice keyboarding on internet sites and software	I	W	M	M	M	M
	Strive to achieve grade-appropriate keyboarding speed and accuracy goal				I	W	M
	Type with hands on their own side of keyboard, curved, fingers on home row			I	W	M	M
	Practice touch typing				I	W	M
	Compose at keyboard by creating classroom-based projects				I	W	M
	Understand speed difference between handwriting and keyboarding				I	W	M
	Select shortkeys instead of toolbar tools when appropriate	I	W	M	M	M	M
	Use correct posture, elbows at sides	I	W	M	M	M	M
	Know parts of keyboard--keys, numbers, F keys, arrows, Esc			I	W	M	M
	Know escape, period key, shift key, spacebar, tab	I	I	I	W	M	M
	Word Processing						
	Know when to use a word processing program, software and online tools			I	W	M	M
	Use principles of grammar, spelling when word processing on computer	I	W	M	M	M	M

©AskaTechTeacher

4th Grade Technology Curriculum: Teacher Manual

		Know basic page layout--heading, title, body, footer			I	W	M	M
		Know how word-wrap works			I	W	M	M
		Know how to highlight a word, sentence, line, select/deselect, doublespace			I	W	M	M
		Know how to add a watermark, bullet list, table, pictures, graphic organizer					I	W
		Know correct spacing after sentences, paragraphs		I	W	M	M	M
		Know how to use grade-appropriate heading on all Word docs				I	W	M
		Know how to use the thesaurus					I	W
		Know how to format a document—i.e., add header, footer, border, cover page, embedded link			I	W	M	M
		Know to put cursor in specific location, i.e., for graphic			I	W	M	M
		Know how to Print Preview before printing			I	W	M	M
		Know how to select and then do--two-step process in editing, formatting			I	W	M	M
		Know how to compose at Keyboard			I	W	M	M
		Can use Ctrl+Enter to force a new page			I	W	M	M
		Know how to write a letter using digital tools	I	W	M	M	M	M
		Can troubleshoot word processing			I	W	M	M
	Google Earth							
		Display familiarity with tools for moving around world	I	W	M	M	M	M
		Know how to find a location, add a picture, placemark, save a picture				I	W	M
		Understand latitudes and longitudes				I	W	M
		Know how to use ruler to measure distances					I	W
		Run a tour of placemarks around the planet				I	W	M	M
2	**Digital Citizen**							
	Students recognize the rights, responsibilities and opportunities of living, learning and working in an interconnected digital world, and they act and model in ways that are safe, legal and ethical.							
		Gather relevant information from print and digital sources, assess credibility of source, and integrate the information while avoiding plagiarism. (CCSS C&CR Writing Anchor Standards)				I	W	M
	Internet privacy and safety							
		Know how to configure privacy settings					I	W
		Understand cyberbullying, use of passwords	I	W	M	M	M	M
		Understand digital footprint and online presence				I	W	M
		Understand how online entities track student activity online				I	W	M
		Understand the appropriate use of the 'digital neighborhood'	I	W	M	M	M	M
	Legal use of online materials							
		Discuss copyright law			I	W	M	M
		Discuss plagiarism and how to cite sources			I	W	M	M
		Discuss 'fair use'			I	W	M	M
		Discuss 'intellectual property', the rights and obligations of using and sharing			I	W	M	M
	Digital Netiquette							
		Understand etiquette in the digital neighborhood	I	W	M	M	M	M
		Know to stay out of other file folders	I	W	M	M	M	M
	Digital Citizenship							
		Understand what a 'digital citizen' is	I	W	M	M	M	M

©AskaTechTeacher

	Exhibit a positive attitude toward tech that supports collaboration and learning	I	W	M	M	M	M
	Demonstrate personal responsibility for lifelong learning	I	W	M	M	M	M
	Exhibit leadership for digital citizenship--set the standard for classmates	I	W	M	M	M	M
Interactions online							
	Address digital commerce						I
	Use safe, responsible and ethical behavior on the internet	I	W	M	M	M	M
	Discuss social media					I	W
	Discuss digital rights and responsibilities	I	W	M	M	M	M
	Recognize irresponsible and unsafe practices on the internet					I	W	M
	Know how to leave a useful comment for a classmate					I	W	M
	Know how online comments follow same rules as speaking and listening					I	W	M

3 Knowledge Constructor

Students critically curate a variety of resources using digital tools to construct knowledge, produce creative artifacts and make meaningful learning experiences for themselves and others.

	Use the internet to build strong content knowledge (CCSS C&CR profile)	I	I	W	M	M	M
	Use technology to produce and publish writing and collaborate with others (CCRA.W.6)	I	I	W	M	M	M
	Use technology strategically and capably (CCSS C&CR profile)	I	I	W	M	M	M
	Comprehend as well as critique. (CCSS C&CR profile)				I	W	M	M
	Value evidence (CCSS C&CR profile)				I	W	M	M
	Compare-contrast documents across digital media (CCSS Anchor Standards)				I	W	M	M
	Gather relevant information from multiple digital sources (CCRA.W.8)				I	W	M	M
	Assess credibility of digital sources (CCSS Anchor Standards)				I	W	M	M
	Integrate and evaluate information from diverse media (CCRA.R.7)				I	W	M	M
	Make strategic use of digital media to express information (CCRA.SL.5)				I	W	M	M
	Use electronic menus and links to locate key facts (RI/)				I	W	M	M
Effective online research strategies							
	Use screenshots to collect information				I	W	M	M
	Locate, organize, analyze, evaluate, and synthesize information from sources	I	W	M	M	M	M
	Evaluate and select information sources and digital tools based on task				I	W	M	M
	Read search results before clicking and know how to identify reliable ones				I	W	M	M
	Guide inquiry by knowing how to choose links and menus	I	W	M	M	M	M
	Know how to search effectively, limit search as needed, and use Ctrl+F					I	W	M
	Know how to effectively use LMS systems and the Cloud					I	W
Technology as knowledge curator							
	Evaluate the accuracy, perspective, relevancy of information, media, data.					I	W	M
	Curate information from digital resources using tools that demonstrate meaningful conclusions (such as outlines, mindmaps).					I	W	M
	Understand the difference between software and webtools and when to use		I	W	M	M	M
	Understand how parts make up a whole in, say, a puzzle or a divided picture	I	W	M			
	Know how to read digitally using both websites and dedicated ereaders	I	W	M	M	M	M
	Know how to evaluate accuracy and relevance of websites					I	W
	Build knowledge by exploring real-world issues, ideas, and solutions.			I	W	M	M

©AskaTechTeacher

4th Grade Technology Curriculum: Teacher Manual

	Online collaborative environments						
		Use blogs for journaling and tracking project progress					I
		Incorporate text, images, widgets to better communicate ideas					I
		Know how to use Discussion boards and forums				I	W	M
4	**Innovative Designer**						
	Students use technology to identify and solve problems by creating new, useful or imaginative solutions.						
		Respond to varying demands of audience, task, purpose, and discipline (CCSS C&CR profile)	I	W	M	M	M	M
		Use glossaries or dictionaries to clarify meaning of key words and phrases (CCSS.L.K.4)		I	W	M	M	M
		Gather, comprehend, evaluate, synthesize, and report on information in order to answer questions or solve problems, (CCSS Key Design Consideration)			I	W	M	M
		Draw on information from print or digital sources, demonstrating the ability to locate answers quickly or to solve a problem efficiently (CCSS. RI.5)				I	W	M
		Reason abstractly and quantitatively (CCSS. Math.Practice.MP2)		I	W	M	M	M
		Use appropriate tools strategically (CCSS. Math.Practice.MP5)	I	W	M	M	M	M
		Attend to precision (CCSS. Math.Practice.MP6)	I	W	M	M	M	M
	Design Process						
		Use planning tools such as mindmaps and brainstorming to organize ideas				I	W	M
		Use presentation tools like graphic organizers, Infographics, screencasts, and videos to share ideas and solve problems in a variety of creative ways				I	W	M
		Use templates and patterns to create new designs (like shapes, letters)	I	W	M	M	M	M
		Select and use digital tools (such as comics) to plan and manage a design process that considers design constraints and calculated risk	I	W	M	M	M	M
		Develop, test and refine prototypes as part of a cyclical design process			I	W	M	M
		Tolerate ambiguity with a capacity to work with open-ended problems.	I	W	M	M	M	M
		Use established patterns and design processes to solve tech problems	I	W	M	M	M	M
		Recognize the part 'failure' plays in solving problems	I	W	M	M	M	M
		Know how to use tables, charts, and why				I	W	M
	Decision Making						
		Identify and define authentic problems and questions for investigation					I	W
		Collect, analyze data to identify solutions and make informed decisions	I	W	M	M	M	M
		Debug programs using sequencing, if-then thinking, logic, or other strategies	I	W	W	W	W	W
		Able to evaluate which program is right for which task	I	W	M	M	M	M
		Students recognize digital designs in the world around them	I					
	Slideshows						
		Know when to use presentation tools			I	W	M	M
		Know how to add/rearrange slides, auto-advance			I	W	M	M
		Know how to add a variety of backgrounds, animations, movies, transitions			I	W	M	M
		Know how to insert pictures from file, internet, clip-art			I	W	M	M
		Know how to insert text, images, slides, multimedia			I	W	M	M
		Understand how to deliver a professional presentation			I	W	M	M
		Can troubleshoot presentation tools	I	W	M	M	M	M

©AskaTechTeacher

		Are familiar with a variety of slideshow tools including software and online tools	I	W	M	M	M	M
	Graphics							
		Use drawing software and web-based tools efficiently	I	W	M	M	M	M
		Know how to insert images, clipart			I	W	M	M
		Know how to import from a file			I	W	M	M
		Know how to resize/move/crop/wrap an image			I	W	M	M
		Know how to mix text and pictures to convey unique message	I	W	M	M	M	M
		Know how to create and annotate screenshots to share information	I	W	M	M	M	M
	Desktop publishing							
		Can identify parts of the desktop publishing screen			I	W	M	M
		Know when to use a desktop publishing program to share information			I	W	M	M
		Know how to make a card, flier, cover page, magazine, trifold, newsletter			I	W	M	M
		Know how to insert a picture, blank page, text box, footer, border			I	W	M	M
		Know how to work with color schemes			I	W	M	M
		Know how to plan a publication				I	W	M
		Can troubleshoot publishing tools			I	W	M	M
		Know how to use greeting cards to reinforce writing and tech skills	I	W	M	M	M	M
	Screencasts, Videos							
		Know how to create screencasts and videos to share information						I
		Know how to upload screencasts and videos to easily-accessible locations						I
		Know how to use the design process to prepare screencasts						I
5	**Computational Thinker**							
	Students develop and employ strategies for understanding and solving problems in ways that leverage the power of technological methods to develop and test solutions.							
		Gather, comprehend, evaluate, synthesize, and report on information to conduct original research in order to answer questions or solve problems, (CCSS Key Design Consideration)	I	W	M	M	M	M
		Draw on information from multiple sources, demonstrating the ability to locate an answer to a question quickly or to solve a problem efficiently (CCSS. RI.5)	I	W	M	M	M	M
		Make sense of problems and persevere in solving them (CCSS. Math.Practice.MP1)	I	W	M	M	M	M
		Reason abstractly and quantitatively (CCSS. Math.Practice.MP2)	I	W	M	M	M	M
		Construct viable arguments and critique the reasoning of others (CCSS. Math.Practice.MP3)	I	W	M	M	M	M
		Model with mathematics (CCSS. Math.Practice.MP4)	I	W	M	M	M	M
		Use appropriate tools strategically (CCSS. Math.Practice.MP5)	I	W	M	M	M	M
		Attend to precision (CCSS. Math.Practice.MP6)	I	W	M	M	M	M
		Look for and make use of structure (CCSS. Math.Practice.MP7)	I	W	M	M	M	M
		Look for and express regularity in repeated reasoning (CCSS. Math.Practice.MP8)	I	W	M	M	M	M
	Critical Thinking							
		Understand how to identify, define authentic problems, questions	I	W	M	M	M	M
		Understand that class computer pod is just like the computer lab	I	W	M	M	M	M
		Know what digital tools are available and how to use them for class and home, including digital calendars, blogs, websites, and annotation tools	I	W	M	M	M	M

4th Grade Technology Curriculum: Teacher Manual

		Understand the part tools, toolbars, menus, taskbars, symbols play in unpacking digital tools	I	W	M	M	M	M
		Always attempt to solve a problem before asking for teacher assistance	I	W	M	M	M	M
		Know how to print to a physical or cloud-based location	I	W	M	M	M	M
		Know how to save work to a local drive and the cloud	I	W	M	M	M	M
		Know how to use programs not yet learned	I	W	M	M	M	M
		Know the difference between save and save-as				I	W	M
		Know the difference between backspace and delete				I	W	M
		Know how to use digital tools to compare-contrast		I	W	M	M	M
		Know why a particular digital tool is suited to a specific need		I	W	M	M	M
		Know how to analyze data digitally and represent data in various ways to facilitate problem-solving and decision-making.			I	I	W	M
	Problem solving							
		Identify, define, and solve authentic problems, questions for investigation	I	W	M	M	M	M
		Know user name and password	I	W	M	M	M	M
		Know how to determine the date, undo	I	W	M	M	M	M
		Learn to use keyboard shortkeys as alternative solutions				I	W	M
		Know what to do if double-click doesn't work	I	W	M	M	M	M
		Know what to do if document or program disappears, or screen freezes	I	W	M	M	M	M
		Can visually compare own screen with instructors	I	W	M	M	M	M
		Follow established procedure when asking for help	I	W	M	M	M	M
		Know what to do when part of computer doesn't work	I	W	M	M	M	M
		Can use Alt+F4 to shut down frozen program				I	W	M
		Can use Task Manager to shut down locked program				I	W	M
		Know how to access work from anywhere in the school	I	W	M	M	M	M
		Know how to solve common hardware problems	I	W	M	M	M	M
		Know what to do if computer doesn't work				I	W	M
		Can trouble shoot a non-working program				I	W	M
		Can recognize and use up to 13 different problem-solving strategies	I	W	W	W	M	M
		Break problems into parts, extract key information, and develop descriptive models to understand complex systems or facilitate problem-solving.				I	W	W
		Able to use graphic organizers to decode problems and automate solutions				I	W	W
	Programming							
		Understand technology contributes to higher-order thinking, DoK, or another	I	W	W	W	M	M
		Understand the cause-effect relationship inherent in actions	I	W	W	W	M	M
		Understand If-then and conditionals in coding	I	W	M	M	M	M
		Understand sequencing, algorithms, loops, functions, and variables	I	W	M	M	M	M
		Eagerly experiment with programming tools	I	W	M	M	M	M
		Understand automation; use algorithmic thinking and a sequence of steps to create and test automated solutions. (i.e., timelines, brainstorming)			I	W	W	W
		Recognize that codes are simply another language			I	W	W	W
		Debug programs using sequencing, if-then thinking, logic, or other strategies	I	W	W	W	W	W
	Scratch							
		Create/add/edit/broadcast sprites						I

©AskaTechTeacher

	Add sound, text bubbles, backgrounds, movement					I
	Complete program task cards for most common skills					I
	Use models created by others; remix to develop unique Scratch video					I
Robotics						
	Contribute to project teams to produce original works or solve problems					I
	Build, program, debug a robot					I
	Trouble shoot simple problems					I
	Use sensors to monitor the environment					I
	Measure distances with robots					I
Spreadsheets						
	Process and sort data by collecting data into Excel and reporting it			I	W	M
	Know how to add text, graphics, data, color		I	W	M	M
	Know how to use paint bucket fill--coordinate drawing		I	W	M	M
	Know how to add, subtract, multiply, divide formulas, and label x/y axis			I	W	M
	Know how to name a chart			I	W	M
	Know how to recolor tabs; rename worksheets			I	W	M
	Explore a business using models/simulations to study complex issues				I	W
	Know how to publish spreadsheet through a widget to blog and/or website				I	W
	Can troubleshoot spreadsheets			I	W	W

6 Creative Communicator

Students communicate clearly and express themselves creatively for a variety of purposes using the platforms, tools, styles, formats and digital media appropriate to their goals.

Use technology and digital media strategically (CCSS C&CR profile)	I	W	W	W	M	M
Use technology to produce and publish writing and interact/collaborate with others (CCSS.ELA-LITERACY.CCRA.W.6)	I	W	M	M	M	M
Explore digital tools to produce and publish writing (CCSS.ELA-Literacy.W)	I	W	M	M	M	M
Explore digital tools to collaborate with peers (CCSS.ELA-Literacy.W)	I	W	M	M	M	M
Use multimedia to aid comprehension (CCSS.ELA-Literacy.W)					I	W
Ask and answer questions from information presented (CCSS.ELA-Literacy.SL)		I	W	M	M	M
Include audio recordings and multimedia to enhance main ideas (CCSS.ELA-Literacy.SL)			I	W	M	M
Integrate and evaluate information presented in diverse media and formats, including visually, quantitatively, and orally (CCSS.ELA-LITERACY.CCRA.SL.2)	I	W	M	M	M	M
Use multimedia to organize ideas, concepts, info (CCSS.ELA-Literacy.WHST)	I	W	M	M	M	M
Interact, collaborate, and publish with peers, experts, or others employing a variety of digital environments and media		I	W	M	M	

Vocabulary

Understand domain-specific vocabulary	I	W	M	M	M	M
Communicate ideas effectively using media (CCSS Anchor Standards)	I	W	M	M	M	M
Use digital tools to decode academic and domain-specific vocab			I	W	M	C

Blogs

Interact, collaborate, publish with peers employing a variety of digital media						I

4th Grade Technology Curriculum: Teacher Manual

	Develop global awareness by engaging learners of other cultures						I
	Contribute to project teams to produce original works or solve problems						I
	Digital Tools						
	Communicate information, ideas effectively to multiple audiences using a variety of media and formats including visual organizers, infographics			I	W	M	M
	Use web-based communication tools to share unique and individual ideas			I	W	M	M
	Learn a variety of tools that address varied communication styles (from written to visual to video) by teaching them to classmates			I	W	M	M
	Know how to use models and simulations to explore complex issues					I	W
	Simulate running a business to identify trends, forecast sales					I	W
	Interact, collaborate, and publish employing digital media including greeting cards for youngers	I	W	M	M	M	M
	Develop cultural understanding by engaging with learners of other cultures	I	W	M	M	M	M
	Digital Storytelling, Quick Writes						
	Compose short stories, quick writes, letters, comics using online tools	I	W	M	M	M	M
	Collaborate and share stories in an online tool		I	W	M	M	M
	Use select digital tools to collaborate and publish with peers employing a variety of digital environments and media	I	W	M	M	M	M
	Participate in a virtual field trip that tells the story of a student's experience	I	W	M	M	M	M
	Speaking and Listening						
	Engage in impromptu speaking such as the Evidence Board					I	W	W
	Create well-prepared presentations such as slideshows with multimedia				I	W	M	M
	Engage in short presentations such as the Presentation Boards						I	W	M
7	**Global Collaborator**						
	Students use digital tools to broaden their perspectives and enrich their learning by collaborating with others and working effectively in teams locally and globally.						
	Understand other perspectives and cultures. (CCSS C&CR profile)	I	W	M	M	M	M
	Respond to the varying demands of audience, task, purpose, discipline. (CCSS C&CR Profile)	I	W	M	M	M	M
	Use digital tools to connect with learners from a variety of cultures engaging with them in ways that broaden mutual understanding and learning	I	W	M	M	M	M
	Explore local and global issues and use collaborative technologies to work with others to investigate solutions	I	W	M	M	M	M
	Know what 'Cloud computing' is					I	W	M
	Collaborate with Others						
	Use digital tools like Padlet to collaborate with peers in projects					I	W	M
	Use technology to work with others, including peers, experts or community members, to examine issues and problems from multiple viewpoints.	I	W	M	M	M	M
	Contribute constructively to project teams, assuming various roles and responsibilities to work effectively toward a common goal.	I	W	M	M	M	M
	Use blogs, forums, Discussion Boards to collaborate and share						I	W
	Use programs like Google Apps to collaborate						I	W

©AskaTechTeacher

4th Grade Technology Curriculum: Teacher Manual

Lesson #1—Introduction

Vocabulary	Problem solving	Skills
• Digital • Embed • Landscape • PC • Portrait • Right-click menu • Right-mouse • Start page • UN-PW • USB port	• Double-click doesn't work (enter) • Monitor doesn't work (power on?) • What if computer doesn't work? (move mouse around) • What's Select-do (select first, and then do what you need done) • How do I change page layout? • What's the difference between 'save' and 'save-as'? • Where do I find class calendar?	**New** Class rules Some posters **Scaffolded** Problem solving Log-ins Digital citizenship Hardware Mouse skills
Academic Applications Tech in life, submitting homework, problem solving	**Materials Required** Posters, after school tech program, last year class rules, Evidence Board, workbooks (if using)	**Standards** CCSS: Anchor standards NETS: 1a, 1b

Essential Question

How do I use technology?

Big Idea

Students develop an awareness of technology and how it enhances educational goals

Teacher Preparation

- Talk with grade-level team so you tie into conversations.
- Have posters up with tech hints.
- Test all equipment.
- Ensure all required links are on student digital devices.
- Be prepared to integrate domain-specific tech vocabulary into lesson.
- Collect words students don't understand for upcoming Speak Like a Geek Board presentations.

Assessment Strategies

- Understood tech in their life, log-ins, and more
- Completed exit ticket
- Joined classroom conversations
- Left room as s/he found it
- Higher order thinking: analysis, evaluation, synthesis
- Habits of mind observed

Steps

Time required: 45 minutes in one sitting or spread throughout the week
Class warm-up: None

_____Before beginning, explain your expectations for the students' time with you—what is the 21st century tech-infused lesson plan (see article at end of lesson)?

_____Clarify the pervasiveness of technology in the lives of your students by drawing a sillhouette of a student on the class screen and ask students what they use technogoy for in their lives. As they mention activities, add them to your drawing. It may look like *Figure 11*:

Figure 11—Digital Student

_____Tour classroom. Show students where everything is. Review important posters, i.e., difference between 'save' and 'save-as', difference between 'backspace' and 'delete', 'save early save often', Mulligan Rule, portrait and landscape (posters in Appendix).
_____Review 'Select-Do' (poster in Appendix). What does that mean? (Hint: You must select something before you can do to it).
_____Collect rules from students to guide classroom actions, including:

Figure 12—Classroom rules

- *No excuses; don't blame others; don't blame computer.*

- *Save early, save often—about every ten minutes.*
- *No food or drink around digital devices. Period.*
- *Respect the work of others and yourself.*
- *Keep hands to yourself. Feel free to help neighbors, but with words only.*

_____You may start with a list like *Figure 12* from the prior year.

_____Make sure to include class discussion guidelines such as 1) listening to others, 2) taking turns while speaking, and 3) waiting to be called on before speaking.

_____Discuss the wide variety of digital tools students will use this year to complete projects. Let students know that you are open to alternative suggestions. For example, if you suggest Wordle, a student can request Tagxedo. Approval is required, but it will be granted if the tool fulfills project needs. Expect students to use evidence to build their case, compare-contrast their tool to your suggestion, and draw logical conclusions.

_____Offer a Keyboarding Club after school two days a week to accommodate students who can't do their homework at home or would like to practice keyboarding. Limit it to 45 minutes so everyone can get home in time for dinner.

_____Also offer after-school help on those same days for students who need assistance with a tech skill or a project involving tech. Request student volunteers who will commit to assisting classmates. You may collaborate with your school's STAR program, where students volunteer for activities as part of their class requirements.

_____Review homework policy (homework in back of this text): due at the end of each month. Students submit homework in the manner that works best for your group (email, Google Apps, or another). Homework is keyboard practice, one row at a time from Popcorn Typer:

- *months 1-3: practice only one row per month*
    - 1st month: homerow
    - 2nd month: QWERTY row
    - 3rd month: lower row

- *months 4-9: practice all rows*
- *too easy? cover hands*

_____Discuss the evidence board (*Figures 13a* and *13b*). This is a bulletin board that celebrates student transfer of knowledge from tech class to home, friends, or other educational endeavors. About once a month, students will have an opportunity to share how they use the tech skills they've learned in other classes, at home, or with friends. They will fill out a badge (like *Figure 13b*) and post it on the Evidence Board by their class. By the end of the year, you want this collection to encircle the classroom.

Figure 13a—Evidence board; 13b—badge

_____Review computer parts. *Figure 14a* is generic. Find the parts on your school's devices (there's a full-size copy at the end of the lesson to use for a study guide and testing) in preparation for the upcoming assessment. For example, if you use iPads, ask students where the 'headphones' are on this device (see full-size assessment at end of lesson)? Or the mouse? How about the USB Port (there is none)? Ask students where the iPad microphone (see *Figure 14b*) is on, say, the PC or Chromebook you use. How about the charging dock? Smartphones—there's a full size assessment at the end of the lesson.

Figure 14a—Parts of computer; 14b—Parts of iPad

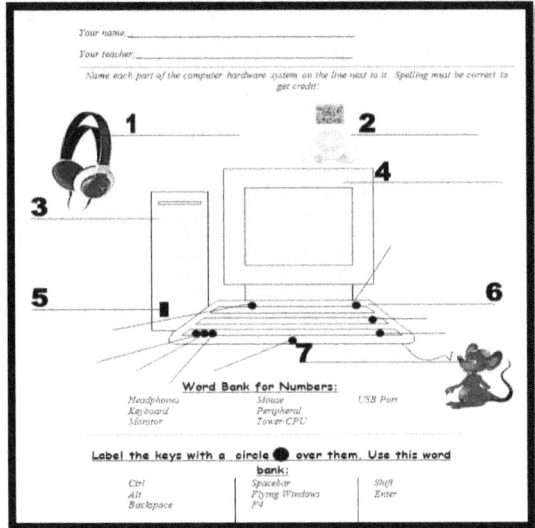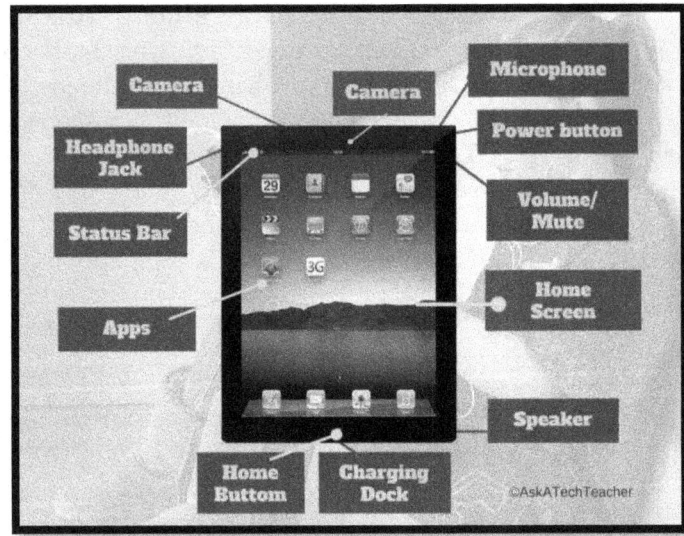

- mouse buttons—left and right, double click, wheel in center
- CPU—power button, CD drive, USB port
- monitor—power button, screen, station number
- headphones—volume, size adjustment, connection to CPU
- keyboard—home row, F-row, enter, spacebar, ctrl, alt, shift

_____Discuss how understanding hardware helps to solve tech problems (*Figure 15*).

Figure 15—Hardware-related problems and solutions

_____Review mouse hold with a neighbor (see *Figure 16*). If this isn't already a habit, make sure students hold the mouse correctly every time they use it:

Figure 16—Mouse hold

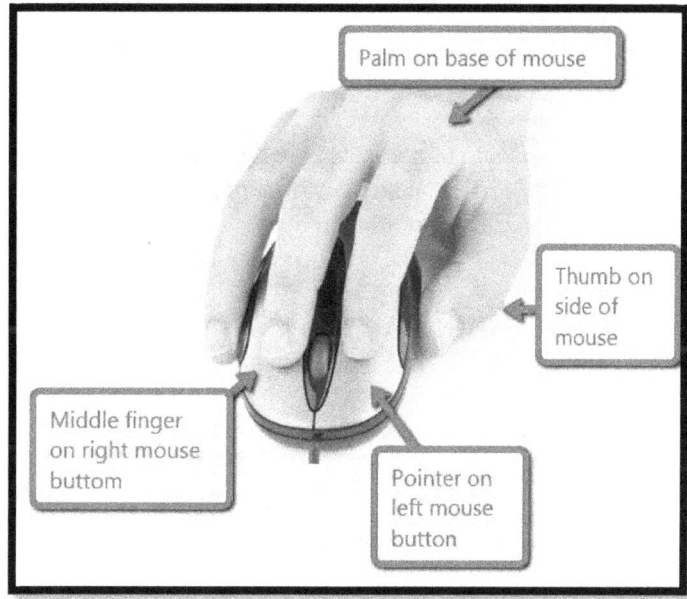

_____Reinforce the importance of students solving their problems. This includes hardware (*Figure 15*). Relate them to your digital device. For example, if sound doesn't work on the Chromebook, what should students do? This will be discussed in depth in the Problem Solving lesson.
_____Review how parts connect—behind CPU, under table, in front ports.
_____Review how to log in. What does 'User Name' and 'Password' mean? How are these unique to each student? More on this later.
_____Provide a template to collect log-ins for programs and websites (*Figure 17*)—more on this later:

Figure 17—UN and PWs

User Name/Passwords		
PROGRAM	**UN**	**PASSWORD**
Keyboard program		
Math program		
Computer		
Class wiki		
Add'l		
Add'l		

_____Discuss **digital citizenship**. You'll cover it in depth throughout the year and in Lesson 6. Remind students any time they visit the internet, they do so safely and legally.

_____Discuss the class internet start page (see article at end of this lesson). An internet start page is a website that comes up when student opens internet. It organizes critical content in a single location and curates links students will use on a weekly basis.

_____Continually throughout the class, check for understanding.

_____Remind students: next week is the first keyboarding speed and accuracy quiz.

Class exit ticket: **Students tack a post-it on Problem Solving Board with a tech problem they faced last week. These will be used for the upcoming Problem Solving Board.**

Differentiation

- *For more assessment strategies, read '5 Authentic Assessment Tools' at lesson end.*
- *Early finishers: visit class internet start page for websites that tie into classwork.*
- *Take a field trip to school server room to see how data is collected and curated.*
- *Have a calendar of class events. You may update it or you may assign this task on a revolving basis to a student. Embed it into class website, wiki, or blog with quizzes, project due dates, and more. Add the upcoming keyboarding speed quiz (next week)*

"A printer consists of three main parts: the case, the jammed paper tray and the blinking red light"

Assessment 1—Hardware Quiz

HARDWARE—PARTS OF THE COMPUTER

Name each part of computer Draw your own lines for the key names. Spelling must be correct to get credit

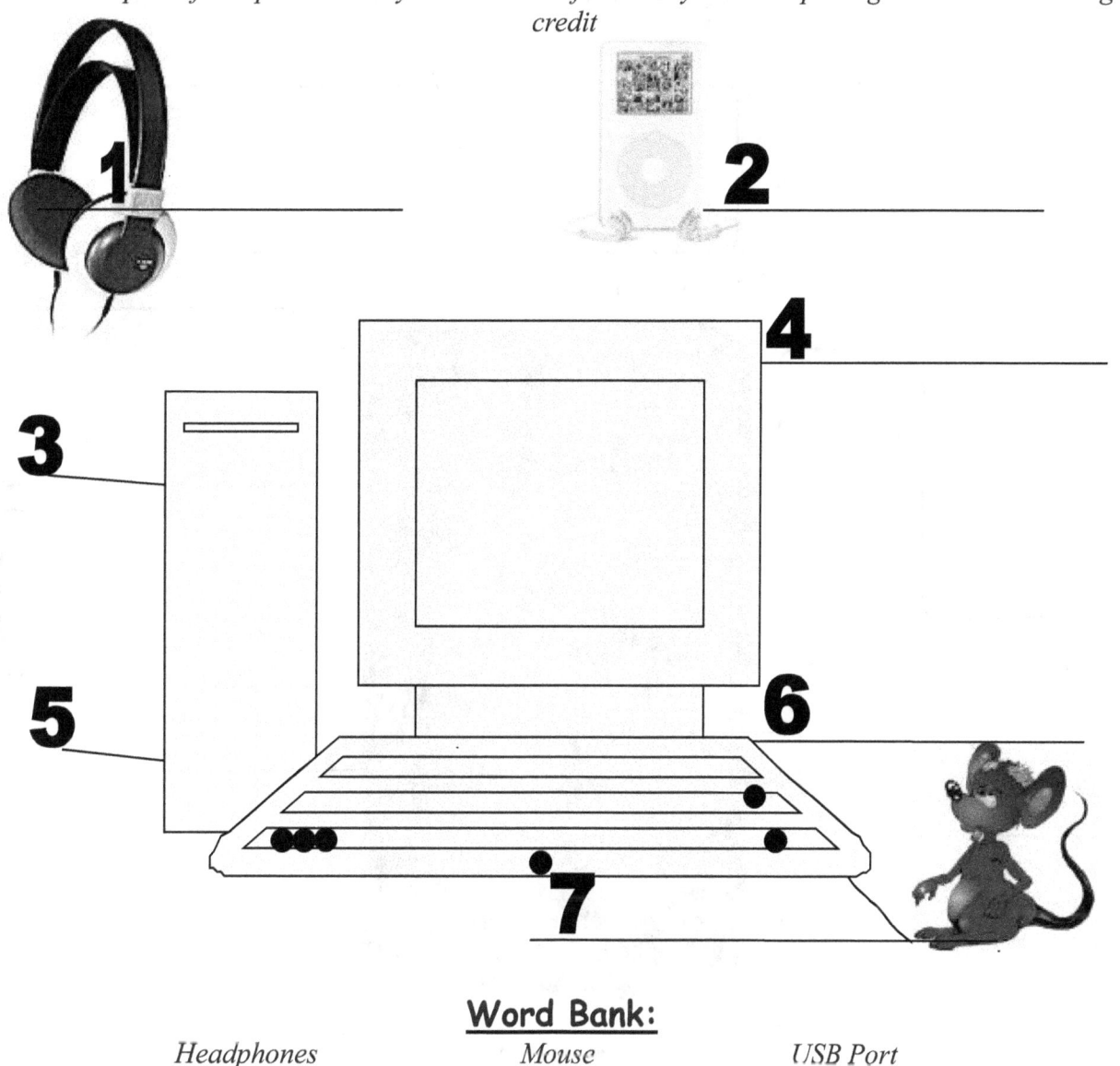

Word Bank:

Headphones	Mouse	USB Port
Keyboard	Peripheral	
Monitor	Tower/CPU	

Label the keys with a circle ● over them. Use this word bank:

Ctrl	Spacebar	Shift
Alt	Flying Windows	Enter
Backspace	F4	

Assessment 2—Parts of Smartphone

HARDWARE—PARTS OF THE SMARTPHONE

Adapt this to your needs

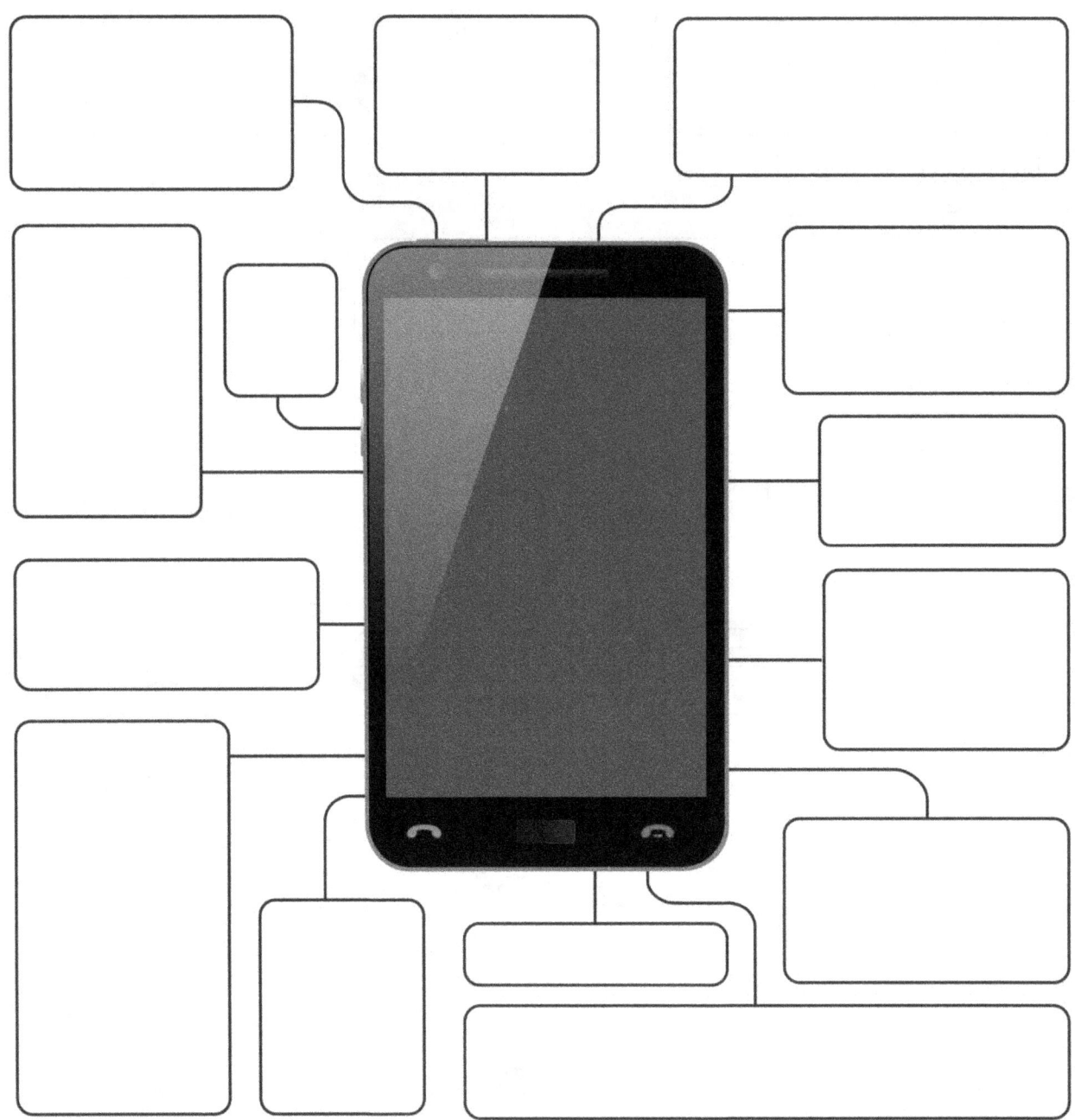

Assessment 3—iPad assessment

IPad Assessment

Assessment 4--Chromebook

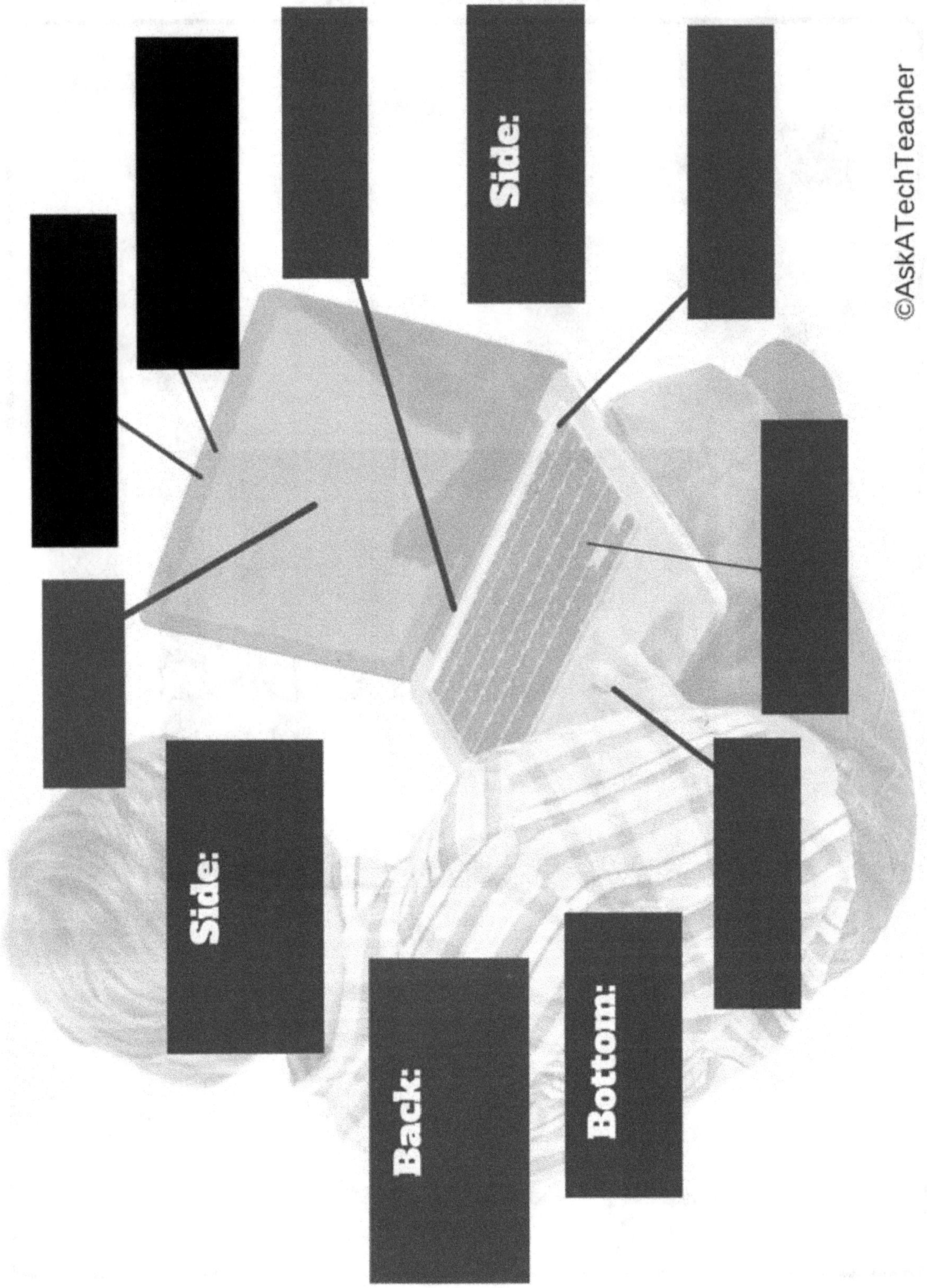

Side:

Side:

Back:

Bottom:

Article 1—21st Century Lesson Plan

21ˢᵗ Century Lesson Plan

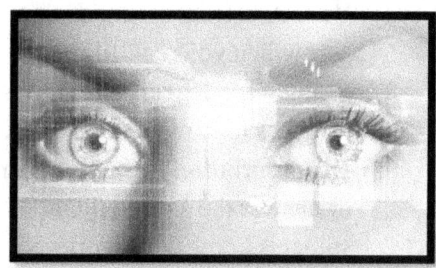

Technology and the connected world put a fork in the old model of teaching—teacher in front of the class, sage on the stage, students madly taking notes, textbooks opened to a particular chapter being reviewed, homework as worksheets based on the text, tests regurgitating important facts. Did I miss anything? This model is outdated **not because it didn't work** (many statistics show students ranked higher on global testing years ago than they do now), **but because the environment changed.** Our classrooms are more diverse. Students are digital natives, already in the habit of learning via technology. The 'college and career' students are preparing for is different so the education model must be different.

Preparing for this new environment requires radical changes in teacher lesson plans. Here are seventeen concepts you'll want to include in your preparation:

1. Students are graduating from high school unable to work in the jobs that are available. It's the teacher's responsibility to insure students **learn over-arching concepts** such as how to speak to a group, how to listen effectively, how to think critically, and how to solve problems. The vehicle for teaching these ideas is history, science, literature, but they aren't the goal.
2. To focus on the over-arching concepts above, make earning **platform-neutral**. For example, when teaching spreadsheets, make the software or online tools a vehicle for practicing critical thinking, data analysis, and evidence-based learning, not for learning one brand of software or a particular spreadsheet tool. Besides, what you use at school may not be what students have at home. You don't want students to conflate your lessons with 'something done at school'. You want them to apply them to their life.
3. **Morph the purpose from 'knowing' to 'understanding'.** Teach the process, not a skill. Students should understand why they select a particular tool, not just how to use it. Why use a slideshow instead of a word processing program? Or a spreadsheet instead of a slideshow? Expect students to be critical thinkers, not passive learners.
4. **Transfer of knowledge is critical.** What students learn in one class is applied to all classes (where relevant). For example, *word study* is no longer about memorizing vocabulary, but knowing how to decode unknown academic and domain-specific words using affixes, roots, and context.
5. **Collaboration and sharing** is part of what students learn. They help each other by reviewing and commenting on projects before submittal to the teacher (Google Apps makes that easy). The definition of 'project' itself has changed from 'shiny perfect student work' to *review-edit-rewrite-submit*. You grade them on all four steps, not just the last one. This makes a lot of sense—who gets it right the first time? I rewrote this article at least three times before submitting. Why expect differently from students? **Plus:** No longer do students submit a project that only the teacher sees (and then a few are posted on classroom bulletin boards). Now, it is shared with all classmates, so all benefit from student work.
6. **Self-help methods** are provided and you expect students to use them. This includes online dictionaries and thesauruses, how-to videos, and access to teacher assistance outside of class. These are available 24/7 for students, not just during classroom hours. This happens via online videos, taped class sessions, the class website, and downloadable materials so students don't worry that they 'left it in their desk'.

7. **Teachers are transparent** with parents. You let them know what's going on in the classroom, welcome their questions and visits, communicate often via email or blogs when it's convenient for them. That doesn't mean you're on duty around the clock. It means you differentiate for the needs of your parents. Your Admin understands that change by providing extended lunch hours, compensatory time off, or subs when you're fulfilling this responsibility.
8. **Failure is a learning tool.** Assessments aren't about 'getting everything right' but about making progress toward the goal of preparing for life
9. **Differentiation is the norm.** You allow different approaches as long as students achieve the Big Idea or answer the Essential Question. You aren't the only one to come up with these varied approaches—students know what works best for their learning and present it to you as an option.
10. The **textbook is a resource**, supplemented by a panoply of books, primary documents, online sites, experts, Skype chats, and anything else that supports the topic. This information doesn't always agree on a conclusion. Students use habits of mind like critical thinking, deep learning, and evidence-based decisions to decide on the right answers.
11. The **lesson plan changes from the first day to the last**—and that's OK. It is adapted to student needs, interests, and hurdles that arise as it unfolds, while staying true to its essential question and big idea.
12. **Assessment** might include a quiz or test, but it also judges the student's transfer of knowledge from other classes, their tenacity in digging into the topic, their participation in classroom discussions, and more.
13. **Vocabulary is integrated into lessons,** not a stand-alone topic. Students are expected to decode words in class materials that they don't understand by using quickly-accessed online vocabulary tools, or deriving meaning from affixes, roots, and context.
14. **Problem solving is integral** to learning. It's not a stressful event, rather viewed as a life skill. Who doesn't have problems every day that must be solved? Students are expected to attempt a solution using tools at their disposal (such as prior knowledge, classmates, and classroom resources) before asking for help.
15. **Digital citizenship is taught,** modeled and enforced in every lesson, every day, and every classroom. It's no longer something covered in the 'tech lab' because every class has as much potential for working online as offline. Every time the lesson plan calls for an online tool or research using a search engine or a YouTube video, teachers review/remind/teach how to visit the online neighborhood safely. It's frightening how students blithely follow weblinks to places most parents wouldn't allow their child to visit in their neighborhood. Just as students have learned how to survive in a physical community of strangers, they must learn to do the same in a digital neighborhood.
16. **Keyboarding skills are granular.** They aren't used only in the computer lab, but in every class students take. If students are using iPads, Chromebooks, laptops, or desktops for learning, they are using keyboarding—which means they must know how to do so efficiently, quickly, and stresslessly. Since keyboarding benefits all classes, all teachers–including the librarian–become partners in this effort. I go into classrooms and show students the broad strokes; the teacher reinforces it every time the student sits down at the computer.
17. **Play is the new teaching.** It is a well-accepted concept for preschoolers and has made a successful leap to the classroom, relabeled as 'gamification'. Use the power of games to draw students into learning and encourage them to build on their own interests. Popular games in the classroom include Minecraft, Mission US, Scratch, and others. If your school is new to this concept, clear it with admin first and be prepared to support your case.

Article 2—Habits of Mind vs. CC vs. IB

Habits of Mind vs. Common Core vs. IB

Pedagogic experts have spent an enormous amount of time attempting to unravel the definition of 'educated'. It used to be the 3 R's—reading, writing, and 'rithmetic. The problem with that metric is that, in the fullness of time, those who excelled in the three areas weren't necessarily the ones who succeeded. As long ago as the early 1900's, Teddy Roosevelt warned:

"C students rule the world."

It's the kids without their nose in a book that notice the world around them, make connections, and learn natively. They excel at activities that aren't the result of a GPA and an Ivy League college. Their motivation is often failure, and taking the wrong path again and again. As Thomas Edison said:

"I have not failed. I've just found 10,000 ways that won't work."

Microsoft founder, Bill Gates, and Albert Einstein are poster children for that approach. Both became change agents in their fields despite following a non-traditional path.

In the face of mounting evidence, education experts accepted a prescriptive fact: student success is not measured by milestones like 'took a foreign language in fifth grade' or 'passed Algebra in high school' but by how s/he thinks. One curated list of cerebral skills that has become an education buzz word is Arthur L. Costa and Bena Kallick's list of sixteen what they call Habits of Mind (Copyright ©2000):

1. *Persisting*
2. *Managing impulsivity*
3. *Listening with Understanding and Empathy*
4. *Thinking Flexibly*
5. *Thinking about Thinking*
6. *Striving for Accuracy*
7. *Questioning and Posing Problems*
8. *Applying Past Knowledge to New Situations*
9. *Thinking and Communicating with Clarity and Precision*
10. *Gathering Data through All Senses*
11. *Creating, Imagining, Innovating*
12. *Responding with Wonderment and Awe*
13. *Taking Responsible Risks*
14. *Finding Humor*
15. *Thinking Interdependently*
16. *Remaining Open to Continuous Learning*

Together, these promote strategic reasoning, insightfulness, perseverance, creativity and craftsmanship.

But they're not new. They share the same goals with at least three other widely-used education systems: 1) Common Core (as close as America gets to national standards), 2) the International Baccalaureate (IB) program (a well-regarded international curriculum, much more popular outside the US than within), and 3) good ol' common sense.

For the rest of the article, visit Ask a Tech Teacher.

Article 3—Which class internet start page is best?

Which Class Internet Start Page is Best?

The internet is unavoidable in education. Students go there to research, access homework, check grades, and a whole lot more. As a teacher, you do your best to make it a friendly, intuitive, and safe place to visit, but it's challenging. Students arrive there by iPads, smartphones, links from classroom teachers, suggestions from friends—the routes are endless. The best way to keep the internet experience safe is to catch users right at the front door, on that first click.

How do you do that? By creating a **class internet start page**. Clicking the internet icon opens the World Wide Web to a default page. Never take your device's default because there's no guarantee it's G-rated enough for a typical classroom environment. Through the 'settings' function on your browser, enter the address of a page you've designed as a portal to all school internet activity, called an 'internet start page'. Sure, this takes some time to set-up and maintain, but it saves more than that in student frustration, lesson prep time, and the angst parents feel about their children entering the virtual world by themselves. They aren't. You're there, through this page. Parents can save the link to their home digital device and let students access any resources on it, with the confidence of knowing you've curated everything.

In searching for the perfect internet start page, I wanted one that:

- *quickly differentiates for different grades*
- *is intuitive for even the youngest to find their page*
- *is customizable across tabbed pages to satisfy changing needs*
- *presents a visual and playful interface to make students want to go there rather than find work-arounds (a favorite hobby of older students)*
- *includes an immediately visible calendar of events*
- *hosts videos of class events*
- *provides collaborative walls like Padlet*
- *includes other interactive widgets to excite students about technology*

Here are four I looked at:

Symbaloo

A logo-based website curation tool with surprising flexibility in how links are collected and displayed. It's hugely popular with educators because collections are highly-visual and easy to access and use. Plus, Symbaloo collections made by one teacher can be shared with the community, making link collections that much easier to curate.

The downside: Links are about all you can collect on Symbaloo.

Only2Clicks

Great for youngers with their big bold buttons, colorful interface.

The downside: Too often, I have technical glitches as I try to set up collections. Maybe it's just me. Another downside: Like Symbaloo, Only2Clicks is focused mostly on link curation. If I want to add widgets, I have to select from their list. With kids, no matter how comprehensive the list, it misses the one I really really need.

Ustart

Offers a good collection of useful webtools for students including links, news, calendar, notes, even weather. It provides tabs for arranging themed collections (like classes) and is intuitive to set up and use. It even includes options for embeddable widgets like Padlet. This is the closest to what I needed of all three.
Overall: This is a good alternative to the one I selected.

Protopage

Protopage did everything on my list. It's flexible, customizable, intuitive, and quick to use with a scalable interface that can be adjusted to my needs (2-5 columns, resize boxes, drag widgets between tabs—that sort). I set up a separate tab for each grade (or you can set up tabs for subjects). The amount of tabs is limited only by space on the top toolbar. Resources included on each tab can be curated exactly as you need. Mine includes:

- *oft-used websites*
- *themed collections of websites*
- *a To Do list*
- *an interactive map*
- *a calculator*
- *a calendar of events*
- *edit-in-place sticky notes*
- *pictures of interest*
- *rss feeds of interest*
- *weather*
- *news*
- *widget for polling the class (Padlet)*

In addition, the Protopage folks are helpful. Whenever I have a problem (which is rare), they fix it quickly.

Article 4—5 Authentic assessment tools

5 Authentic Assessment Tools

Assessments have become a critical piece to education reform. To prepare students well for college and career means they must deeply learn the material and its application to their lives and future learning. That means assessing student knowledge authentically and accountably.

A well-formed assessment is not always measured by a grade. Sometimes it derives evidence of learning from anecdotal observation, watching students apply prior learning, working in groups, or participating in classroom discussions.

Thanks to technology, there are lots of fun and effective ways to assess learning in ways that transform your classroom. Here are seven ideas:

Polls

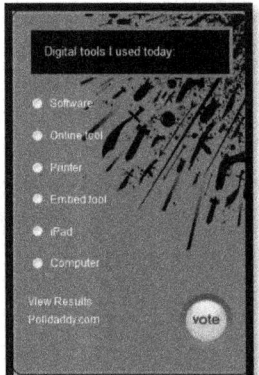

Polls are quick ways to assess student understanding of the goal of your daily teaching. It measures student learning as much as lesson effectiveness. Polls are fast—three-five minutes—are anonymously graded and shared immediately with students. It lets everyone know if the big idea of the lesson is understood and if the essential questions have been answered.

These can be graded, but are usually used formatively, to determine organic class knowledge before moving on to other topics.

Quick Quizzes

These are one-two question checks during class to measure understanding. They are either delivered at an assigned time during class (where everyone participates at once) or are questions students answer when they gain that knowledge from a lesson. Both approaches are a great way for a teacher to determine if she has explained a topic clearly enough that students have a useful understanding of it.

A nice by-product of letting students answer questions when they're ready is they get a topic much faster than you expect. That means you know when to move on to more challenging information.

Gameshows

Team students up with study materials and prep time. This may be fifteen minutes or an entire class—you decide. Encourage them to strategize how to work best as a team. For example, they may decide to assign experts on topics or all be generalists. They may also select a captain, depending upon what type of 'gameshow' is being played.

When prep time is completed, review gameshow rules. They will differ depending upon the gameshow you select. Then get started! They'll think it's a game as you see what they really know on a subject.

Virtual Wall

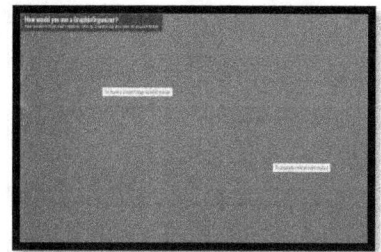

Ask students a question and have them add their answer to a virtual wall.

Virtual walls are also great ideas for reviewing a subject prior to a summative assessment. Have each student post an important idea they got from the unit with significant required details.

Brainstorm

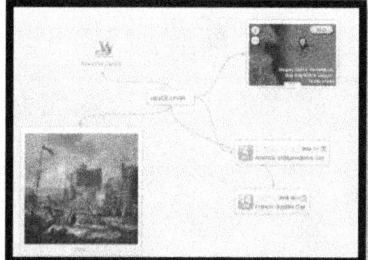

Create a group mindmap to evaluate what the class knows on the subject. This is well-suited to informing you what the class as a whole understands from your teaching, but also creates an excellent study guide for students.

Assessments that work best are those that are fresh and new to students, requiring they think critically and creatively as they share knowledge. What do you use to organically assess student learning?

For more assessment ideas, Education.com has a good discussion on the importance of assessment.

Lesson #2—Keyboarding

Vocabulary	Problem solving	Skills
• Ctrl+P • Digital • Digital portfolios • Log-on • Shortkeys • Systray • Toolbar • Wpm	• Dance Mat won't play flash version (does digital device allow Flash?) • Computer doesn't work (check hardware) • How do I spell-check? • What are red/green/blue squiggles? • Why shortkeys (they're faster and easier)	**New** **Scaffolded** Keyboarding Posture at computer
Academic Applications Academic classes, many parts of life	**Materials Required** speed quiz, keyboarding program, hardware study guides, student workbooks (if using)	**Standards** CCSS.ELA-Literacy.W.4.6 NETS: 1d, 6a

Essential Question

How do I use a keyboard to share ideas?

Big Idea

Students connect keyboarding and classwork authentically

Teacher Preparation

- Keyboarding speed and accuracy quiz is available.
- Talk with grade-level team so you tie into conversations
- Ensure that all required links are on student computers.
- Have student digital accounts and portfolio ready.
- Know which tasks weren't completed last week.
- Integrate domain-specific tech vocabulary.
- Know if you need extra time to complete this lesson.
- Upload Hardware Quiz to class website so students can study at home (if available).
- Include grade-level team, administration, and parents to build keyboarding skills.
- Collect words students don't understand for Speak Like a Geek Board presentations.

Assessment Strategies

- Took keyboarding quiz, paying attention to good habits
- Understood why keyboard
- Signed up for Board
- Worked independently
- Completed warm-up, exit ticket
- Joined classroom conversations
- [tried to] solve own problems
- Decisions followed class rules
- Left room as s/he found it
- Higher order thinking: analysis, evaluation, synthesis
- Habits of mind observed

Steps

Time required: 45 minutes in one sitting or spread throughout the week with a block of 15 minutes set aside for speed/accuracy quiz

Class warm-up: *Keyboarding, to prepare for today's speed and accuracy quiz. Pay attention to posture and good keyboarding habits*

_____ Review parts of computer (or digital device) for quiz next week (study guide in prior lesson). Sound out, roots, prefixes and suffixes. Spelling counts.

_____ As with the mouse, check posture of a neighbor. Sit this way everywhere they use a computer—home, school, the library, everywhere:

Figure 18a—Computer position; 18b—posture

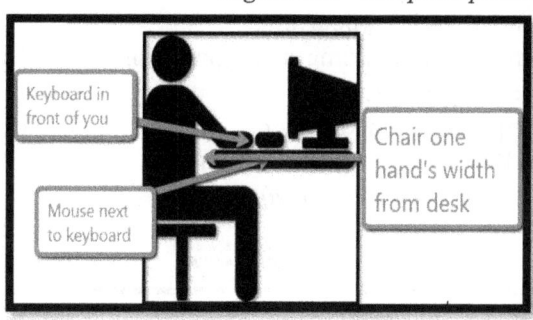
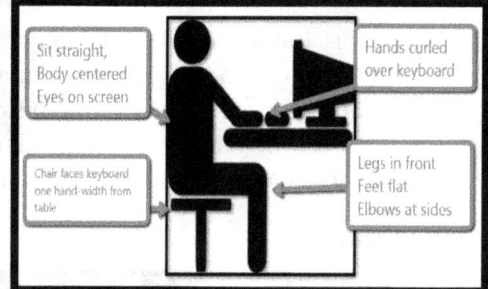

_____Review how student hands should look (*Figure 19*):

Figure 19—Hand position

_____Review the keyboarding hints poster in *Figure 20a* (full size poster in Appendix).

Figure 20a—Keyboarding hints; 20b—keyboarding curriculum map

_____These came directly from the classroom, tested on hundreds of students a year. These are the most common fixes that help students excel at keyboarding.

_____This lesson builds on kindergarten pre-keyboarding skills preparing for 2nd grade two-hand typing and increased tech demands (*Figure 20b*--full size poster in Appendix). All relevant information is collected into this one place so you know where to look when you need it.

_____Review Important Keys and Blank Keyboard templates for quizzes (see *Assessments* at end of lesson for templates) students will take in a few weeks (*Figure 21*):

Figure 21—Important keys

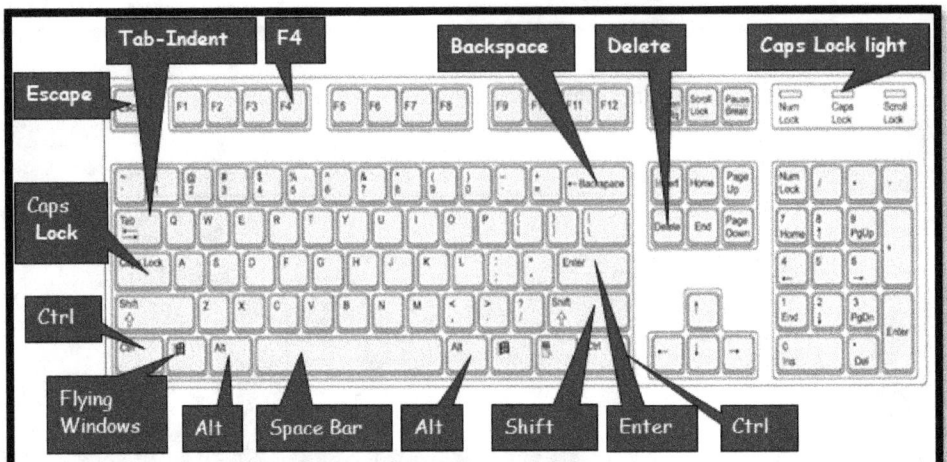

_____Today is the first speed and accuracy quiz of the year. They will take one per grading period.

_____Keyboarding goal this year:

- *Sufficient command of keyboarding skills to type one page in a single sitting*
- *Speed of 25 wpm—about as fast as students handwrite*

_____*Figure 22* is criteria to evaluate keyboarding technique (full size *Assessment* at end of lesson):

Figure 22—Keyboard assessment I

Student_____					
Keyboarding Technique Checklist (3rd – Middle School Grades)					
Technique	Date	Date	Date	Date	Date
Feet placed for balance and sits up straight.					
Body centered to the middle of keyboard.					
Eyes on the screen.					
Types with correct fingering.					
Types with a steady, even rhythm.					
Keeps fingers on home row keys.					
Has a good attitude and strives for improvement.					
WPM (words per minute)					
Accuracy percent					

4 pts = Mastery level 2 pts = Partial Mastery level
3 pts = Near Mastery level 1 pt = Minimal Mastery level

_____Load a digital copy for each student onto your iPad and then annotate to assess.

_____If your students have just started to practice keyboarding, pick only a few of these criteria to assess. As the K-3rd graders get more practice, they'll come to 4th grade with a greater facility and you can expect more. If you use iPads for keyboarding, adapt this list to that digital device. There is a small amount of research that shows iPad keyboarding is as fast as traditional—especially when users have grown up with that sort of keyboard.

_____The speed quiz can be delivered in several ways:

- *Place a page from a book being read in class on the class screen. Students copy it for the quiz. This method forces their heads up rather than on their hands.*
- *Print a page from a book being read in class or a sample document for each student. They place it to the side of their keyboard and type from it.*
- *Use an online typing test like TypingTest.com.*

_____Students type for three-five minutes, then save/share/print.

_____This first quiz is a benchmark—to evaluate skills. The rest of the quizzes will be based on improvement. If students do their homework and tenaciously use good keyboarding habits whenever they sit at the digital device, they'll do fine.

_____Here's the scale for the rest of the year (*Figure 23*):

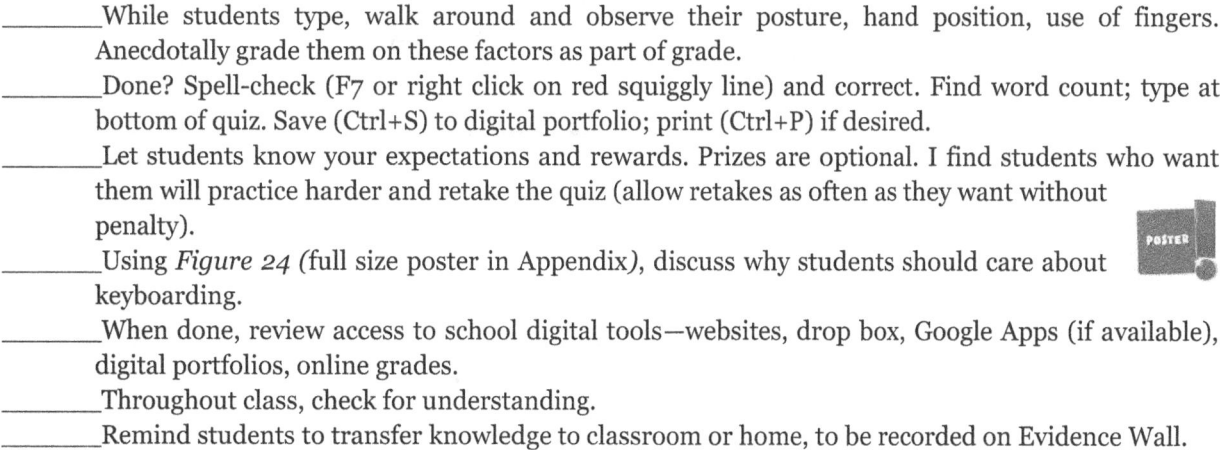

Figure 23—Keyboard assessment II

_____While students type, walk around and observe their posture, hand position, use of fingers. Anecdotally grade them on these factors as part of grade.

_____Done? Spell-check (F7 or right click on red squiggly line) and correct. Find word count; type at bottom of quiz. Save (Ctrl+S) to digital portfolio; print (Ctrl+P) if desired.

_____Let students know your expectations and rewards. Prizes are optional. I find students who want them will practice harder and retake the quiz (allow retakes as often as they want without penalty).

_____Using *Figure 24* (full size poster in Appendix), discuss why students should care about keyboarding.

_____When done, review access to school digital tools—websites, drop box, Google Apps (if available), digital portfolios, online grades.

_____Throughout class, check for understanding.

_____Remind students to transfer knowledge to classroom or home, to be recorded on Evidence Wall.

4th Grade Technology Curriculum: Teacher Manual

_____One more note: Keyboarding skills include more than typing. Now, 'good keyboarding' includes many of the basics required to excel at summative year-end testing. This includes drag-and-drop, highlighting, copy-paste, and stamina. See How to Prepare Students for PARCC/SBA Testing at the end of this Lesson.

Figure 24—Why learn to keyboard

Class exit ticket: *Create a poll using PollDaddy or Google Forms (or another digital tool) and ask students which of the reasons listed on Figure 24 resonate with them? Put it on the class screen so students can vote as they leave.*

Differentiation

- Discuss what's inside computer—motherboard, etc.
- Add Hardware quiz to class calendar.
- Use mental math to figure out keyboard quiz words per minute from word count.
- Early finishers: visit class internet start page for websites that tie into classwork.

Assessment 5—Keyboarding quiz

Student _____

Keyboarding Technique Checklist
Duplicate for each student

Technique	Date	Date	Date	Date	Date
Feet placed for balance and sits up straight.					
Body centered to the middle of keyboard.					
Eyes on the screen.					
Types with correct fingering.					
Types with a steady, even rhythm.					
Keeps fingers on home row keys.					
Has a good attitude and strives for improvement.					
WPM (words per minute)					
Accuracy percent					

4 pts = Mastery level		2 pts = Partial Mastery level
3 pts = Near Mastery level		1 pt = Minimal Mastery level

Keyboarding Technique Checklist
Duplicate for each student

Technique	Date	Date	Date	Date	Date
Feet placed for balance and sits up straight.					
Body centered to the middle of keyboard.					
Eyes on the screen.					
Types with correct fingering.					
Types with a steady, even rhythm.					
Keeps fingers on home row keys.					
Has a good attitude and strives for improvement.					
WPM (words per minute)					
Accuracy percent					

4 pts = Mastery level		2 pts = Partial Mastery level
3 pts = Near Mastery level		1 pt = Minimal Mastery level

4th Grade Technology Curriculum: Teacher Manual

Assessment 6—Important Keys

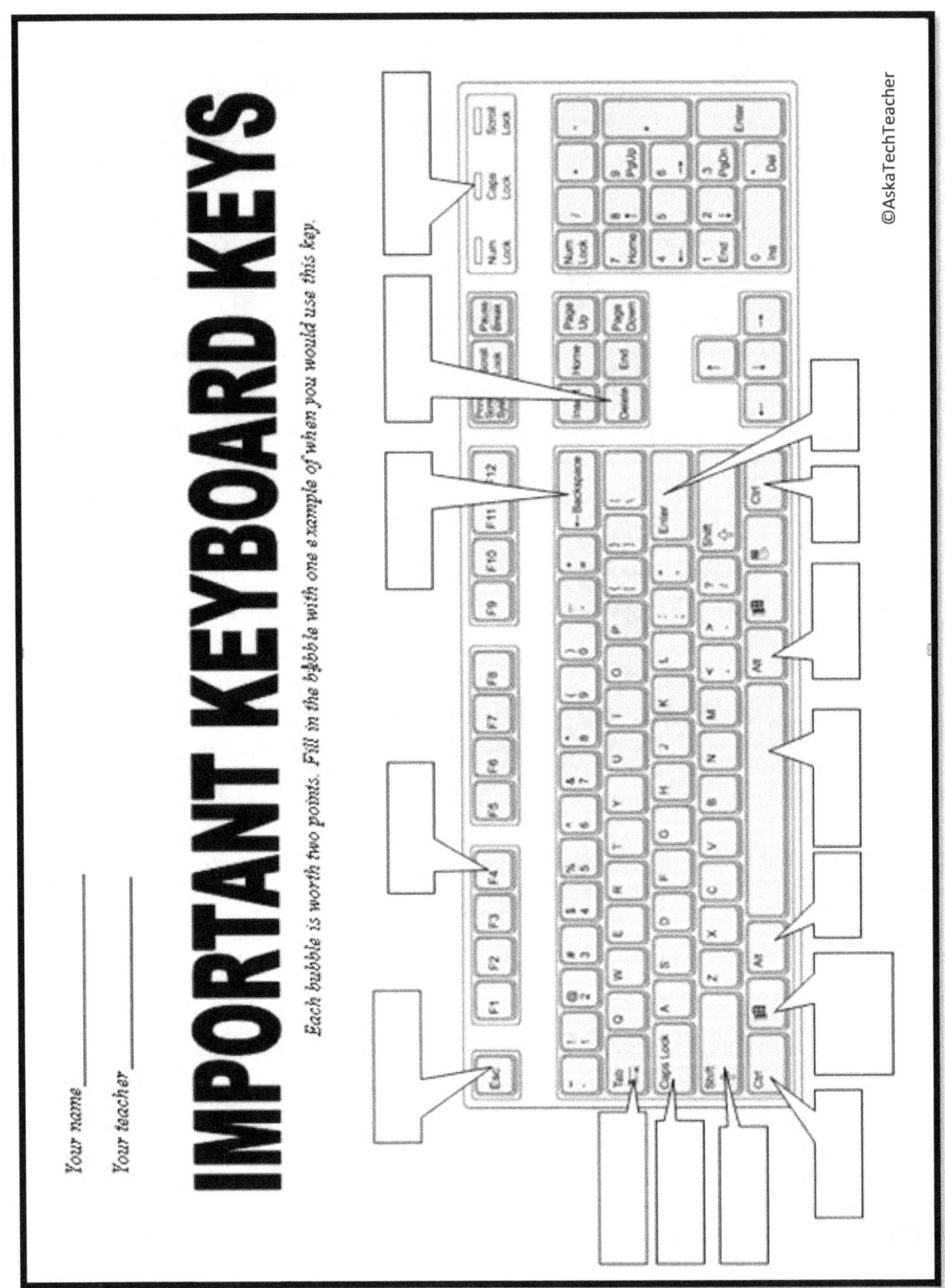

Assessment 7--Blank Keyboard quiz

Blank Keyboard

Name: _____

Assessment 8--Blank Chromebook keyboard

Blank Keyboard--Chromebook

Name _____

©AskaTechTeacher

Article 5—5 Ways to make classroom keyboarding fun

5 Ways to Make Classroom Keyboarding Fun

When you teach typing, the goal isn't **speed and accuracy**. The goal is that students type well enough that it doesn't disrupt their thinking.

Let me say that again:

The goal of keyboarding is students type well enough that it doesn't disrupt their thinking.

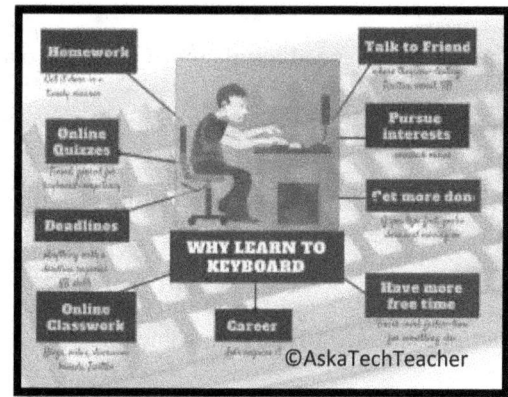

Much like breathing takes no thought and playing a piano is automatic, students want to be able to think while they type, fingers automatically moving to the keys that record their thoughts. Searching for key placement shouldn't interfere with how they develop a sentence. Sure, it does when students are just starting, but by third grade students should be comfortable enough with key placement to be working on speed.

To type as fast at the speed of thought isn't as difficult as it sounds. When referring to students in school, 'speed of thought' refers to how fast they develop ideas that will be recorded. 30 wpm is the low end. 45 wpm is good.

Students used to learn typing in high school, as a skill. Now, it's a tool for learning. So much of what we ask students to do on the way to authentic learning requires typing. Consider the academic need to:

- *write reports*
- *comment on Discussion Boards and blogs*
- *journal in blogs and online tools like Penzu*
- *research online (type addresses into a search bar)*
- *take digital notes (using Evernote, OneNote and similar)*
- *collaborate on Google Apps like Docs, Sheets, Presentations*
- *take online quizzes (like PARCC, SB)*
- *use online tools for core classes (Wordle, Animoto, Story Creators)*

If you're a Common Core state, keyboarding shows up often in the Standards, but can be summarized in these three ways:

- *Keyboarding is addressed **tangentially**–students must be able to type *** pages in a single sitting (see CCSS.ELA-Literacy.W.4.6 for example. The 'pages in a single sitting' starts in 4th grade with one page and continues through 6th where it's increased to three–see CCSS.ELA-Literacy.W.6.6)*
- *By 3rd grade, Common Core discusses the **use** of keyboarding to **produce** work, i.e., CCSS.ELA-Literacy.W.3.6 which specifically mentions 'use technology to produce and publish writing (using keyboarding skills)'*
- *Keyboarding is required to take **Common Core Standards assessments** in the spring.*

The myth is that students will teach themselves when they need it. That's half right. They will teach themselves, but it won't necessarily be in time for their needs. If you're in a tech-infused school, it's your obligation to teach them the right way to type so they can organically develop the tools to support learning.

Most teachers roll out typing with a graduated program like Type to Learn or Typing Club. In September of the new school year, students start Lesson 1. Sometime around May, they are through all the lessons and considered trained. Everything is on auto-pilot with little intervention from the teacher. That works for about ten percent of students. Those are the ones who are intrinsically motivated to learn and nothing gets in their way.

The other 90% need a little more help. Here are six ideas to make your typing lessons fun and effective:

Drill

Drill is part of every granular typing program. Students must learn key placement, finger usage, posture, and all those other details.

There are a lot of options for this—both free like Typing Web and fee-based like QwertyTown. Students usually start enthusiastically, which wanes within a few months as it becomes more of the same rote practice.

Games

When your organic typing program shows signs of wearing on students, throw in a sprinkling of games that teach key placement, speed and accuracy. Big Brown Bear is great for youngers; NitroTyping for olders, and Popcorn Typer for the in-between grades of 2nd-5th.

Offer games sporadically, not on a schedule. Make it a reward for keyboarding benchmarks.

Team Challenge

Students work in teams to answer keyboard-related questions in a game show format. You can use a Jeopardy template that includes not only keyboard questions, but shortkeys that students use often.

Integrate into Class Inquiry

Within a month of starting a keyboarding program, have students use their growing skills authentically in class projects. This can be book reports, research, a brochure for history class, or a collaborative document through Google Apps. The keyboarding is a tool to communicate knowledge in a subject, much like a pencil, an artist brush or a violin. The better their keyboarding skills, the easier it is to complete the meat of the project, like a blog response, trading cards on characters in a book, or a family tree.

Remind students to use the keyboarding skills they've learned to make this real-life experience easier—hands on their own side of the keyboard, use all fingers, good posture, elbows at their sides. Let their team of grade level teachers know what traits to look for as students research in class or the library. Get parents to reinforce it at home.

ASCII Art

ASCII Art uses keyboarding skills to create artistic representations of class learning. This is a fun way to use keyboarding in other classes. All students do is find a picture that represents the class inquiry topic being addressed, put it as a watermark into the word processing program, type over the washed out image with a variety of keys, then delete the watermark. This takes about thirty minutes usually and always excites students with the uniqueness of their work.

Article 6--How to Prepare Students for End-of-year Tests

How to Prepare Students for End-of-year Tests

As part of my online tech teacher persona, I get lots of questions from readers about how to make technology work in an educational environment. This one from Terry is probably on the minds of thousands of teachers:

Any help for identifying and re-enforcing tech skills needed to take the online PARCC tests (coming in 2014-15)? Even a list of computer terms would help; copy, cut, paste, highlight, select; use of keys like tab, delete, insert; alt, ctrl and shift.

There does not seem to be any guidelines as to prepping students on the "how to's" of taking an online test and reading and understanding the directions. It would be great to take advantage of the time we have before the PARCC's become a reality. Thanks!

Between March 24 and June 6, more than 4 million students in 36 states and the District of Columbia will take near-final versions of the PARCC and Smarter Balanced efforts to test Common Core State Standards learning in the areas of mathematics and English/language arts. Tests will be administered via digital devices (though there are options for paper-and-pencil). The tests won't produce detailed scores of student performance (that starts next year), but this field-testing is crucial to finding out what works and doesn't in this comprehensive assessment tool, including the human factors like techphobia and sweaty palms (from both students and teachers).

After I got Terry's email, I polled my PLN to find specific tech areas students needed help with in preparing for the Assessments. I got answers like these:

"They had to drag and drop, to highlight, and they had to compare and contrast. They had to write a letter. They had to watch a video, which meant putting on headphones. They had to fill in boxes on a table. There were a lot of different mouse-manipulation tasks."

"Students are asked to retype a paragraph to revise. My students can't type fast enough!"

"...questions [are] a mix of multiple-choice, problem solving, short-answer responses, and other tasks. Students had to drag and drop answers into different boxes."

It boils down to five tech areas. Pay attention to these and your students will be much more prepared for Common Core assessments, be it PARCC or Smarter Balanced:

Keyboarding

Students need to have enough familiarity with the keyboard that they know where keys are, where the number pad is, where the F row is, how keys are laid out. They don't need to be touch typists or even facilely use all fingers. Just have them comfortable enough they have a good understanding of where all the pieces are. Starting next school year, have them type fifteen minutes a week in a class setting and 45 minutes a week using keyboarding for class activities (homework, projects--that sort). That'll do it.

Basic computer skills

These skills--drag-and-drop, keyboarding with speed and accuracy, highlighting, and playing videos--are not easy for a student if they haven't had an instructive course in using computers. It won't surprise any adult when I say using and iPad isn't the same as using a computer. The former has a bunch more buttons and tools and the latter more intuitive. And typing on an IPad virtual keyboard is not the same as the reassuring clackity-clack of a traditional set-up. Will students get used to that? Yes, but not this month.

Make sure students are technologically proficient in their use of a variety of digital devices, including computers and iPads. This means students have an understanding of what defines a digital device, how it operates, what type of programs are used on various types (for example, apps are for iPads and software for laptops) and how do they operate, and what's the best way to scaffold them for learning? Being comfortable with technology takes time and practice. Make digital devices and tech solutions available at every opportunity--for note-taking, backchannel communications, quick assessments, online collaboration, even timing an activity. Make it part of a student's educational landscape.

This includes the safe and effective use of the internet. Students should understand how to maneuver through a website without distraction.

One area Terry asks about is vocabulary. The words she mentioned--*copy, paste, cut, highlight*--these are domain-specific. Use the correct terminology as you teaching, but observe students. If they don't understand what you're saying, help them decode it with context, affixes, or an online dictionary for geek words. Keep a list of those words. Soon, you'll have a vocabulary list for technology that's authentic and specific to your needs.

Stamina

Expect students to type for extended periods without complaint. Common Core requires this. That's what 'one page in a sitting in 4th grade, 2 pages in a sitting in 5th grade, 3 pages in a sitting in 6th grade' means. The Assessments expect students have that sort of stamina. They're long tests with lots of keyboarding and other tech skills. Make sure your students have practiced working at computers for extended periods.

A good idea is to have students take some online assessments prior to this summative one. These can be created by the teacher using any number of online tools like Google Forms or use already-created tests like those that follow BrainPop videos.

Problem Solving

Make sure students know what to do when a tech problem arises. They should be able to handle simple problems like 'headphones don't work' or 'caps lock won't turn on' or 'my document froze'. This is easily accomplished by having students take responsibility for solving tech problems, with the teacher acting as a resource. They will soon be able to differentiate between what they have the ability to handle and what requires assistance.

A great starting point when teaching problem solving are Common Core Standards for Mathematical Practice. These are aligned with the Math Standards, but apply to all facets of learning.

Teacher Training

Make sure teachers administering the online tests are familiar with them and comfortable in that world. They should know how to solve basic tech issues that arise without calling for outside help. This is effectively accomplished by having teachers use technology in their classroom on a regular basis for class activities, as a useful tool in their educational goals. Helps teachers make this happen.

4th Grade Technology Curriculum: Teacher Manual

Lesson #3—Digital Tools in the Classroom

Vocabulary	Problem solving	Skills
• Alt+F4 • Attachments • Bcc • Cc • Cells • F4 • Fields • Flag • Netiquette • Wpm	• How do I close a program (Alt+F4) • Can I save without sending (yes) • Can I format (click 'Rich formatting') • Typing is hard (it gets easier) • Why is 'transfer' important (we want you to use tech skills to excel in life) • I can't log in (what's your UN/PW?) • I won a free ** • How is the internet unsafe—I'm anonymous?	**New** Email Class calendar Blogging **Scaffolded** Digital citizenship Log-ins Digital tools Digital portfolio Class website
Academic Applications Writing, speaking and listening, digital citizenship	**Materials Required** Internet, Evidence Board, keyboarding program, email program, websites that tie into inquiry	**Standards** CCSS.ELA-Literacy.W.4.6 NETS: 1b, 4b

Essential Question

How does technology make learning easier and more authentic?

Big Idea

Learn digital tools to communicate and collaborate

Teacher Preparation

- Have all classroom digital tools ready to use.
- Talk with grade-level team so you tie into conversations.
- Know if you need extra time to complete this lesson.
- Know which tasks weren't completed last week.
- Integrate domain-specific tech vocabulary into lesson.
- Collect words for Speak Like a Geek Board presentations.

Assessment Strategies

- *Followed directions*
- *Practiced email using appropriate writing style*
- *Used good keyboarding habits*
- *Completed warm-up, exit ticket*
- *Joined class conversations*
- *[tried to] solve own problems*
- *Decisions followed class rules*
- *Left room as s/he found it*
- *Higher order thinking: analysis, evaluation, synthesis*
- *Habits of mind observed*

Steps

Time required: 45 minutes in one sitting or spread throughout the week
Class warm-up: Keyboard homerow with Popcorn Typer or another tool that focuses on one row. Observe student position.

_____How do students use what they learned in class in their lives and other classes? Add this to Evidence Board. Ask several times a month.

_____This Lesson covers three topics. Cover as many as are relevant to your group:

- o *Log-ins*
- o *Online Communication*
- o *Class Digital Tools*

_____Review the importance of digital citizenship from the last lesson (*Figure 25*).

63

Figure 25—Internet safety

Log-ins

_____Review how students log into digital devices using user names and passwords (*Figure 26*):

Figure 26—How to log in

_____Have a method for tracking them. It might be as simple as a 3.5 card (*Figure 27*):

- *Keep a physical copy by the student's seat or in their personal binder.*
- *Keep a digital copy in the student's digital portfolio.*
- *Take a snapshot of it to keep on their digital device for quick reference.*

Figure 27—Track UN and PW

User Name/Passwords		
PROGRAM	UN	PASSWORD
Keyboarding Program		
Math Program		
Computer		
Class wiki		
Add'l		

_____If using workbooks, make sure students know how to annotate *Figure 27* in their workbook, using a tool like iAnnotate or Adobe.

_____Have students log into school digital portfolios—website, class pages, other.

Online Communication (Email)

_____Discuss each digital communication tool, though you'll focus on email:

- *Blogs*
- *Comments*
- *Email*
- *Forums*
- *Texting*
- *X/Twitter*

_____Compare and contrast how these communicate. What level of security can you expect of each?

_____To use any form of digital communication requires the habits of digital citizenry. It is a concept you will return to over and over throughout the year.

_____What is email? Who has their own email account? Watch BrainPOP's video on email or select another from Ask a Tech Teacher's resource pages.

_____People want an email program that:

- *is intuitive to use*
- *can be accessed from any digital device, any location*
- *is 'up' 99.99% of the time (What does that mean?)*
- *alerts user when a message arrives*

_____Discuss email etiquette (*Figure 28*—full size in Poster appendix):

Figure 28—Email etiquette

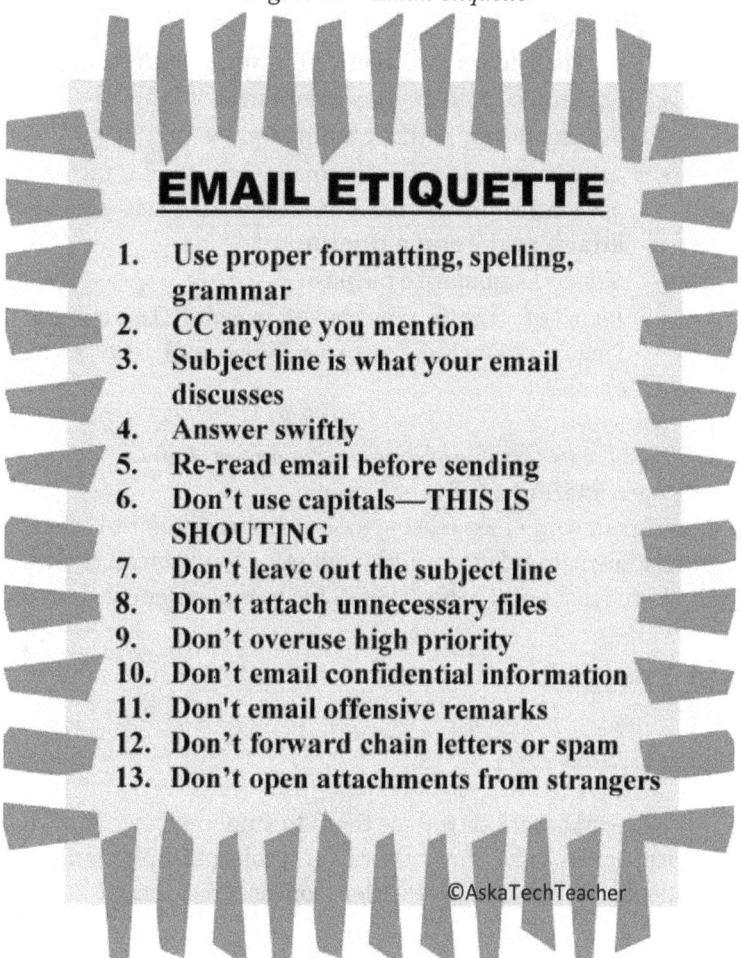

_____How might the structure of an email message differ based on its purpose? Should it be long or short? Formal or informal? What tasks is it best suited for—stories? Opinion pieces? Informative discussions? For the conveyance of information and data? Persuasive pieces? Go through the types of writing students will work on this year.

_____There are many email programs. What you have at home may be different from school. Compare Outlook in *Figure 29a* to Gmail in *Figure 29b*:

Figures 29a-b—Email programs

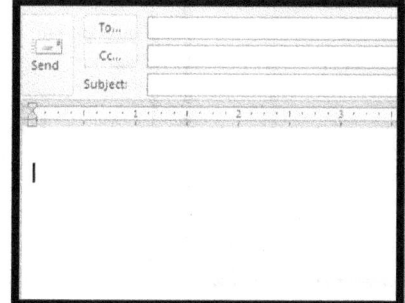 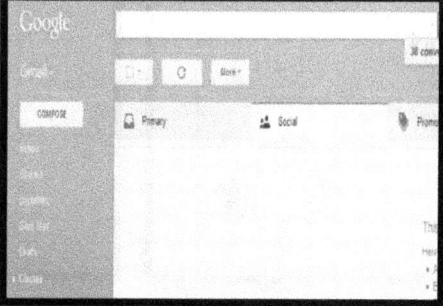

_____Open school email program. Review layout. Use tab to move between fields. **Correct spelling** of address is important. Otherwise, your message will 'bounce'. What's that mean?

_____Find:

- *To:* spell address correctly or it won't reach recipient
- *Cc:* send copy to anyone mentioned
- *Bcc:* send copy without telling sendee
- *Attach:* include a file in email. Only send attachments to people who know you. Only open attachments from the same. Discuss email security and spam. Review how to **attach and open a document**.
- *Subject:* summarize purpose
- *Body of email:* concise, thorough. Use correct grammar/spelling (not 'texting' language). Include pictures, links, and text. **Avoid attachments.** Why? What's a 'virus'?

_____Review how to attach and open a document. Only send attachments to people who know you. Only open attachments from the same.

_____Experiment with email editing tools—they're similar to others students already use.

_____Have students send you or a classmate a sample email (if available).

_____Show students how to check 'Sent' file to be sure email went out.

Class Digital Tools

Student workbooks

_____If using workbooks, introduce them to students now. Show how to open them from their digital device, access links, find rubrics and project samples, and take notes using the annotation tool. Students can circle back to review concepts or forward to preview upcoming lessons.

Annotation Tool

_____If you're using student workbooks, show students how to annotate their copies with a tool such as iAnnotate (*Figure 30a*), Notability (*Figure 30b*), Adobe Acrobat (free—*Figure 30c*)) or another tool available in your school.

_____If students are sharing the PDF (for example, it's loaded on a class computer that multiple grade-level classes visit), show how to select their own color that's different from other students.

Figure 30a--Notability; 30b--Adobe Acrobat; 30c--iAnnotate

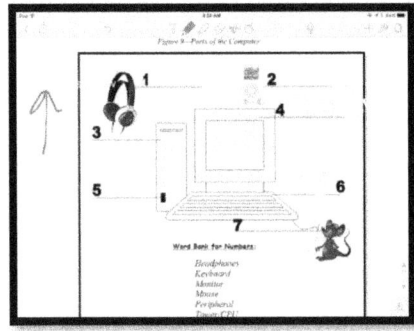  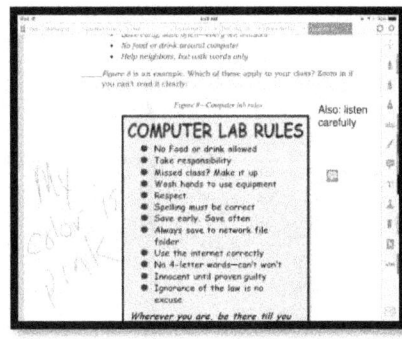

_____Review options available in the annotation tool you use, such as:

- *highlighting*
- *text*
- *note*
- *freeform*

_____Discuss all the class digital tools students will use this year such as:

- *Class calendar*
- *Class internet start page and student portfolios*
- *Class website and student blogs*
- *Google apps*
- *Class webtools*
- *Vocabulary decoding tools*

_____Add your specific tools as needed.

Class Internet Start Page

_____An internet start page is a website that comes up when students open the internet. It organizes content into a single location and curates links students will use weekly. See *Figure 32*.

Class website

_____Websites encourage reflection, organization, logical thinking, and embedding of sharable projects i.e., Tagxedos and Animotos. If your school doesn't have Google Apps, free websites can be created at Weebly, Wix, or a blog account like Wordpress (Google for addresses).

Student blogs

_____If you use student blogs in 4th grade, review these with your class.

Class Calendar

_____Have a class calendar that tracks due dates, class events, and other important information.
_____This can be done in Google Calendar (*Figure 31a*), Office 365 (*Figure 31b*), Padlet, or another option of your choice (i.e., Publisher). If possible, embed into class website or student blogs.

Figure 31a-c—Class calendars

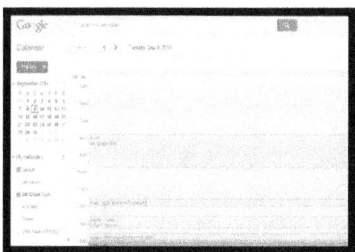  

_____ Demonstrate how to edit calendar by adding a homework assignment.
_____ Assign a student each month to be responsible for adding events to the class calendar.

Google Apps

_____ Everything created in Google Apps is backed up instantly in the Cloud. Importantly, it enables collaboration and sharing anywhere—two cornerstones to Common Core and ISTE. This facilitates a shift from software-based, print-centric programs to a more open, equitable and green to education (Microsoft has a version called Office 365—Google for address).

_____ Show students how to use student accounts—log in, use Drive, and share documents with others. Demonstrate similarity between Google Docs/Sheets/Presentation and Office if students are more familiar with MS Office.

Student digital portfolios

_____ Discuss how students use Digital Portfolios (also known as digital lockers or digital binders):

- *store work (in Cloud) required in other classes or at home*
- *interact, collaborate, and publish with peers, experts, or others*
- *contribute to project teams*
- *edit or review work in multiple locations*
- *submit class assignments*

_____ There are a variety of approaches to digital portfolios that satisfy some or all of the above uses: 1) folders on school network, 2) fee-based programs from companies such as Richer Picture 3) cloud-based storage like Dropbox or Google Apps, 4) online collaborative sites like Google Classroom (Google names for addresses if interested), or 5) an LMS like Otus.

_____ Have students practice by uploading something to their digital portfolio.

Figure 32—Class internet start page

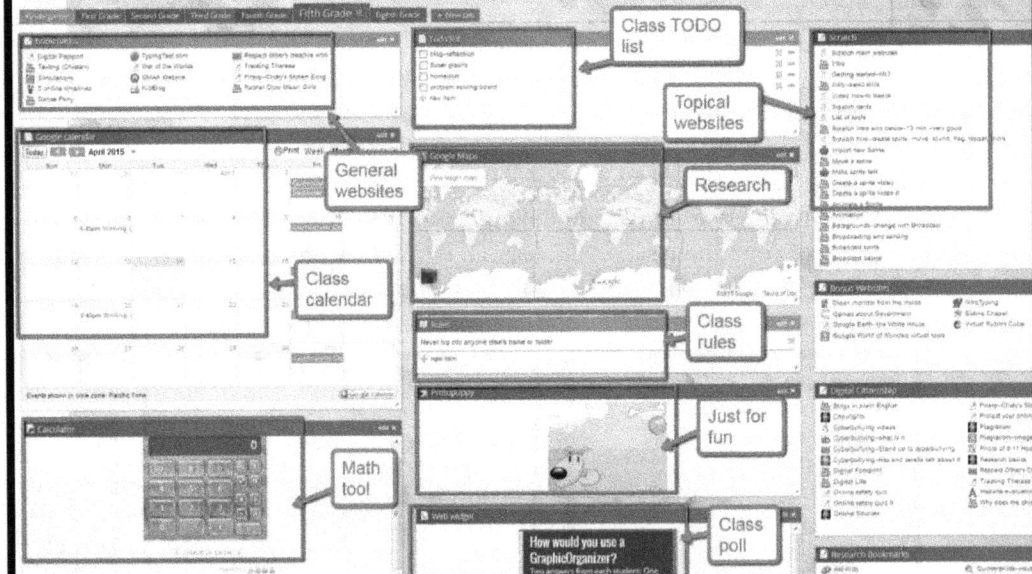

_____Include what students visit daily (i.e., guidelines, calendar, 'to do' list, typing websites, research locations, sponge sites, calculator) as well as info specific to current project.

Class Webtools

_____Discuss the wide variety of digital tools students will use this year to complete projects. Let students know that you are open to alternative suggestions. For example, if you suggest Wordle, a student can request Tagxedo. Approval is required, but it will be granted if the tool fulfills project needs. Expect students to use evidence to build their case, compare-contrast their tool to your suggestion, and draw logical conclusions.

Vocabulary Decoding Tools

_____Show students how to access the native apps or webtools available on the digital devices that can be used to decode vocabulary students don't understand. Depending upon the device, these will be on the homepage, the browser toolbar, a shortkey, or a right click. Show students how to quickly look up words from any of their classes rather than skipping over content that includes the word. Let them practice with several of the words in this lesson's *Vocabulary* list.

_____Options for dictionary tools include (find websites with an internet search):

- *Kids Wordsmyth*
- *Merriam-Webster for Kids*
- *Picture Dictionary*
- *right click on a word in MS Word and select 'Look up'*
- *right click in Google Apps (i.e., Google Docs) and select 'research'*
- *one created by students in prior years—they find a word they don't understand, add it with a definition to a webpage you've set up for that purpose (maybe on the class blog or website)*

_____Have students attempt to access all school digital tools.

Class exit ticket: **Have students vote in a poll for which tool they think they'll use the most this year.**

Differentiation

- *Sometime at start of school year, visit classroom and explain how class digital devices are the same as tech lab digital devices—on a smaller scale (see directions at end of lesson, "Take Tech to Classroom"). The visual of you in their classroom well conveys that message.*
- *Add homework due date to calendar—once a month.*
- *Offer additional websites that tie into class conversations.*

4th Grade Technology Curriculum: Teacher Manual

Lesson #4—Problem Solving

Vocabulary	Problem solving	Skills
• Cerebral • Inductive reasoning • Irrelevant • Life skill • Relevant	• I tried to solve the problem, • I asked for help and the person didn't know the answer • Nothing works!	**New** Using a poll **Scaffolded** Problem solving Keyboarding
Academic Applications Any class, school and life, college and career	**Materials Required** keyboard program link, Problem Solving Board rubrics, Evidence Board badges	**Standards** CCSS Standards for Math. Practice NETS: 4a, 5c

Essential Question

How do I solve a problem I've never seen before?

Big Idea

Problem solving is 'cerebrally-stimulating—and fun!

Teacher Preparation

- Know which tasks weren't completed last week.
- Verify all required links are available.
- Be prepared to integrate domain-specific tech vocabulary.
- Know if you need extra time to complete this lesson.
- Collect words students don't understand for Speak Like a Geek Board beginning later. Use a physical Vocabulary Wall (i.e., a bulletin board) or a virtual wall like Padlet. Students independently add words.
- Commit one after-school session per week to help students problem solve. You may use student helpers.

Assessment Strategies

- Anecdotal
- Committed to solving problems
- Decisions followed class rules
- Left room as student found it
- Completed warm-up, exit ticket
- Joined class conversations
- Higher order thinking: analysis, evaluation, synthesis
- Habits of mind observed

Steps

Time required: 45 minutes in one sitting or spread throughout week
Class warm-up: Set up hardware problems around the room. As students enter, they solve the one related to their station before starting class.

_____Start Hardware Quiz (*Assessment 1, 2 or 3*). Give students 5-10 minutes. Remind them spelling counts. They can retake for full credit. This is called the Mulligan Rule, taken from golf (Appendix).
_____When students finish, practice keyboarding using Popcorn Typer or Dance Mat Typing or another tool that **focuses on one row at a time** while the rest of the class finishes. Students used these last year so they should begin independently. Observe posture and use proper hand position with no flying hands.
_____Turn music on to establish a typing rhythm for students. Encourage them to type to the beat.

_____Review speed and accuracy quiz from last week. Any common problems—hunt-and-peck? Using a finger for spacebar? Flying elbows?

_____Any evidence of learning to post on Evidence Board?

_____Review Problem Solving corner of classroom—where you collect common tech problems students will be expected to solve wherever they use digital devices (see *Figure 33*).

Figure 33—Problem-solving board

_____Reinforce the importance of students solving their own problems. This includes hardware. For example, if sound doesn't work on the Chromebook, what should students do? What if it's an iPad? This will be circled back on throughout the year.

_____Sign up for Problem-solving Board—starts next week. Remember 3rd grade? This is the first of three Presentation Boards this year:

1. *Problem-solving board*
2. *Speak Like a Geek*
3. *Google Earth Board*

_____All three Board presentations are independent investigation, risk-taking for cautious students, and presentation skills practice. Here's how this Board works:

- *Post sign-up sheets by the class door where they're easily found. Include slips of paper (Figure 34) that students can track important information:*

Figure 34—Board info required

My name: _____
My question: _____
My presentation date: _____

- *Alternatively, have sign-ups online where they can be shared through:*

    o *Office 365*
    o *Padlet (using calendar template)*
    o *SignUp Genius*

- *Each student signs up for a date and a problem to present.*
- *Student gets solution from family, friends, or even teacher as a last resort.*
- *Presentation date: Student tells classmates problem, how to solve it, takes questions.*
- *Entire presentation takes about three minutes.*

_____*Assessment 9* is an example of the Board assessment to share with students:

Assessment 9—Problem-solving board rubric

PROBLEM SOLVING BOARD
Grading Rubric

Name: _____

Class: _____

Knew question
Knew answer
Asked audience for help if didn't know answer
No umm's, stutters
Look audience in eye
No nervous movements (giggles, wiggles, etc.)
No nervous noises (giggles,)
Overall

_____Load a copy of *Assessment 9* for each student onto your iPad. As students make their presentations, annotate your grading onto the form and save/share/publish.

_____Students may sign up in groups, as long as there is one problem per group member.

_____A little background: Problem-solving Board covers tech issues faced in class. As you move through the year, collate a list of problems for next year's Board. Start with the problems students posted as a class exit ticket after Lesson 1. Include problems students had with tech in homework, at home as they used tech for a school assignment, with classroom digital devices—from all parts of their life. *Figure 35* is a sample list of common tech problems:

Figure 35—Common computer problems

Common Computer Problems	
What if the double-click doesn't work	What is protocol for email subject line
What if the monitor doesn't work	What does 'CC' mean in an email
What if the volume doesn't work	How do I exit a screen I'm stuck in
What if the computer doesn't work	How do I double space in Word
What if the mouse doesn't work	How do I add a footer in Word
What's the right-mouse button for?	How do I add a watermark in Word
What keyboard shortcut closes program	How do I make a macro in Word
How do I move between cells/boxes?	How do I add a border in Word
How do I figure out today's date?	How do I add a hyperlink in Word
What if the capital doesn't work	Keyboard shortcuts for B, I, U
What if my toolbar disappears	What if the program disappears
What if the document disappears	What if the program freezes
Keyboard shortcut for 'undo'	What is the protocol for saving a file

_____Include shortkeys like *Figure 36*:

Figure 36—Common shortkeys

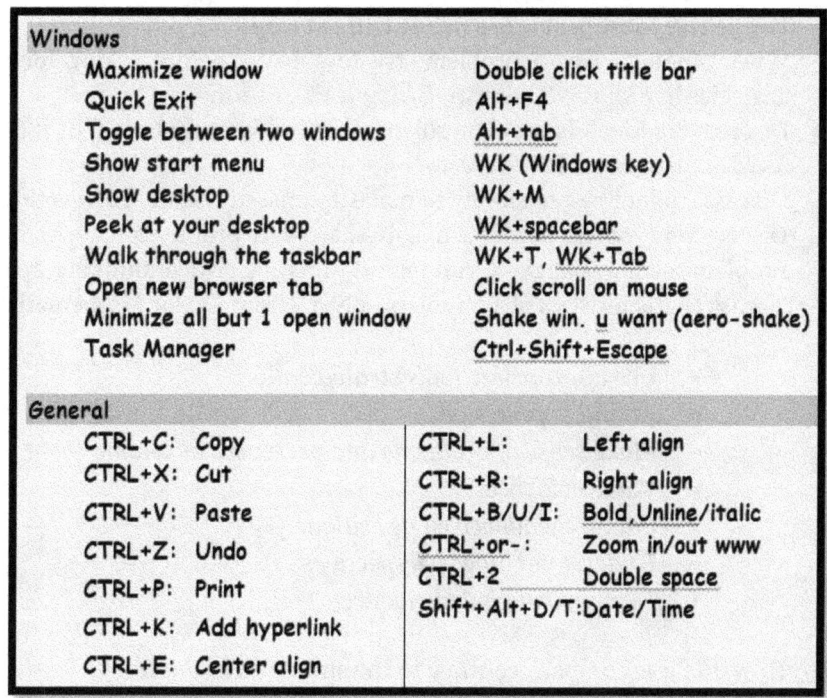

_____Why are shortkeys considered in the category 'problem solving'?
_____See *Figures 37a* and *37b* for examples of platform-specific shortkeys:

Figure 37a—iPad shortkeys; 37b—Chromebook shortkeys

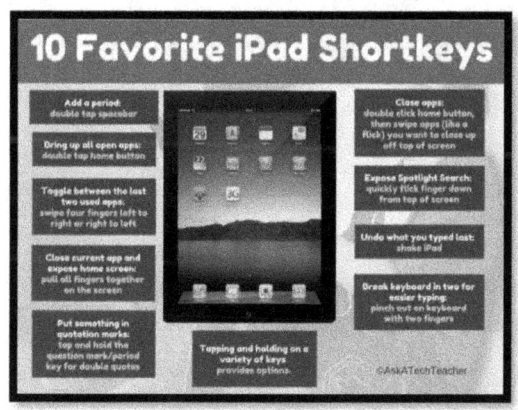 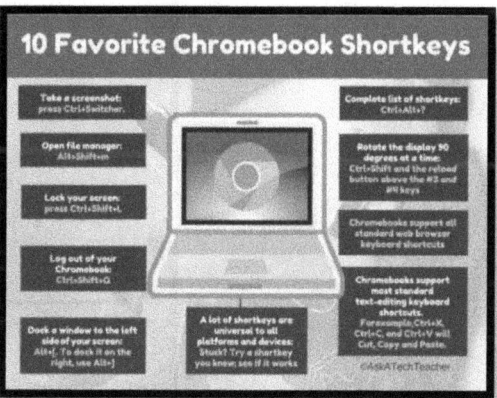

_____If you can't read these posters, zoom in (if you have a digital copy of this book) or find most of them in the back of the book.
_____Board presentations provide an authentic method of practicing presentation skills discussed in Common Core under 'Speaking and Listening'.
_____While students are signing up, classmates can practice keyboarding or visit inquiry-based websites you've listed on the class internet start page (or wherever you collect links for class use).
_____Remind students that *Important Keys* quiz is next week.
_____Discuss Problem Solving, life skill that transcends a subject.

_____Review article at lesson end: *"How to Teach Students to Solve Problems"*.

_____Discuss what it means to be a 'problem solver'. Who do students go to when they need a problem solved? Do students believe that person gets it right more often than others? Would they believe most people are wrong half the time?

_____When students face a problem, try to solve it before asking for assistance. Use strategies in *Figure 38* How to Solve a Problem.

_____Discuss 'Big Idea': Is problem solving 'cerebrally-stimulating? Is it fun? Why or why not? Discuss quotes in *Figure 39*.

_____Discuss student responsibility to make up missed classes. How is this 'problem solving'?

_____Discuss why you ask students to solve hardware problems independently.

_____Problem solving is aligned with logical thinking, critical thinking, reasoning, and habits of mind. Discuss characteristics of a 'problem solver' (from CC for Mathematical Practice):

- *Use appropriate tools strategically.*
- *Attend to precision.*
- *Make sense of problems and persevere in solving them.*
- *Value evidence.*
- *Comprehend as well as critique.*
- *Understand other perspectives.*
- *Demonstrate independence.*

_____How do these compare-contrast to the strategies in *Figure 38*, How to Solve a Problem.

_____Discuss these strategies with students. Asks them for personal examples of each. If they don't have any, prod them gently with your personal experiences. What is the overlap between solving math problems and solving life problems?

Figure 38—How to solve a problem

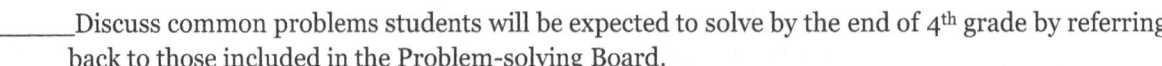

_____Discuss common problems students will be expected to solve by the end of 4th grade by referring back to those included in the Problem-solving Board.

_____Problems at the beginning of each weekly lesson relate to the activities they will complete during the week. They may or may not be different/the same as those on the Problem-solving Board. By the end of each lesson, expect students to solve these independent of assistance.

_____For your own problem-solving skills: Read the article at the end of this lesson, *"What Happens When Technology Fails"*?

Figure 39—Problem-solving quotes

Great Quotes About Problem Solving

"In times like these it is good to remember that there have always been times like these."
— Paul Harvey *Broadcaster*

"Never try to solve all the problems at once — make them line up for you one-by-one.
— Richard Sloma

"Some problems are so complex that you have to be highly intelligent and well-informed just to be undecided about them."
— Laurence J. Peter

"Life is a crisis - so what!"
— Malcolm Bradbury

"You don't drown by falling in the water; you drown by staying there."
— Edwin Louis Cole

"The significant problems we face cannot be solved at the same level of thinking we were at when we created them."
— Albert Einstein

"It is not stress that kills us. It is effective adaptation to stress that allows us to live."
— George Vaillant

"The most serious mistakes are not being made as a result of wrong answers. The truly dangerous thing is asking the wrong questions."
— Peter Drucker *Men, Ideas & Politics*

"The problem is not that there are problems. The problem is expecting otherwise and thinking that having problems is a problem."
— Theodore Rubin

It's not that I'm so smart, it's just that I stay with problems longer.
—Albert Einstein

No problem can stand the assault of sustained thinking.
—Voltaire

The problem is not that there are problems. The problem is expecting otherwise and thinking that having problems is a problem.
—Theodore Rubin

Problems are only opportunities with thorns on them.
—Hugh Miller

_____Remember: Bring science book next week.

Class exit ticket: ***Take a poll that asks students to choose problem-solving strategies they are most likely to use in the future.***

Differentiation

- *If homework is due, make sure it's added to class calendar.*
- *Add next week's Important Keys quiz (template in Appendix) to class calendar.*
- *Unplug hardware so students must fix the problem before they start the day's lesson.*
- *Early finishers: visit class internet start page for websites that tie into classwork.*

Article 7—How to teach students to solve problems

How to Teach Students to Solve Problems

Of all the skills students learn in school, **problem solving** arguably is the most valuable and the hardest to learn. It's fraught with uncertainty—what if the student looks stupid as he tries? What if everyone's watching and he can't do it—isn't it better not to try? What if it works, but not the way Everyone wants it to? When you're a student, it's understandable when they decide to let someone tell them what to do.

But this isn't the type of learner we want to build. We want risk-takers, those willing to be the load-bearing pillar of the class. And truthfully, by a certain age, kids want to make up their own mind. Our job as teachers is to provide the skills necessary for them to make wise, effective decisions.

It's not a stand-alone subject. It starts with a habit of inquiry in all classes—math, LA, history, science, any of them. I constantly ask students questions, get them to think and evaluate, provide evidence that supports process as well as product. Whether they're writing, reading, or creating an art project, I want them thinking what they're doing and why.

Common Core puts problem solving front and center. It comes up in ELA ("*Students will be challenged and asked questions that push them to refer back to what they've read. This stresses critical-thinking, problem-solving, and analytical skills that are required for success in college, career, and life.*"), but is inescapable in Math. In fact, students cannot fully meet the Math Standards without understanding how to effectively approach the unknown. Consider the Standards for Mathematical Practice that overlay all grade levels K-12:

- *Make sense of problems and persevere in solving them*
- *Reason abstractly and quantitatively*
- *Construct viable arguments and critique the reasoning of others*
- *Model*
- *Use appropriate tools strategically*
- *Attend to precision*
- *Look for and make use of structure*
- *Look for and express regularity in repeated reasoning*

Do these sound like great strategies for everything, not just math? How about deciding what classes to take? Or whether to make a soccer or basketball game on the weekend? Or which college to attend? Using these eight tools strategically, with precision, and tenaciously is a great first step.

The question becomes: How do students **learn to use them**? Certainly, as they accomplish their grade-level math curriculum, you as teacher remind them they aren't doing a multiplication problem (or an Algebra one); rather they're reasoning abstractly or using appropriate tools strategically, or expressing regularity in repeated reasoning. But for deep learning, hands-on authentic experience is required. Let's say, for example, the class is investigating the purchase of an MP3 player. Should they purchase an IPod, a smartphone, a dedicated use MP3 player, or a different option? How do students arrive at a decision—solve that problem? Ask students to work through the steps below as they address a decision. Ask them to note where they accomplish one or more of the Standards for Mathematical Practice above:

1. What do you want in an MP3 player? Should it play music, show videos, pictures, communicate with others, be a phone also? Make that list so you know how to evaluate information as you collect it (**compare/contrast**).
2. What do you know about the topic (**evidence**)? Have you seen some you liked or didn't like? What have you heard about those on your list? You are a good resource to yourself. Don't discount that. You'll be surprised how much you know on a variety of topics. This step is important to college and career. Future employers and schools want you to think, to use your intelligence and your knowledge to evaluate and solve problems.

3. What advice do knowledgeable friends have (**perspective taking, collaboration**)? You want the input of MP3 users. Your friends will think whatever they own is the best, because they're vested in that choice, but listen to their evidence and the conclusions they draw based on that. This is important to a team-oriented environment. Listen to all sides, even if you don't agree.
4. **Dig deeper (close reading)**. Check other resources (**uncover knowledge**). This includes:
    - *people who don't like the product*
    - *online sources. Yep, you might as well get used to online research if you aren't yet. Statistics show more people get their news from blogs than traditional media (newspapers, TV) and you know where blogs are.*
    - *your parents who will bring up topics friends didn't, like cost, longevity, reliability*
5. **Evaluate your resources (integration of knowledge)**. How much money do you have? Eliminate the choices that don't fit your constraints (money, time, use, etc.) If there are several choices that seem to work, this will help you make the decision. You might have to save money or get a job so you can afford the one you've chosen. Or, you might decide to settle for a cheaper version. Just make sure you are aware of how you made the choice and are satisfied with it.
6. What are the **risks involved** in making the decision (**reflection**)? Maybe buying an MP3 player means you can't do something else you wanted. Are you comfortable with that choice?
7. **Make a decision (transfer learning)**. That's right. Make a decision and live with it knowing you've considered all available information and evaluated it logically and objectively.

Optionally, you might have students evaluate problem solving in their favorite game, say, Minecraft. All it requires is that they think about what they're doing as they play:

- *What is the goal of Minecraft? How is it best achieved*
- *What does the student know about playing the game that can be used in achieving the goal?*
- *Does working with friends and gaining feedback make life easier in Minecraft?*
- *How does experience in the game affect progress?*
- *And so on...*

This is how students become the problem solvers required of their Future. When the day comes that how they solve a problem affects the direction their life takes (college, career, marriage, children, a tattoo), they'll be happy to have strategies that make it easier.

Article 8—What happens when technology fails?

What Happens When Technology Fails?

Has this happened to you? You spend hours rewriting an old lesson plan, incorporating rich, adventurous tools available on the internet. You test it the evening before, several times, just to be sure. It's a fun lesson with lots of activities and meandering paths students undoubtedly will adore. And it's student-centered, self-paced. Technology enables it to differentiate authentically for the diverse group of learners that walk across your threshold daily.

Everyone who previewed it is wowed. You are ready.

Until the day of, the technology that is its foundation fails. Hours of preparation wasted because no one could get far enough to learn a d*** thing. You blame yourself—why didn't you stick with what you'd always done? Now, everyone is disappointed.

Implosions like this happen every day in tech-centric classrooms. Sometimes it's because the network can't handle the increased traffic, or students can't log in due to a glitch, or the website server goes upside down—nothing a teacher can do about that. Really, the reason doesn't matter. All that matters is an effort to use technology to add rigor and excitement to an old and tired lesson plan fails, leaving the teacher more technophobic than ever. With the pride of place iPads and Chromebooks and 1:1 programs are getting in curriculum decisions, tech problems will be common, varied, frustrating, show-stopping, and nauseating. They will be wide-ranging, everything from a student's device not having required software to the classroom systems not hooking up to the school's network or WiFi. Students will look to their teacher for solutions and the teacher will become best friends with a colleague in thick glasses and the pasty tan of someone rarely away from their computer, whose conversation includes domain-specific words like *gig, server,* and *modem* rather than the score of the weekend football games.

To many, 'tech problem' equates to the mind-numbing, bone-chilling feeling of 'I have no idea what to do'.

In a word: Failure. Not a feeling veteran teachers like. As a culture, we eulogize those who go bravely through gates of fire, can think under pressure, are never beaten down, and who can connect the dots even when they're bouncing all over the landscape:

> *No problem can stand the assault of sustained thinking. (—Voltaire)*

> *Success consists of going from failure to failure without loss of enthusiasm. (—Winston Churchill)*

> *Far better is it to dare mighty things, to win glorious triumphs, even though checkered by failure... than to rank with those poor spirits who neither enjoy nor suffer much, because they live in a gray twilight that knows not victory nor defeat. (—Theodore Roosevelt)*

I've learned you can tell a lot about a teacher by the way s/he handles three things: a rainy day, parents who drop in unexpectedly, and a lesson plan that explodes.

It doesn't stop with the teacher, either. What about when we ask our students to use one of the gazillion available internet tools to communicate-collaborate-share-publish—those exciting Common Core words that are code for 'technology-rich'. Now, when students don't turn in homework, their entirely believable excuse is 'the computer ate my homework' because most everyone has had it happen to them. When I attempt to unravel what happened with questions like: *Where did you save it?* I get the deer-in-the-headlights-look that says: *How am I supposed to know the answer to THAT question?*

Having said all this, I am willing to stipulate: Tech failure is inevitable. There are too many moving parts. Too many circuits and algorithms and scripts and wires shoved under a desk to expect it to go right all the time or even most of the time. Exorcise any thought of *perfection* in the same sentence as *tech* from your syntax. But if fear of failure is a reason NOT to use technology, no one would ever cross that digital threshold. So let's ignore the absolute inevitability of failure, and address the question: *What do I do when it happens?*

I have three ideas:

Prepare for it

I'm not fatalistic. I'm realistic. Technology—be it phones, scanners, your house's water meter, your child's online report cards, the Smart TV you just purchased—fails often and will continue to do so into the foreseeable future. In that way, it is very human. Perfection is well outside of its programming.

Knowing that, bone up on the **Law of Technology Failures**: *The reliability of technology is directly proportional to your needs.* To decode that: Tech fails most often where it is needed most. Prevent failures by having back-ups—not just of data, but devices, hardware, systems. For example, if you're trying to get to Disneyland from Arkansas with three friends, each with Google Maps (or my new favorite, Waze) on their phones, said phones will never run out of battery power. Ever. Redundancy. Install three browsers on your computer so if Firefox won't work, Chrome will. Build in time for system reboots (because that solves at least half the tech problems that plague a classroom). Pre-test relevant systems to become familiar with glitches. Sure, tech will still fail, but not in areas in which you are prepared.

Having said that, keep in mind the **corollary to the Law of Technology Failures**: *The better technology works, the safer you'll feel with it, the less redundancy you will activate.*

Be a problem solver

Dylan Thomas said this as well as anyone in history:

> *Do not go gentle into that good night. Rage rage against the dying of the light.*

Embrace problems. Own them. Here are three basics that will get you through many a stressful tech day:

1. **Know the basics.** My job requires tech every day so I've solved a lot of problems. I've found there are only about twenty that account for 80% of the downtime. The top two: If the digital device won't start, check to see if it's plugged in. If power isn't the problem, reboot. Those two solve about half of the tech traumas I face in the classroom. There are eighteen more I'm equally prepared for. Track yours by writing each down as it happens. Soon, you'll find it's the same ones over and over. The tech version of Groundhog Day.
2. **Google the problem.**
3. **Be a risk-taker.** Sure we mouth that to our students and Common Core expects it in college- and career-ready students, but does that mean teachers too? Well, yes. Make that who you are. Grin in the face of problems. Model solutions. As Edwin Cole famously said, *"You don't drown by falling in the water; you drown by staying there."* Don't drown. Don't stay there. Stand up and you may discover it's only an inch deep.

Build in alternatives

Many times this year during the nation's premiere tech-in-ed conference—ISTE—the internet didn't work. Lots of reasons why—all that mattered was that presenters couldn't access their presentations. Most handled this with aplomb either with screenshots or animated descriptions of what might have been. No one quit and walked off the stage.

Let's face it: If you're over the age of ten, you know life runs off of Plan B.

What else can you do?

- **Don't expect technology to remain unchanged**—Links die, by some counts, about 4% a year. The website you used last week can be 404—not working today (for example: Nimble Fingers for keyboarding). The favorite software you've used for years could be incompatible with system updates (i.e., Oregon Trail). Your new digital device won't run a handful of the programs you use regularly. Prior to presenting, go through the tool you're going to use or the process you're teaching—see if it actually works as it used to.
- **Use it as a teachable moment**—show students how you handle stress, problems, frustration. It's a learning experience. It's an opportunity to stretch that magnificent big brain and devise a solution. It's a chance to ask students, *"What would you do?"*
- **Don't apologize**—save apologies for something you caused. Tech failures are the cause of the Universe.

Tech is the third leg to the 'inevitable experiences' stool, along with death and taxes. Personally, I don't know anyone who hasn't had a major tech failure. You know it's coming. That's out of your control. The only thing you can control is how you react to it.

Lesson #5—Outline in Word Processing

Vocabulary	Problem solving	Skills
• Alignment • Alt+F4 • Bullets • Ctrl+Z • Icons • Indent/exdent • Mulligan Rule • Shortkey • Title	• Numbers disappeared (backspace into outline; push enter for next number) • I can't find tool (use Search) • Outline won't work (try shortkeys) • How do I indent (tab) • I can't find tool on ribbon (try shortkey) • I can't find the answer to my problem and my parents can't help • I was sick last quiz (retake for full credit)	**New** Outlining **Scaffolded** Word processing Keyboarding Speaking and listening
Academic Applications Any class that needs to organize thoughts, ideas, research, reading, writing	**Materials Required** textbook, word processing program, graded quizzes, Important Keys quiz, sign-up for Problem-solving Board, Evidence Board badges, workbooks (if using)	**Standards** CCSS.ELA-Literacy.RI.4.9 NETS: 3c-d, 5b-c

Essential Question

How do I use technology to organize information efficiently?

Big Idea

Outlining aids understanding and organization of information

Teacher Preparation

- Remind students to bring science book.
- Talk with grade-level team so you tie into conversations.
- Ensure all required links are on student digital devices.
- Know which tasks weren't completed last week.
- Know if you need extra time to complete this lesson.
- Integrate domain-specific tech vocabulary.
- Collect words students for Speak Like a Geek Board.

Assessment Strategies

- Completed Important Keys quiz
- Signed up for Board
- Brought science book
- Followed directions
- Used good keyboarding habits
- Completed warm-up, exit ticket
- Joined class conversations
- [tried to] solve own problems
- Decisions followed class rules
- Left room as s/he found it
- Higher order thinking: analysis, evaluation, synthesis
- Habits of mind observed

Steps

Time required: 45 minutes in one sitting or spread throughout the week with a block of 30 minutes set aside for outlining
Class warm-up: Keyboard home row

_____Warm up with keyboarding practice using Popcorn Typer or Dance Mat Typing or another tool that **focuses on one row at a time**. Students used these last year so should be able to begin independently. Observe student ability to maintain correct posture, keep elbows at sides, use proper hand position and all fingers with no flying hands.

_____These are the same websites students will use for homework. Have them practice using these websites so they know how to get there and where 'homerow' exercises are located.

_____While keyboarding, students can sign up for the Problem-solving Board. It starts next week.
_____Preview Problem-solving Board. Students can get solution from family, friends, neighbors or even teacher as a last resort. Point out class problem-solving board with common problems and solutions. Students teach classmates how to solve the problem. It takes about three minutes.
_____Review Hardware Quiz. Remind students of Mulligan Rule.
_____Important Keys quiz today. *Figure 40* is a thumbnail—full size at end of lesson 2:

Figure 40—Important Keys quiz

_____This includes fifteen non-letter keys they should know. They can work in groups.
_____Flip all keyboards over so no one is tempted. Give no more than seven minutes.
_____Review grading (same as the keyboarding speed-accuracy quiz).
_____When done, remind them that the Blank Keyboard quiz is next week.
_____Any evidence of learning for Evidence Board?
_____Why outline? How does it benefit a student's understanding of a topic? How does it assist in organizing information? Consider:

- *to encourage a better understanding of a topic*
- *to organize ideas*
- *to promote reflection on a topic*
- *to assist analysis of a topic*

_____How students access an outline tool will be slightly different if they use a computer (PC, Mac, even a Chromebook) or an iPad. Be familiar with the app you plan to use so you can adapt instructions as needed.
_____Today, you'll outline one chapter in a book you've brought from class. You'll be expected to find the main topics and supporting points to be included in the outline. Your outline will look something like *Figures 41a-c*:

Figure 41a—Outline in Word; 41b—in Google Docs; 41c—in Workflowy

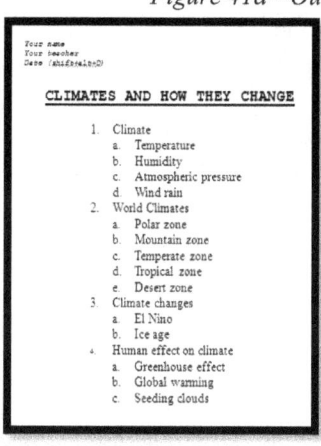 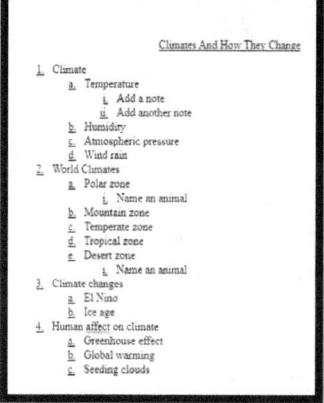 

_____Open a word processing program like MS Word or Google Docs.
_____If you don't use Word or Docs, try (find websites with an Internet search):

- *OneNote—software, web, or an iPad app*
- *Workflowy – online outliner (Figure 41c)*

_____If these don't work on your Chromebook, try:

- *Outliner of Giants*

_____If you're an iPad school, try one of these:

- *Google Docs or MS Word app*
- *Quicklyst – quick notes and list on iPads*
- *OmniOutliner –for iPads and online*

_____Any time students go online, remind them to do so safely.
_____Bring outline up on class screen. Put heading at top (name, teacher, date). What's the purpose of the heading? Add date with shortkey.
_____Center title beneath heading. What's the purpose of a 'title'?
_____Use three ribbon tools—or adapt for the toolbar in the word processing program you use: 1) bullet or numbered list, 2) indent—push text to right (subpoint), and 3) exdent—push text to left (more important point). See *Figure 42 (in MS Word)*:

Figure 42—Outline tools

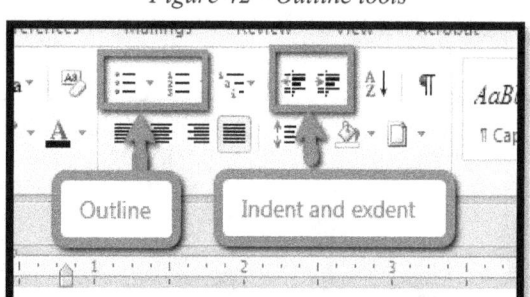

_____Or, use tab to indent and Shift+tab to exdent—I like this better.
_____Outline chapter headings, subheadings in the book students brought to class. Summarize and/or paraphrase relevant points in text.
_____Work individually or in small groups.
_____Done? Now edit. As a group, suggest information on this topic learned from other resources (library books, videos, personal experience) and integrate it into the right spot by adding points and subpoints, even images. How does this contribute to overall understanding of topic? How does this enable student to more knowledgeably discuss subject?
_____Remind students: Every time they use computers, practice keyboarding skills.
_____Remind students: Save early save often. Why? How often?
_____If printing, preview to be sure outline takes only one page. Save or save-as? Which is right for this situation?
_____Review how students save (*Figure 43* is a thumbnail of a poster in Appendix):

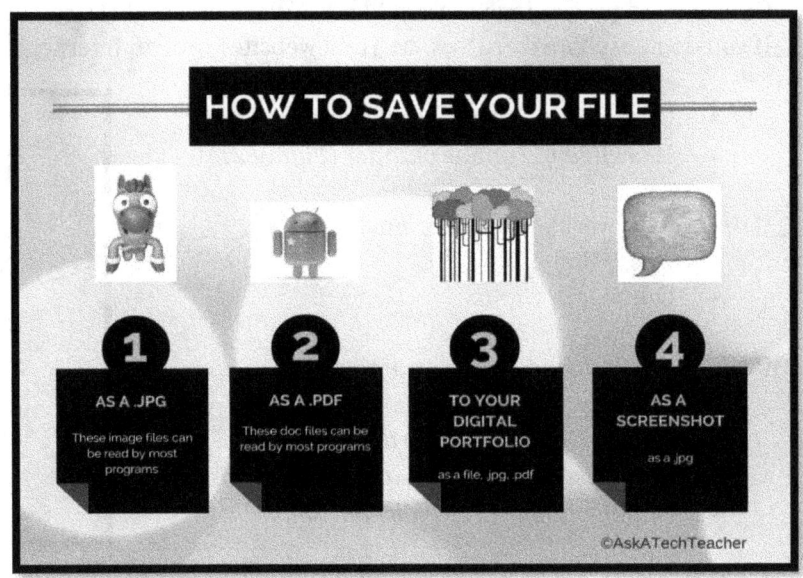

Figure 43—How to save your file

_____Why is it important to put student name in file name? Demonstrate a search of student name. See how a file shows up even if they didn't save it right—as long as they saved it 1) with their last name in file name, and 2) to school network (if using that approach).
_____Print/save/share/publish—you decide.
_____Throughout class, check for understanding.

Class exit ticket: **Students tack a post-it on a virtual or physical Vocabulary Wall with a tech word they don't know. Use these for upcoming Speak Like a Geek.**

Differentiation

- Add start of Problem-solving Board to calendar—next week
- Add next week's Blank Keyboard quiz to calendar.
- Students who finish visit class internet start page for websites connected to inquiry.

Lesson #6—Digital Citizenship

Vocabulary	Problem solving	Skills
• Cyberbully • Digital footprint • Fair use • Format • Forums • Netiquette • Online presence • Plagiarism • Social media • Texting • Virus	• Aren't all images on Google free (no—they're to view, not steal) • I'm anonymous. Why worry about my actions (your true measure is how you act when no one looks) • Why doesn't 'fair use' cover everything when I'm a student (it only covers academic stuff) • I can't find the copyright • No one will guess my password (yes, they will)	**New** Digital footprint Digital rights and responsibilities **Scaffolded** Digital citizenship Cyberbullying Digital privacy Plagiarism
Academic Applications Science, history, social studies, any classes that use internet for resources	**Materials Required** word processing/keyboard program, Problem-solving Board sign-ups and rubric, Evidence Board badges, email program, workbooks (if using)	**Standards** CCSS.ELA-Literacy.W.4.4 NETS: 2a-d

Essential Question

How do I use technology efficiently to communicate?

Big Idea

Use online resources safely.

Teacher Preparation

- Talk with grade-level team so you tie into conversations.
- Ensure all required links are on student digital devices.
- Know which tasks weren't completed last week.
- Integrate domain-specific tech vocabulary into lesson.
- Collect words for Speak Like a Geek Board.
- Know if you need extra time to complete this lesson.

Assessment Strategies

- Completed presentation
- Shared evidence of learning
- Completed blank keyboard quiz
- Used good keyboarding habits
- Emailed appropriate message
- Completed warm-up, exit ticket
- Joined class conversations
- [tried to] solve own problems
- Decisions followed class rules
- Left room as s/he found it
- Higher order thinking: analysis, evaluation, synthesis
- Habits of mind observed

Steps

Time required: 45 minutes in one sitting or spread throughout the week and year
Class warm-up: Keyboard QWERTY row

_____Warm up with Popcorn Typer or another tool that focuses on one row at a time.
_____Review important keys quiz from last week.
_____Any evidence of learning to post on Evidence Board?
_____Give students blank keyboard quiz (*Figure 44*—full-size *Assessment* is at the end of *Keyboarding* lesson). They can work in groups. Flip keyboards over so no one is tempted. Students get ONLY seven minutes. They should know key placement.

Figure 44—Blank keyboard

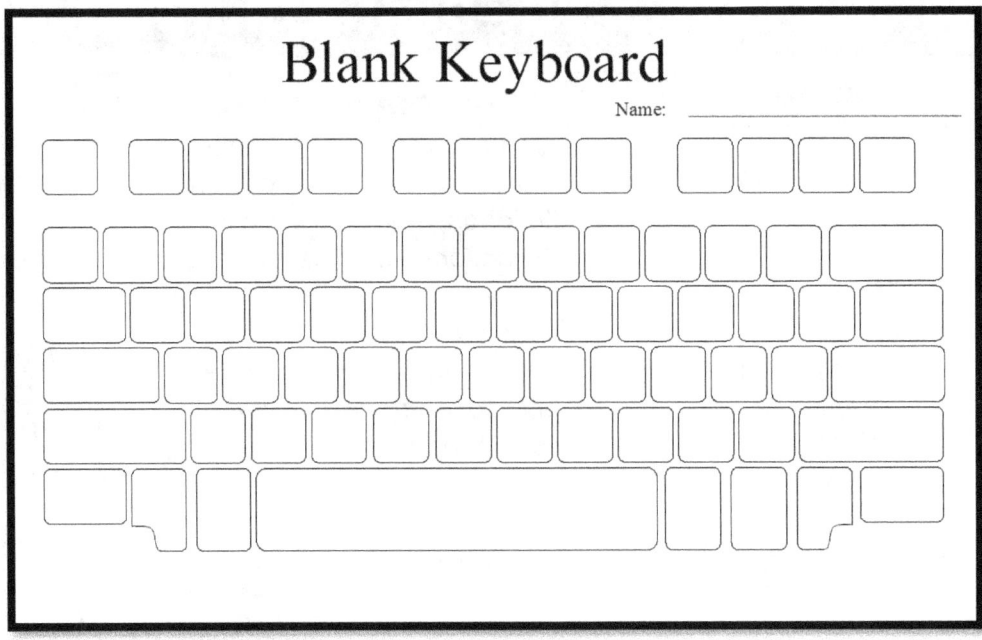

_____Remember: Homework due end of each month. Remind students the entire years' worth of assignments is in the back of their student workbook (if you use those).
_____Start Problem-solving Board. Review. Be encouraging to students. It's difficult to be 'teacher'.

Digital Citizenship

_____Discuss *digital citizenship*. You'll cover it in depth throughout the year.
_____As a group, throughout the school year where relevant, discuss the topics listed in this curriculum map table under '4th grade' (*Figure 45*). If you haven't covered topics listed under K-3, discuss those first before moving into 4th-grade material. They will scaffold learning for students, making your lessons more authentic and relevant.

For an in-depth digital citizenship curriculum (including projects that reinforce learning, definitions, and scores of websites), refer to Structured Learning's K-8 Digital Citizenship curriculum. It's a companion to this tech curriculum:

Figure 45—DigCit topics

Digital Citizenship Topics	K	1	2	3	4	5	6
Cyberbullying	x	x	x	x	x	x	x
Digital citizenship	x	x	x	x	x	x	x
Digital commerce						x	x
Digital communications					x		x	x
Digital footprint and Online presence				x	x	x	x	x
Digital law					x		x	x
Digital privacy					x	x	x	x
Digital rights and responsibilities	x	x	x	x	x	x	x
Digital search and research					x	x	x	x

Fair use, Public domain				X	x	x	x	x
Image copyright					x		x	x	x
Internet safety		x	x	x	x	x	x	x
Netiquette			x	x	x	x	x	x
Online Plagiarism						x	x	x	x
Passwords		x	x	x			x	x
Social media							x	x
Stranger Danger		x	x	x				

_____Post the pyramid in *Figure 46* on the wall in your classroom (there's a full-size poster in the appendix). Every time you've discussed a topic, mark it off:

Figure 46—Digcit topic pyramid

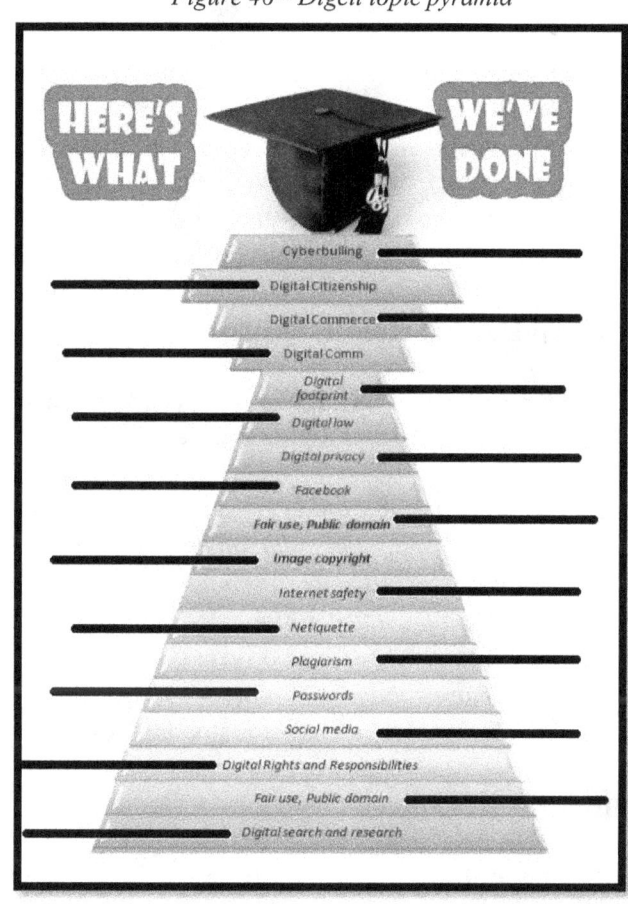

_____Your goal: Cover the following topics. Preview to be sure they're appropriate for your group.

General discussion of Digital Citizenship

- Review last year's digital citizenship discussion. Solicit ideas from students.
- Discuss X/Twitter (see the article at the end of the lesson) and hashtags—watch Hashtag, you're it! (available on YouTube).
- Discuss blogs (see article at end of lesson).
- Discuss texting (see the article at the end of the lesson). Watch video on Jennette McCurdy's "Chicken" Commercial for Safe Kids USA (available on YouTube).

Cyberbullying

- What is **cyberbullying**? What does 'cyber' mean? What is the same/different about bullying and cyberbullying?
- Use tools employed to deal with neighborhood bullies on cyberbullies.
- Watch cyberbullying videos such as those from Common Sense, or check the Ask a Tech Teacher resource pages.

Digital footprint

- Discuss. Why is it important? Reiterate the last phrase—that we are influenced by what we find on a digital footprint.
- Watch the video, *The Digital Footprint* (available on YouTube).

Digital privacy

- Introduce **Digital Privacy**. Discuss how **passwords** protect privacy. Remind students they never share passwords, even with friends.
- Discuss password guidelines and rules.
- Watch the NetSmartzKids video on passwords (available on YouTube).

Digital rights and responsibilities

- What are the **digital rights and responsibilities** of a fourth grader? Watch this YouTube video "Digital Rights and Responsibilities". Discuss these concepts:

    - *Act the same online as you'd act in your neighborhood.*
    - *Don't share personal information. Don't ask others for theirs.*
    - *Be aware of your surroundings. Know where you are in cyberspace.*
    - *Always show your best side online.*
    - *Anonymity doesn't protect the individual.*
    - *Share knowledge online.*
    - *If someone is 'flaming', stop it if possible or walk away.*

Netiquette

- What is '**netiquette**' to a fourth grader (see the poster in the appendix)?

Online search/research

- covered in other lessons

Plagiarism

- What does '**plagiarism**' mean? Why give credit to original authors/artists?
- Watch this Common Craft video on Plagiarism.
- Discuss plagiarism concepts like image copyrights, fair use, public domain.

Class exit ticket: *Send an email to the teacher listing the top three digital tools the student is excited to use.*

Differentiation

- Review home row. Repeat keys together several times while waving finger to use.
- Add homework due date to class online calendar for each month.
- Encourage students to check email on a regular basis by sending them emails and providing incentives for responding such as:
  - students ask a teacher for secret password to email back to you
  - take a silly picture using Photo Booth and email it to you
  - respond to your email
  - forward an email to a friend
  - send students online game link and have them respond with their best score
  - send students on a scavenger hunt around campus for specific items
  - wear a school t-shirt next Tuesday
- Early finishers: visit class internet start page for websites that tie into classwork.

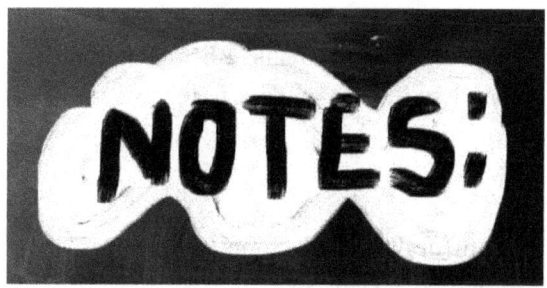

_____
_____
_____
_____
_____
_____
_____
_____

Article 9—11 Ways Twitter improves education

Ways X/Twitter Improves Education

A teacher must communicate with students in a way they will hear. Twitter might be perfect for your class.

Twitter can easily be dismissed as a waste of time in the elementary school classroom. Students get distracted. They might see inappropriate tweets. How does a teacher manage a room full of Tweeple?

But, you've read a lot about Twitters usefulness in writing skills and sharing information so you—of the Open Minded Attitude—want to try it. Here's ammunition for what often turns into a pitched, take-sides verbal brawl as well-intended educators try to reach a compromise on using Twitter (in fact, many Web 2.0 tools—blogs, wikis, discussion forums, and websites that require registrations and log-ins—can be added to the list) that works for all stakeholders:

Students learn manners
Social networks are all about netiquette. People thank others for their assistance, ask politely for help, and encourage contributions from others. Use this framework to teach students how to engage in a community—be it physical or virtual. It's all about manners.

Students learn to focus
With few characters, you can't get off topic or cover tangential ideas. You have to save those for a different tweet. Tweeple like that trait in writers. They like to hear the writer's thoughts on the main topic, not meanderings. When forced to write this way, students will find it doesn't take a paragraph to make a point. Use the right words, people get it. Consider that the average reader gives a story seven seconds before moving on. OK, yes, that's more than a tweet, but not much.

Students learn to share
Start a tweet stream where students share research on a topic. Maybe it's Ancient Greece. Have each student share their favorite website (using a #hashtag — maybe #ancientgreece) and you've created a resource others can use. Expand on that wonderful skill learned in kindergarten about sharing personal toys. Encourage students to RT (retweet) posts they found particularly relevant or helpful.

Writing short messages perfects the art of "headlining"
Writers call this the title. Bloggers and journalists call it the headline. Whatever the label, it has to be cogent and pithy enough to pull the audience in and make them read the article. That's a tweet.

Tweets need to be written knowing that tweeple can @reply
This is a world of social networks where people comment on what you say. That's a good thing. It's feedback and builds an online community, be it for socializing or school. Students learn to construct their arguments

expecting others to respond, question, and comment. Not only does this develop the skill of persuasive writing, students learn to have a thick skin, take comments with a grain of salt and two grains of aspirin.

#Hashtags develop a community
Create #hashtags that will help students organize their tweets—#help if they have a question, #homework for homework help. Establish class hashtags to deal with subjects you want students to address.

Students learn tolerance for all opinions
Why? Because Tweeple aren't afraid to voice their thoughts. Because the Twitter stream is a public forum (in a classroom, the stream can be private, visible to only class members), students understand what they say is out there forever. That's daunting. Take the opportunity to teach students about their public profile. Represent themselves well with good grammar, good spelling, and well-chosen tolerant ideas. Don't be emotional or spiteful because it can't be taken back. Rather than shying away from exposing students to the world, use Twitter to teach students how to live in it.

Twitter, the Classroom Notepad
I tried this out after I read about it through my PLN. Springboarding off student engagement, Twitter can act as your classroom notepad. Have students enter their thoughts, note, and reactions while you talk. By the time class is done, the entire class has an overview of the conversation with extensions and connections that help everyone get more out of the inquiry.

Twitter is always open
Inspiration doesn't always strike in that 50-minute class period. Sometimes it's after class, after school, after dinner, even 11 at night. Twitter doesn't care. Whatever schedule is best for students to discover the answer, Twitter is there. If you post a tweet question and ask students to join the conversation, they will respond in the time frame that works best for them. That's a new set of rules for classroom participation, and these are student-centered, uninhibited by a subjective time period. Twitter doesn't even care if a student missed class. S/he can catch up via tweets and then join in.

Article 10—Will texting destroy writing skills?

Will Texting Destroy Writing Skills?

Across the education landscape, student text messaging is a bone of contention among teachers. It's not an issue in the lower grades because most K-5 schools successfully ban cell phones during school hours. Where it's a problem are grades 6-12, when teachers realize it's a losing battle to separate students from their phones for eight hours.

The overarching discussion among educators is texting's utility in providing authentic experiences that transfer learning from the class to real life. Today, I'll focus on a piece of that: Does text messaging contribute to 1) shortening student attention span, or 2) destroying their nascent writing ability

Let's start with attention span. TV, music, over-busy daily schedules, and frenetic family life are likely causes of a student's short attention span. To fault text messaging is like blaming the weather for sinking the Titanic. Texting has less to do with the inability to spit out a full sentence than a student's 1) need for quickness of communication, 2) love for secrecy, and 3) joy of knowing a language adults don't.

What about writing? In the thirty years I've been teaching everyone from kindergarteners to college, I can tell you with my hand on a Bible that children are flexible, masters at adjusting actions to circumstances (like the clothes they wear for varying events and the conversations they have with varying groups of people). There is no evidence to support that these elastic, malleable creatures are suddenly rigid in their writing style, unable to toggle between casual texting shorthand with friends and a professional writing structure in class.

In general, I'm a fan of anything that encourages student writing, and there are real benefits to giving students the gift of textual brevity rather than the stomach-churning fear of a five-paragraph structured essay. I've done quite a few articles on the benefits of Twitter's approach to writing and my teacher's gut says the same applies to text messaging. Truth, studies are inconclusive. Some suggest that because young students do not yet have a full grasp of basic writing skills, they have difficulty shifting between texting's abbreviated spelling-doesn't-matter language and Standard English. But a British study suggested students classify 'texting' as 'word play', separate from the serious writing done for class so it results in no deterioration of writing skills. Yet another study found that perception of danger from texting is greater than reality: 70% of the professionals at one college believed texting had harmful effects on student writing skills. However, when analyzed, the opposite was true: Texting was actually beneficial.

It's interesting to note that texting can be a boon to children who struggle with face-to-face situations. These 'special needs' students flourish in an environment where they can write rather than speak, think through an answer before communicating it, and provide pithy conversational gambits in lieu of extended intercourse. In the texting world, socially-challenged children are like every other child, hidden by the anonymity of a faceless piece of metal and circuits

To blame texting for student academic failures is a cop-out by the parents and teachers entrusted with a child's education. Treated as an authentic scaffold to academic goals, teachers will quickly incorporate it into their best-practices pedagogy of essential tools for learning.

9 Things My Blog Taught Me

When I started blogging four years and 957 posts ago, all I knew was I wanted to connect with other tech teachers. Now, thanks to the 1,000,000+ people who have visited, I know much more of what I get from blogging:

How to write

Bloggers are divided into two categories: 1) those who write short, under-1000-word posts and 2) those who write in-depth, lengthy articles. I've chosen the former. I like pithy ideas that readers can consume in the time it takes to drink a cup of coffee. As a result, I've learned to be frugal with words. I choose verbiage that conveys more than one-word's-worth of information and I leave tangential issues for another post. Because I realize readers are consuming on the run, I make sure to be clear–no misplaced pronouns or fuzzy concepts like 'thing' or 'something'.

Prove my point

This part of writing transcends what print journalists must do. Yes, they do it, but blog readers expect ideas to include links to sources. If I'm reviewing a tech ed concept, I link to other websites for deeper reading. That's something that can't happen in paper writing. Sure, they can provide a link, but to put the paper down, open the laptop, copy that link–I mean, who does that? In a blog, I get annoyed if someone cites research and doesn't provide the proof.

Listen

When I write an article, I cross post it to other parts of my international PLN. And then I listen.

What are readers saying? What are their comments to me? Often, I learn as much from readers as what I thought I knew when I wrote the article.

For example, I get many emails from tech ed professionals with questions about the field. I used to answer them based on my experience. Now, I have my Dear Otto series where I share my thoughts and solicit input from readers. Wow–have I learned a lot! The flipped blog–teacher becomes student.

How to work through the dry times

I rarely have writer's block, but when I do, I jump into the blogosphere and see what my colleagues are writing. In my fiction writing, researching waters down the dry spells. The same works for blogging. I visit my favorite tech ed blogs, get inspired, research the pedagogy/topic, and often come up with my own take on it, based on my unique classroom experience.

How to persevere

Four years of blogging and I'm still waiting to make it big. What's that mean to me? I want that knock on my virtual door from *Byte* or *PC Magazine* asking me to come on board as a paid house blogger. Truth, that probably won't happen and by now, I've stuck it out so long I wouldn't know what to do if I stopped blogging.

There are lots of opinions out there

When I share thoughts on tech ed, sometimes I'm surprised at comments I get. They might touch a corner of the idea I hadn't thought of or be 180 degrees from my conclusions. It forces me to think bigger, consider how people who aren't me will read my words. That's humbling and empowering.

There are a lot of smart people in the world

In a previous lifetime when I built child care centers for a living, I read lots of data that said people thought the education system was broken–but not in their area. Well, as I meander through life, I realized that applies to everything. People are happy with what their status quo and frightened/suspicious of change. Through blogging, I get to delve into their reality because we are efriends. I've found that lots of people are smart, intuitive, and looking to improve the world. I'm glad I learned that.

How to be responsible

Yes, blogging is demanding. I have to follow through on promises made in my profile and posts. When I say I'll offer tech tips weekly, I have to do that even if I'm tired or busy with life. It's not as hard as it sounds. If you're a mom, you've got the mindset. Just apply it to blogging.

How to be a friend

My readers visit my posts and comment or poke me with a 'like'. Maybe, on good days, they repost. Those are nice attaboys. I always return the favor by dropping by their blogs to see what they're up to. It takes time, but like any relationship, is worth it. I have online friends I've never met who I feel closer to than half the people in my physical world. I've seen them struggle with cancer, new jobs, unemployment, kid problems. I've learned a lot about life from them.

4th Grade Technology Curriculum: Teacher Manual

Lesson #7—Google Earth

Vocabulary	Problem solving	Skills
• F4 • Grid • Interactive • Lat • Long • Mulligan rule • Power button • Tour	• How do I zoom in to Google Earth? • Students have difficulty dragging globe? Introduce arrow keys. • How do I play a Google Earth tour? • How do I move between cells (tab) • Where's 'bcc'? • What if I retake a quiz and get a lower score? (keep the highest)	**New** **Scaffolded** Google Earth basics Keyboarding
Academic Applications Geography, history, literature	**Materials Required** quiz results, Google Earth sample tour, lat-long practice, student workbooks (if using)	**Standards** CCSS.ELA-Literacy.RI.4.7 NETS: 1b, 3d, 5a, 6a

Essential Question

How can I understand my world more authentically?

Big Idea

Seeing the planet is so much more exciting than reading about it

Teacher Preparation

- Talk with grade-level team so you tie into conversations.
- Ensure that all required links are on student computers.
- Know which tasks weren't completed last week.
- Integrate domain-specific tech vocabulary.
- Collect words students for Speak Like a Geek Board.
- Know whether you need extra time to complete lesson.

Assessment Strategies

- Used good keyboarding habits
- Completed Board presentation
- Completed Google Earth project using prior years skills
- Understood GE contributes uniquely to understanding
- Worked well in a group
- Completed warm-up, exit ticket
- Joined classroom conversations
- [tried to] solve own problems
- Left room as s/he found it
- Higher order thinking
- Habits of mind observed

Steps

Time required: 45 minutes in one sitting or spread throughout the week with a block of 30 minutes for Google Earth

Class warm-up: Keyboarding—QWERTY row

_____Review blank keyboard quiz. Review **Mulligan Rule**: If student didn't do as well as they hoped on a quiz, they can retake for full credit. Few will and those that do will work to do better.

_____Any evidence of learning to post on Evidence Board?

_____Open Google Earth on your computer. IPads: Access app, but be aware there are differences between app and full-featured program. Know these and accommodate project requirements.

___Ask students what they remember about Google Earth from prior years—if you've used the SL technology curriculum (*Figure 47a* is kindergarten, *Figure 47b* is 1st grade; *Figure 47c* is 2nd grade, *Figure 47d* is 3rd grade).

Figure 47a—Google Earth project in K; 47b—1st; 47c—2nd; 47d—3rd

   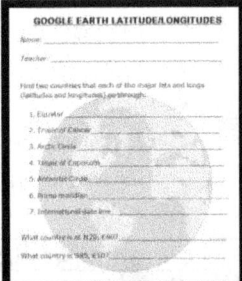

___Open Google Earth. Ask for a student volunteer to review what they remember about the program, using class screen. Include how to:

- *maneuver*
- *access layers*
- *search*

___Give students a few minutes to reacquaint themselves.

___Discuss latitudes and longitudes—nicknamed 'lats' and 'longs'. What have students discussed about these in class? What are they (*Hint: a way to identify anything on planet*)?

___Show students how to activate lats and longs (*Figure 48*). Ask students to identify yellow grid lines—equator, Tropic of Cancer/Capricorn, Arctic/Antarctic Circle, Prime Meridian.

Figure 48—Google Earth lats and longs

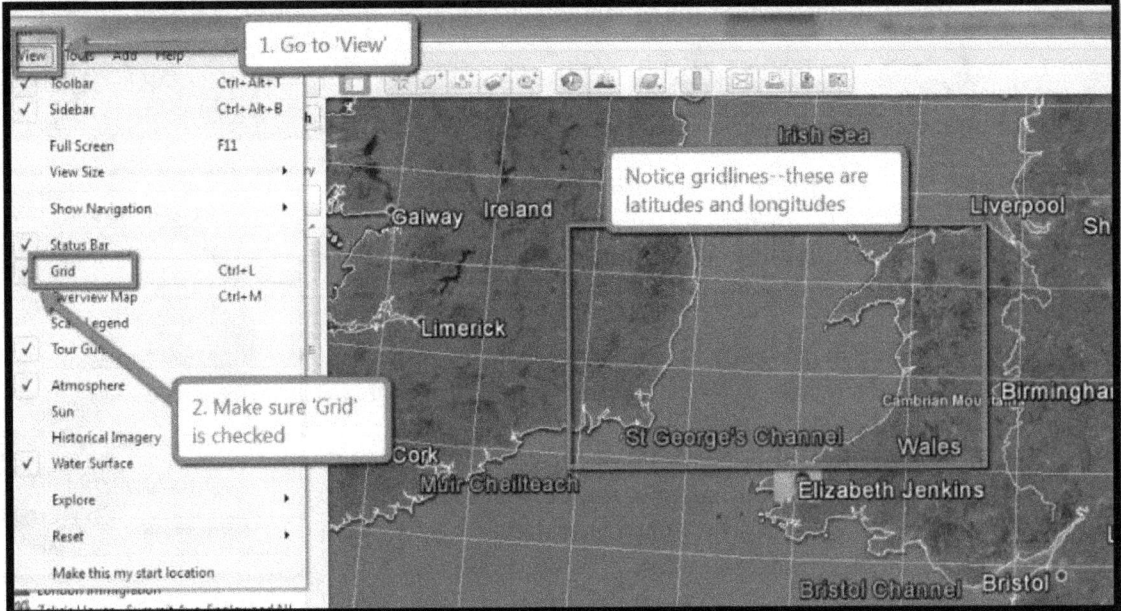

Assessment 10--Google Earth Practice

Name: _____ Teacher: _____

Latitude Practice

Open Google Earth. Find two countries or cities that cross each of the major Latitudes. Write names on the line next to that latitude.

If time, take Google Earth tour of a topic that ties into class discussion, i.e., habitats or landforms. Write down two examples of the topic for each continent. Click on the item for more information and/or watch included videos.

1. Equator 1)_____ 2)_____
    a. Option #1:_____
    b. Option #2:_____

2. Tropic of Cancer 1)_____ 2)_____
    a. Option #1:_____
    b. Option #2:_____

3. Arctic Circle 1)_____ 2)_____
    a. Option #1:_____
    b. Option #2:_____

4. Tropic of Capricorn 1)_____ 2)_____
    a. Option #2:_____
    b. Option #1:_____

5. Antarctic Circle 1)_____ 2)_____
    a. Option #1:_____
    b. Option #2:_____

_____Work in groups to *Assessment* worksheet. Worksheet can be loaded onto student iPads and filled out with an annotation tool or printed.
_____Hints:

- be sure 'Borders and Labels' layer is active
- zoom in or out until you can read the place location name
- drag globe until you find the place name

_____Take time to explore locations. Make sure '*3D Buildings*' layer is active so you can better see the local highlights.
_____Walk around and help when needed.
_____Submit sheet at end of class in the manner that works best for your class.
_____Throughout class, check for understanding. Expect students to solve problems as they maneuver through lessons and make decisions that follow class rules.

Class exit ticket: *Provide a list of features, continents, locations that tie into class discussions, places students will visit this year, and/or field trips coming up. Ask students to visit one on Google Earth and share a screenshot in the easiest manner available to your classroom (blog post, wiki page, or class online photo curator). Depending upon your digital devices, here are ideas for screenshots:*

- **Windows**: *the Snipping Tool*
- **Chromebook**: *hold down the control key and press the window switcher key*
- **Mac**: *Command Shift 4 to take a partial screenshot*
- **Surface tablet**: *hold down volume and Windows button at the same time*
- **iPad**: *hold Home button and power button at same time*
- **Online**: *a screenshot tool*

Differentiation

- Open sheet in word processing tool. Complete it digitally and submit via email.
- Add Google Earth lat/long project to class calendar.
- Have students play Google Earth tours created by last year's students or one you've installed that ties into class discussion. Encourage students to pause tour to explore an interesting location or feature.
- Early finishers: visit class internet start page for websites that tie into classwork.

All I need now is a computer and a ten year old kid to teach me how to use it.

— *Fletch in FLETCH LIVES*

Lesson #8—Coding

Vocabulary	Problem solving	Skills
• Coding • Debug • Hotkey • If-then • Macro • Programming • Sequence • Shortkey • Symbolism	• I don't know how to use the programming tool (experiment; be a risk-taker) • I don't like coding (why?) • My partner does lots of the work (that's OK if you do your part also) • I couldn't debug my program, (start at the beginning)	**New** Coding/programming Macros Hotkeys Programming shortkeys **Scaffolded** Problem solving Coding
Academic Applications Math, critical thinking, habits of the mind	**Materials Required** Coding links and memberships in onsite program (i.e., Code.org)	**Standards** CCSS: Standards for Math. Practice NETS: 4a-b, 5c-d

Essential Question

How do I use a program I've never seen before?

Big Idea

By thinking critically and using information from other parts of my life, I can create something new and useful.

Teacher Preparation

- Talk with grade-level team so you tie into inquiry.
- If you're the lab teacher, arrange with stakeholders to extend this lesson to one hour and fifteen minutes, to accommodate the nation-wide Hour of Code.
- Test Macro to be sure shortkey is not used for another function.
- Know which tasks weren't completed last week and whether they are necessary to move forward.
- Integrate domain-specific tech vocabulary into lesson.
- Collect words students don't understand to include in Speak Like a Geek Board presentations.
- If you offer afterschool tech help and it's manned by students, verify they will be there.

Assessment Strategies

- Anecdotal
- Completed exit ticket
- Worked well with partner
- Completed one hour of coding
- Joined classroom conversations
- Higher order thinking: analysis, evaluation, synthesis
- Habits of mind observed

Steps

Time required: 15 minutes to discuss problem solving, critical thinking, coding. 60 minutes for hands-on coding (75 minutes preferred).

Class warm-up: None

_____Skip presentations and Evidence Board this week.
_____Discuss critical thinking, problem solving.
_____Coding **teaches children to think.** Discuss programming concepts:

- *abstraction and symbolism—variables are common in math, but also in a student's education. Tools, toolbars, images—these all represent something bigger.*
- *creativity—think outside the box; develop solutions no one else has*
- *debugging—write-edit-rewrite; problem-solve; when you make a mistake, you don't throw your hands into the air or call for an expert. You look at what happened step by step and fix where it went wrong*
- *if-then thinking—actions have consequences*
- *logic—thinking through a problem from A to Z, understanding the predictability of movements*
- *sequencing—knowing what happens when; mentioned in Common Core standards for grades 1 through 5*

_____Share this with students and get their thoughts:

"In 1997, the New York Times reported, 'It may be a hundred years before a computer beats humans at Go.' It took 16 years."

_____December will host the **Hour of Code**, a one hour introduction to students on coding, programming, and why they should love it. It's designed to demystify code and show that anyone can learn to be a maker, a creator, and an innovator.
_____This unit may be done individually or in small groups.
_____Most people—students and adults—think programming looks like *Figure 49a* when it actually looks like *Figure 49b*:

Figure 49a-b—Programming

 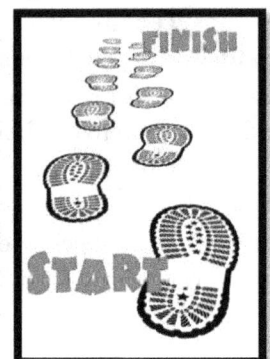

_____Do students remember previous years' activities—if you used the SL curriculum (*Fig. 50a-d*):

Figures 50a-d—Coding in K through 3rd grade

_____There are five approaches. Pick one that works for your student group:

1. Finding Language-specific Symbols
2. Using Alt Codes
3. Programming Shortkeys
4. Hour of Code lessons
5. Miscellaneous coding websites

Finding Language-specific Symbols

_____Shortkeys are two-three-key combinations that create a symbol, like *Figure 51*:

Figure 51—Popular unusual shortkeys

Desired Symbol	Shortcut Key Combination
à, è, ì, ò, ù, À, È, Ì, Ò, Ù	CTRL+` (ACCENT GRAVE), *the letter*
á, é, í, ó, ú, ý, Á, É, Í, Ó, Ú, Ý	CTRL+' (APOSTROPHE), *the letter*
â, ê, î, ô, û, Â, Ê, Î, Ô, Û	CTRL+SHIFT+^ (CARET), *the letter*
ã, ñ, õ, Ã, Ñ, Õ	CTRL+SHIFT+~ (TILDE), *the letter*
ä, ë, ï, ö, ü, ÿ, Ä, Ë, Ï, Ö, Ü, Ÿ	CTRL+SHIFT+: (COLON), *the letter*
å, Å	CTRL+SHIFT+@, a or A
æ, Æ	CTRL+SHIFT+&, a or A
œ, Œ	CTRL+SHIFT+&, o or O
ç, Ç	CTRL+, (COMMA), c or C
ð, Ð	CTRL+' (APOSTROPHE), d or D
ø, Ø	CTRL+/, o or O
¿	ALT+CTRL+SHIFT+?
¡	ALT+CTRL+SHIFT+!
ß	CTRL+SHIFT+&, s

_____*Figure 51* is for Word, but there are similar lists for Macs and Chromebooks. Most of these can also be invoked with Alt Codes (see next section).

Using Alt Codes

_____A coding secret is 'Alt codes'. These are symbols you invoke by typing Alt+[a number] on most digital devices. Have your students try out those that would be useful for them. For example:

Alt+0191 = ¿
Alt+0128 = €

_____Students who are writers or photographers will like the copyright symbol:

Alt+0169 = ©

_____Tip: Press the ALT key. While it is pressed, put in the numbers from your NUMBER PAD. It doesn't work using the numbers at the top of the keyboard). Make sure the NUM LOCK is ON.

Programming Shortkeys for Actions, Programs, Tools

_____Creating a shortkey will quickly become a favorite with your students. A popular use is to activate the screenshot program for the digital device you use.
_____Adapt the following directions for the device you use. These are for the windows platform:

- *Go to Start*
- *Right click on the desired program*
- *Select 'properties'*
- *Click in 'shortcut'*
- *Push key combination you want to use, say, Ctrl+Alt+S*
- *Save*

_____*Figure 52* is a video on how to create a shortkey (available on YouTube).

Figure 52—Create a shortkey

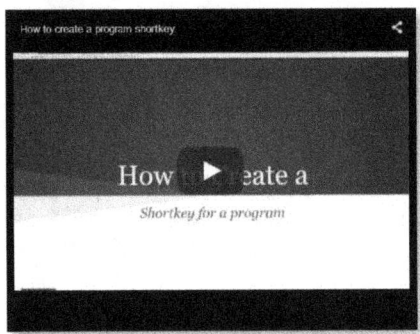

_____If you use iPads, these are called 'hotkeys':

- *Go to Settings > General Settings > Keyboard Settings.*
- *Scroll down and click "add new shortcut."*

Follow one of the free online Hour of Code programs

_____Websites like Code.org offer full lesson plans for Hour of Code. This is the easiest way to get involved in programming as they do all the planning for you. This may be exactly what you need.
_____Before trying this option, review digital citizenship –especially privacy and safety.

Miscellaneous websites

_____If you don't want to teach a specific skill, try these websites:

- Khan Academy Computer Science
- Scratch
- Snap!—runs in your browser

- Tinkercad–3D modeling–fee–perfect for 3D printing
- Wolfram Alpha widgets

_____Here are apps that take coding to an iPad if you're a 1:1 iPad school:

- MIT's App Inventor–build Android apps on a smartphone
- Cargo-Bot—logic iPad game
- Hopscotch (for up to intermediate–more complicated than Kodable)

_____Coding is a great tie-in to Common Core Math Standards. Any time you can show students how to use their math skills outside of math, it surprises them. They don't expect a discussion on problem solving or modeling to come from math.

_____Review the Common Core Standards for Mathematical Practice. If you are not a Common Core school, review the similar guidelines from your Standards:

- CCSS.Math.Practice.MP2
  Reason abstractly and quantitatively
- CCSS.Math.Practice.MP3
  Construct viable arguments; critique reasoning of others
- CCSS.Math.Practice.MP4
  Model with mathematics
- CCSS.Math.Practice.MP5
  Use appropriate tools strategically
- CCSS.Math.Practice.MP6
  Attend to precision
- CCSS.Math.Practice.MP7
  Look for and make use of structure
- CCSS.Math.Practice.MP8
  Look for and express regularity in repeated reasoning

_____Remind students to transfer knowledge to classroom or home.

_____Introduce this option after an overview of digital citizenship –especially privacy and safety.

Class exit ticket: ***Have students send you a screenshot of what they programmed. They can use any screenshot option they'd like, such as:***

- ***Windows****: the Snipping Tool*
- ***Chromebook:*** *hold control key and press the window switcher key*
- ***Mac****: Command Shift 4 to take a partial screenshot*
- ***Surface tablet****: hold down volume and Windows button at the same time*
- ***iPad****: hold Home button and power button at same time*
- ***Online****: a screenshot tool*

Differentiation

- *Early finishers: visit class internet start page for websites that tie into classwork.*

Article 12—Want to code on an iPad? 3 apps

Want to Code on an iPad? Here are 3 Great Apps

Coding has become the poster child for a tech-infused classroom. Over 15 million kids participated in Hour of Code this past December. So many teachers took students to Code.org's curriculum offerings, the website crashed.

So what is 'coding'? According to the Urban Dictionary, it's another word for 'programming' which means:

The art of turning caffeine into Error Messages

Let's go to Webster's definition instead:

The act or job of creating computer programs

Not much better. To techies, 'programming' or 'coding' is

a series of symbols, used synonymously as text and grouped to imply or prompt the multimedia in the games and programs that happen on computers, websites, and mobile apps.

This complicated definition is why—historically—programming, IT, and Computer Science have been of interest only the geekiest of kids. But there are good reasons why kids should like this activity. According to Computer Science Education Week:

- There will be 1 million more computing jobs than students over the next 10 years (adding up to $500 billion in salaries)
- More than 50 percent of all projected math and science occupations are in computing occupations.
- Computing occupations are among the highest-paying jobs for new graduates. Yet fewer than 3% of college students graduate with a degree in computer science.

But, the reason educators embrace coding is purer: **It teaches children to think.** Fundamental programming concepts include:

- *abstraction and symbolism—variables are common in math, but also in a student's education. Tools, toolbars, images—these all represent something bigger.*
- *creativity—think outside the box; develop solutions no one else has*
- *debugging—write-edit-rewrite; problem-solve; when you make a mistake, you don't throw your hands into the air or call for an expert. You look at what happened step by step and fix where it went wrong.*
- *if-then thinking—actions have consequences*
- *logic—thinking through a problem from A to Z, understanding the predictability of movements*
- *sequencing— what happens when; mentioned in Common Core standards for grades 1 through 5*

When kids learn to code, they also learn to thrive in the 21st Century world. No surprise the United Kingdom took the bold step of adding coding to the core school curriculum.

Most programming classes, training, and games take place on websites, but with the popularity of iPads, developers created apps to put the learning where kids live. As I evaluated three to share with you today, I measured them against the minimum standards for any app—be it coding or reading—used for education. These guidelines include:

- *support the '4 C's'—creativity, critical thinking, communication, collaboration*
- *offer compelling content (although this is subjective; 'compelling' varies teacher-to-teacher and student-to-student)*
- *are not distracting or overwhelming in colors, music, or activity*
- *offer levels that differentiate for student needs*
- *include few ads—and those that are there do not take up a significant portion of the screen*
- *are intuitive to use with a short learning curve*
- *don't collect personal information other than user credentials or data required to operate the app*
- *rated 'for everyone' or 'low maturity'*
- *include no in-app purchases or billing*

Based on these criteria, here are my top three:

Kodable

Kodable bills itself as a programming curriculum for grades K-2 that can be accomplished in twenty minutes a week. The main character is a chinless blue fuzzball with big eyes and a small mouth. The goal is to move him/her along a short track littered with coins by providing commands to indicate which direction the creature should go. Players use logical thinking and sequencing to complete the maze and win gold coins. As they improve, they level up, adding if-then analysis to their decision matrix, and the course gets more complicated.

Hopscotch

Hopscotch teaches basic computer programming concepts to children between the ages of 8 and 12. It uses no typing or syntax, just drag and drop blocks. The interface is simple, colors vibrant, and moves intuitive (at least as you start). Using it, students create games, animations, drawings and more while learning to make their characters do simple (and not-so-simple) moves.

Tynker

Free, Fee for upgrade bundles

Tynker, both the website and the companion app, teaches programming with puzzles to ages 3-8. You get twenty puzzles with the free app and can purchase more as needed. They are solved by stringing together commands in sequences using a drag-n-drop interface. No internet connectivity is required.

—*for an extended version of this article, including links, visit Ask a Tech Teacher.*

4th Grade Technology Curriculum: Teacher Manual

Lesson #9—Internet Research I

Vocabulary	Problem solving	Skills
• Address bar • Digital neighborhood • Extensions • Hits • Limiters • Netiquette • Right-click	• Password doesn't work? (Is it spelled correctly?) • How do I open a program • I forgot I was presenting today (is there room a later week?) • All the hits are .coms (add .org to the limiters)	**New** Website evaluation Searching the internet **Scaffolded** Digital citizenship Keyboarding
Academic Applications Research, quick research on a topic of interest	**Materials Required** Evidence Board badges, Problem-solving Board rubrics, links to internet sites	**Standards** CCSS.ELA-Literacy.W.4.7 NETS: 1c, 3a-d

Essential Question

How can I refine internet searches so I get information I need?

Big Idea

Students focus research on websites that address their interests

Teacher Preparation

- Have links to Digital Citizenship sites available.
- Talk with grade-level team so you tie into conversations.
- Ensure all required links are on student digital devices.
- Know which tasks weren't completed last week.
- Be prepared to integrate domain-specific tech vocabulary.
- Know if you need extra time to complete this lesson.
- If you are using Common Sense Digital Passport, have class log-ins available.
- Collect words students don't understand for Speak Like a Geek Board presentations.

Assessment Strategies

- Worked independently
- Used good keyboarding habits while typing
- Completed warm-up, exit ticket
- Joined classroom conversations
- [tried to] solve own problems
- Decisions followed class rules
- Left room as s/he found it
- Higher order thinking: analysis, evaluation, synthesis
- Habits of mind observed

Steps

Time required: 45 minutes in one sitting or spread throughout the week with a block of 30 minutes set aside for internet research project

Class warm-up: Keyboarding QWERTY row

_____Anything to post on Evidence Board? Anyone have tech problems they'd like help with?
_____Continue Problem-solving Board. Be encouraging—this can be difficult.
_____Before beginning a discussion of internet research, take SafeKids online quiz.
_____Why do we research? Encourage students to move beyond broad responses such as 'for classwork' or 'to find out something I don't know'. Overarching reasons include:

- *To build knowledge*
- *To present knowledge*

_____Discuss website address parts (see *Figure 53*).

Figure 53—Parts of a website

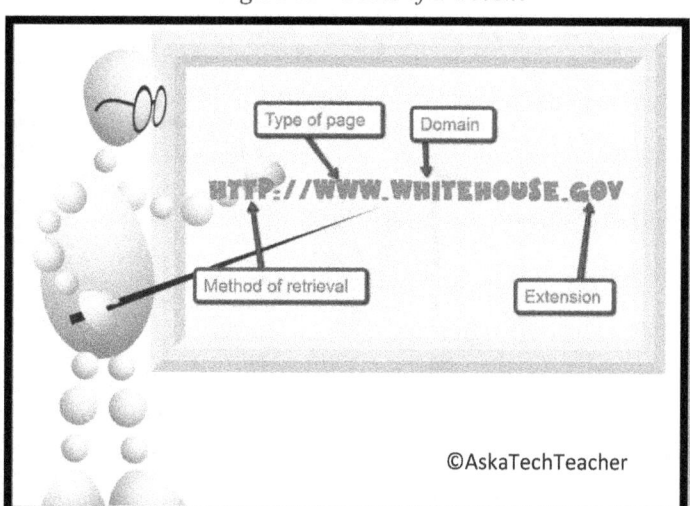

_____Discuss the types of extensions including foreign extensions:

- *Gov (government entities)*
- *Edu (colleges/universities)*
- *net*
- *org*
- *com*
- *foreign*

_____What do these extensions mean? Who can get them? Discuss how extensions relate to reliability and believability of material on the site. Does it matter if you're looking for a place to buy backpacks? How about if you're writing a research paper?

_____Consider why this is important:

- *How can you use websites to locate an answer to a question quickly or to solve a problem efficiently if you don't know the website is reliable?*
- *How can you explain how an author uses reasons and evidence to support particular points, and/or identify which reasons and evidence support which point(s) if you aren't convinced the reasons and points are accurate?*
- *How can you integrate information from several texts in order to write or speak about the subject knowledgeably if you don't know that the websites are knowledgeable?*

_____Watch and discuss BrainPOP's *Internet search video* together. If you don't have a subscription, choose another from the Ask a Tech Teacher resource pages.

_____Understand what contributes to successful internet searches:

- *keywords (using a + in front of a word to refine the search)*
- *knowing enough about the topic to pick strong keywords*
- *quotes ("")*

_____Practice with a topic students are discussing in class. Type *California Missions* (or one that fits your students)—no quotes—into the search bar. Notice the high number of hits.

_____ Now type "California missions" (with quotes)—you get less hits.
_____ Now type "California missions" Indians—adding a word refines hits.
_____ Now type "California missions" –'Santa Barbara'—the 'minus' sign leaves out sites.
_____ Throughout class, check for understanding.

Figure 54—Steps for internet research

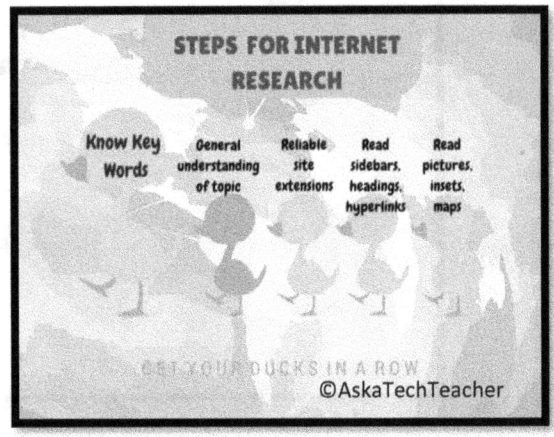

Class exit ticket: *In two minutes, ask students to post 4-5 words about that topic to a collaborative document (a Padlet wall, a Google Form, Google Spreadsheet, or another option that works for your student group).*

Figure 55a—Group research in Padlet; 55b—Google forms; 55c—Google Spreadsheets

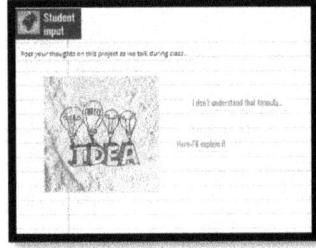  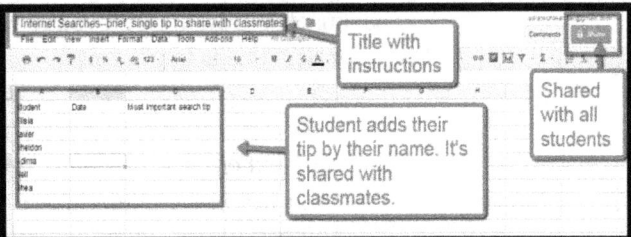

Differentiation

- Use Common Sense's Digital Passport 'Search Shark' to practice/teach internet searches.
- Search student name. Tie into discussion on online identities and reputations.
- Gamify search skills by adapting this Google Drive search game from Alice Keeler's website. Search 'Gamify Searching Google Drive.
- Keep track of digital citizenship topics covered with check list at end of lesson.
- Full digital citizenship curriculum for K-8 available from Structured Learning.
- Early finishers: visit class internet start page for websites that tie into classwork.

Lesson #10—Internet Research II

Vocabulary	Problem solving	Skills
• Diagram • Digital citizen • Fill • Flash drive • Hits • Limiters • Netiquette • Organizer • Save as • Taskbar • Toggle	• What is today's date?(Shift+Alt+D) • I can't find my document/folder (Start button-search) • Internet menu bar disappeared (F11) • My screen's too small (double click blue bar at top of window) • I have too many hits (Use "", +, -) • What's the difference between save and 'save as'? • How do I save to flash drive (save as) • Why are there shortkeys?	**New** Reliability of website **Scaffolded** Keyboarding skills Internet searches Digital citizenship
Academic Applications Research, writing, reading	**Materials Required** Board rubrics and badges, research questions, inquiry websites, student workbooks (if using)	**Standards** CCSS.ELA-Literacy.W.4.7 NETS: 1c, 3a-d

Essential Question

How do I share with classmates?

Big Idea

Focus research on websites that closely address interests

Teacher Preparation

- Talk with grade-level team so you tie into conversations.
- Ensure all required links are on student digital devices.
- Know which tasks weren't completed last week.
- Know if you need extra time to complete this lesson.
- Integrate domain-specific tech vocabulary.
- Have research skills worksheet and question list available online or hard copy.
- Collect words students don't understand for Speak Like a Geek Board presentations.

Assessment Strategies

- Completed evaluation questions
- Used good keyboarding habits
- Completed warm-up, exit ticket
- Completed project with partner
- Joined classroom conversations
- [tried to] solve own problems
- Decisions followed class rules
- Left room as s/he found it
- Higher order thinking: analysis, evaluation, synthesis
- Habits of mind observed

Steps

Time required: 45 minutes in one sitting or spread throughout the week with 30 minutes set aside for web evaluation exercise

Class warm-up: Keyboarding lower row (or QWERTY—whichever you've reached)

_____ Continue Problem-solving Board. Be encouraging—it's difficult to be the 'teacher'.
_____ Any problems students would like solutions to? Any evidence of learning for Evidence Board?
_____ Remember: Homework due end of each month.
_____ Remind students to safely travel the digital neighborhood (*Figure 56*—full size in Appendix):

Figure 56—Rules of digital neighborhood

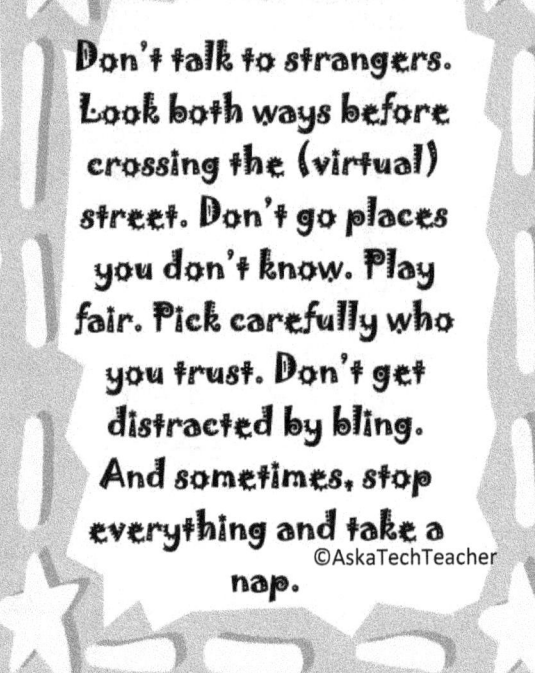

- *Stay on assigned websites*
- *Don't click ads*
- *Don't get distracted by bling*
- *Don't talk to strangers*
- *Follow netiquette rules*

_____Remind students about limiters that assist a search:

- " "
- +
- -

_____Once limiters are applied, evaluate websites based on content criteria:

- *Is author(s) credible/knowledgeable on subject?*
- *Is website publisher credible*
- *Is content accurate based on what you know? One mistake—be careful. Two—move on.*
- *Does content include depth in your topic*
- *Is information up to date*
- *Is website unbiased?*
- *Is website age-appropriate? Can students understand verbiage?*

_____Continue the conversation with this BrainPop video Research—online sources (search their site for the topic). Take the quiz together. If you don't have a BrainPop subscription, complete the web evaluation from Acadia University (find it with an internet search) as a group or in small groups. Complete questions, then discuss as a class.

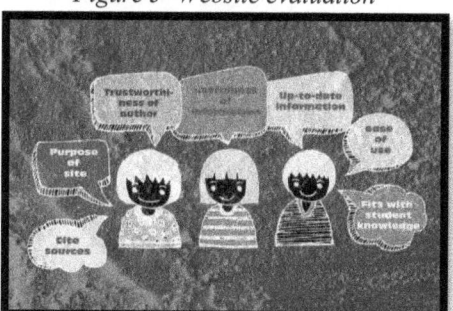

Figure 3--Website evaluation

_____Have a list of websites that tie into classroom discussion on a topic (it might be the same topic you used during the last lesson). Today, you'll evaluate one as a class and then small groups of students will evaluate another.

_____Before going to these: Discuss how some websites are hoaxes, how students can identify a 'spoof' website. Show students a fake website such as Zapatopi's tree octopus or Urban Legends doctored pictures. Are they real? Why? Don't reveal truth until everyone has had their say.

_____Most libraries evaluate websites based on:

- *purpose of the site*
- *trustworthiness of the author*
- *usefulness of the information*
- *up-to-date information*
- *ease of use*

_____Why is website reliability and credibility important?

- *How can websites answer a question if you don't know the website is reliable?*
- *How can you explain how an author uses reasons and evidence to support particular points in a text, and/or identify which reasons and evidence support which point(s) if you aren't convinced the reasons and points are accurate?*
- *How can you integrate information from several texts in order to write or speak about the subject knowledgeably if you don't know that the websites are knowledgeable?*

_____Demonstrate how to make decisions using the checklist on class screen.
_____Now students will work in groups to evaluate a website using the checklist.

- *Use search skills to find websites on a topic being discussed in class. For example, for Mars, select a website that looks interesting to your group.*
- *Evaluate the website using the checklist.*
- *If it does not meet requirements, select a different website hit.*

_____When you find a reliable website, complete a worksheet answering questions about your topic using the selected website. *Figure 58 is a sample—full-size Assessment at end of lesson*):

Figure 58—Sample website questions

Research Skills

Team members:

1_____ 2_____ 3_____

What is the largest valley on Mars?

    Keywords:_____

    Answer:_____

How does gravity affect satellites?

    Keywords:_____

    Answer:_____

What do rocks tell us about life on Mars?

    Keywords:_____

    Answer:_____

What else did you discover that interested you:

_____

_____

_____Remind students to transfer knowledge to classroom or home.

Class exit ticket: *Display a Padlet wall, a Google Form, or a Google Spreadsheet on class screen. As each student leaves, ask them to share one element of a website that makes the student trust the information.*

Differentiation

- *Fill out worksheet on computer rather than printing.*
- *Google student name. Tie this into inquiry into online identities.*
- *Anytime you can inject tech into the class, do it! For example—take a video of students working at their computers and upload to class website/blog/wiki.*
- *Students who finish can visit class start page for websites that go along with classwork.*

Assessment 11—Research Skills worksheet

Research Skills

Team members:

1_____ 2_____ 3_____

What is the largest valley on Mars?

Keywords: _____ _____

Answer: _____ _____

How does gravity affect satellites?

Keywords: _____ _____

Answer: _____

What do rocks tell us about life on Mars?

Keywords: _____ _____

Answer: _____ _____

What else did you discover that interested you?

_____

_____

4th Grade Technology Curriculum: Teacher Manual

Lesson #11—Halloween Greetings

Vocabulary	Problem solving	Skills
• Blinking • Clip-art • Ctrl+P • Cursor • Font • Format • Highlighter • Log-on • Save-as • Squiggles • Watermark	• Double-click doesn't work? (enter) • Program disappeared (check taskbar) • Save early, save often • It's hard to highlight a word (click inside word and then format) • How do I save to a flash drive? • How do I add a footer?(Double click space at bottom of page) • Do I save or save-as? (What are you saving and why?)	**New** Adding citations **Scaffolded** Word processing Keyboarding Adding images
Academic Applications Writing, literacy	**Materials Required** Problem-solving Board rubrics, Evidence Board badges, word processing program. Rubrics, student workbooks (if using)	**Standards** CCSS.ELA-Literacy.W.4.3 NETS: 4b, 6a

Essential Question

How do I tell a story so the reader gets wrapped up in it?

Big Idea

Write a narrative to develop real or imagined experiences using effective technique and descriptive details

Teacher Preparation

- Remind grade team students need a story they've written for tech lesson.
- Talk with grade team to tie into their writing lessons.
- Know which tasks weren't completed last week.
- Integrate domain-specific tech vocabulary.
- Collect words students don't understand for Speak Like a Geek Board presentations.
- Know if you need extra time to complete this lesson.

Assessment Strategies

- Completed rubric and project
- Showed evidence of learning from prior lessons
- Followed directions
- Used effective technique, event sequences, descriptive details
- Used good keyboarding habits
- Completed warm-up
- Joined classroom conversations
- [tried to] solve own problems
- Decisions followed class rules
- Left room as s/he found it
- Higher order thinking: analysis, evaluation, synthesis
- Habits of mind observed

Steps

Time required: 45 minutes in one sitting or spread throughout the week with a block of 30 minutes for writing project

Class warm-up: Keyboarding lower row

_____ Continue Problem-solving Board presentations.
_____ Any evidence of learning to post on Evidence Board?

_____ Do students have a story written during core classroom time? If not, go get it.
_____ Open the word processing program you use at your school—MS Word, Office 365, Open Office, Google Docs, Notes. Review layout with students if necessary.
_____ If you have iPads, you can use the free Microsoft and Mac apps, but be familiar with these as they will have differences from the fully-functioning software or online tools.
_____ Remind students of their many word processing projects—if you've been using the SL technology curriculum in past years (*Figures 59a-d*):

Figure 59a—WP project in 2nd; 59b—2nd; 59c—3rd; 59d—3rd

  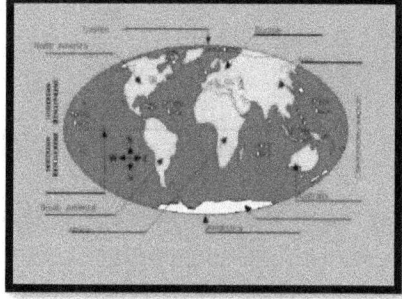

Once there was a ghost, a   and a pumpkin. They lived in a haunted house.

Guess what their favorite holiday was?

_____ Review tips in articles at the end of the lesson on MS Word and Google Docs.
_____ Students take the next half hour to type and format a story they've written. It will:

- *orient the reader by establishing a situation and introducing a narrator and/or character*
- *organize an event sequence that unfolds naturally*
- *use narrative techniques, such as dialogue, description, and pacing, to develop experiences and events or show the responses of characters to situations*
- *use a variety of transitional words, phrases to manage the sequence of events*
- *use concrete words and phrases and sensory details to convey events precisely*
- *provide a conclusion that follows from the narrated experiences or events*

_____ It should take less than fifteen minutes to type. Do the math with students:

300 words per page
WPM rate of 25 WPM
300 /25 = 12 minutes

_____ When done typing, provide evidence of student tech skills as included in *Assessment 12*:

- *heading page*
- *title*
- *story with various fonts, colors, sizes, writing details*
- *pictures to support writing*
- *border*
- *professional appearance*
- *'The End' in Word Art or another title font and appearance*

Assessment 12—Word processing rubric

HALLOWEEN STORY—GRADING RUBRIC

Name_____

Date_____

Teacher's Name_____

1. Heading with name, date, teacher   _____
2. Strong title   _____
3. Several lines of story   _____
   a. 5 different fonts   _____
   b. 5 different size fonts   _____
   c. 5 different colors   _____
   d. Descriptive details   _____
   e. Clear event sequences   _____
   f. Effective technique   _____
   g. Spell-check   _____
   h. Grammar check   _____
   i. Writing skills   _____
   j. Details highlighted   _____
4. Well-thought-out WordArt title   _____
5. 5 pictures   _____
6. Story fills page, but not more   _____
7. Professional appearance   _____
8. A festive border   _____
9. Footer (extra credit)   _____
10. Watermark (extra credit)   _____

Q: What was the witch's favorite subject in school?

A: Spelling
   http://www.kidsdomain.com/holiday/halloween/games/jokes.html

---

_____Remind students that picture goes where cursor is blinking. Resize as needed. If using online images, discuss copyright protections and citations.

_____Before adding title, discuss how to come up with one. It must:

- *be concise and pithy*
- *draw the reader in*
- *be exciting*

_____If you haven't discussed adding citations to a document before, do so today (*Figure 60*):

- *in a Word doc*
- *in a Google Doc*
- *using a different digital device you use in your school*

Figure 60—Images in word processing

_____Remind students: Every time they use digital device, practice good keyboarding.

_____Here are two samples: *Figure 61a* in MS Word (or Office 365) and *Figure 61b* in Google Docs:

Figure 61a—Word processing in Word; 61b—in Google Docs

_____When finished, work with a partner to be sure story includes required elements from the assessment rubric as well as:

- Use technology to spell- and grammar-check (red and green squiggly lines). Explain to students that grammar-check is often wrong so students must decide themselves whether to accept corrections.
- Use synonym finder (right click) to add descriptive detail and replace repetitive words.

_____Use program highlighter to create a legend of writing skills used in story:

- *Descriptive details*
- *Clear event sequences*
- *Effective dialogue*
- *Conventions being emphasized in 4th grade writing*

_____Student reads neighbor's story. Highlight passages that fulfill the requirements of the legend they created. *Figure 62* is an example:

Figure 62—Highlighting in word processing

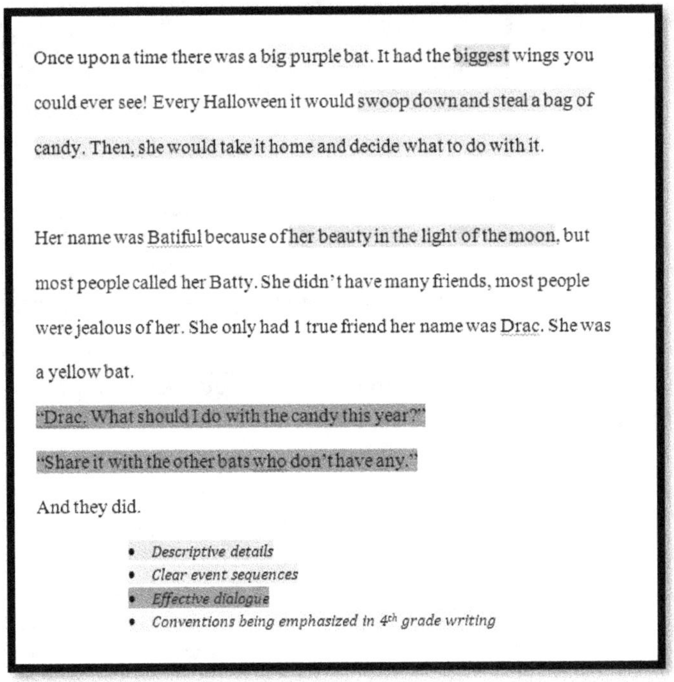

> Once upon a time there was a big purple bat. It had the biggest wings you could ever see! Every Halloween it would swoop down and steal a bag of candy. Then, she would take it home and decide what to do with it.
>
> Her name was Batiful because of her beauty in the light of the moon, but most people called her Batty. She didn't have many friends, most people were jealous of her. She only had 1 true friend her name was Drac. She was a yellow bat.
> "Drac. What should I do with the candy this year?"
> "Share it with the other bats who don't have any."
> And they did.
> - *Descriptive details*
> - *Clear event sequences*
> - *Effective dialogue*
> - *Conventions being emphasized in 4th grade writing*

_____Look at neighbor's highlights. Discuss.
_____When done, save to digital portfolio; save-as to flash drive (if available). Why 'save' once and 'save-as' the second time? What's the difference?
_____Print preview—does story fit on one page? Resize images and fonts as needed.
_____Mulligan Rule in effect.
_____Throughout class, check for understanding.

Class exit ticket: None

Differentiation

- Insert watermark that says 'Happy Halloween' (or similar).
- Insert footer with student name. Explain the purpose of a footer. This story doesn't need one, but you want students to learn the skill.
- Add Story to class calendar.
- Students who finish can visit class internet start page for class-themed websites.

> "I have traveled the length and breadth of this country and talked with the best people, and I can assure you that data processing is a fad that won't last out the year."
>
> - The editor in charge of business books for Prentice Hall, 1957

Article 13—7 MS Word Tricks

7 MS Word Tricks Every Teacher Should Know

Computers are a foreign language. Even with small class sizes, the more students can do for themselves, the more fun they have learning the intricacies of technology.

The good news: Students love independence. It's cool to know something no one else can. In my class, students love showing off their problem-solving skills by helping neighbors. Here are 7 tricks that cover common problems students face with MS Word:

1. Ctrl+Z–undo
   This will be your favorite. There are too many times I've had a frantic student, almost in tears because s/he thought s/he'd lost his/her document, and I retrieved it in two seconds. I was a hero for a period.

2. Macro for a heading
   This is great for students who have to remember MLA rules. What goes in a heading? How big are margins? Where's a page number go? No worries. Create a macro and save as a template.

3. How to find lost documents
   It takes a while to get accustomed to saving files on a network. Often, documents end up lost. My students learn early to use 'search' on the start menu.

4. How to insert data
   The 'insert' key is so confusing it's disappearing from newer keyboards. If students complain they lose data as they type, this is probably why. Show them how to push 'insert' and all will be fixed.

5. Show-hide tool.
   *Kids try to strong-arm Word into doing their will–often the wrong way. My favorite is 'enter enter' to double space. It seems to work until they have to edit, and then everything gets messed up. Have students push **show-hide** to see if they're using the double space tool.*

6. Tables—they work so much better than columns and tabs.
   *Teach it to kids **early and use it often**. It will save you miles of distress.*

7. How to insert the date
   *It takes until Middle School for students to remember the date. Until then, show them **Shift+Alt+D to insert** current date.*

Article 14—9 Google Docs tricks

9 Google Docs Tricks Every Teacher Should Know

The list below highlights tools that are available only in Google Docs and in my estimation make a big difference in an academic setting. See if you agree:

1. **Revision History**
   Use revision history to track student involvement and go back in time to a version that worked better

2. **Share/Collaborate**
   Multiple students can use the same document and it is automatically saved to their Google account. Take advantage of that for note-taking, projects, wherever it's suited. The document is automatically shared with all stakeholders (rather than 'save as' to multiple accounts).

3. **Research**
   Use the 'Research function to insert graphics so citations are seamless

4. **Don't worry about saving**
   Google does that for you—constantly. Once a document is created it is automatically saved to the cloud

5. **Spell-check on only the red line**
   There's no 'spell check tool' or F7. Find the red squiggle, right click, pick the correct spelling (or use Research to assist)

6. **Download As**
   Create the document in Google Docs, but download it in any format—Office, Open Office, whatever works for stakeholders. Some users may not be comfortable with Google Docs—help them out by sending the doc as an MS Word

7. **Embed**
   Once a document is created in Google Apps, it can be embedded into a student blog, class website, a wiki, or any number of online locations. Called 'publishing', this is simple, requires an html code that is automatically generated by the program.

8. **Copyright-free images**
   Available through Google, Life, and stock images. This is similar to MS Office's clipart gallery, but a different selection of images

9. **Easily insert comments**
   Add notes to a collaborative document so stakeholders can see ideas from other members. These are automatically created and shared with involved parties. This is possible in MS Word, but not as smoothly.

Lesson #12—Word Processing Tables I

Vocabulary	Problem solving	Skills
• 4x5 • Categories • Cells • Columns • Handles • Rows • Shift-tab • Table	• I deleted my work (Ctrl+Z) • What's today's date (Shift+Alt+D) • I ran out of rows! (click in the last cell of table and push tab) • There's not enough room (keep typing; cell increases in size) • Column is too narrow (drag margin to resize)	**New** **Scaffolded** Table skills Keyboarding skills Digital citizenship Problem-solving strategies
Academic Applications Research, writing, speaking and listening	**Materials Required** word processing program with table facility, Board rubrics, Evidence Board badges	**Standards** CCSS.ELA-Literacy.SL.4.4 NETS: 4b, 5b

Essential Question

How do tables help me present information clearly?

Big Idea

Tables allow information to be organized neatly and effectively

Teacher Preparation

- Talk with grade-level team so you tie into conversations.
- Ensure all required links are on student digital devices.
- Know which tasks weren't completed last week.
- Integrate domain-specific tech vocabulary into lesson.
- Collect words for Speak Like a Geek Board presentations.
- Know if you need extra time to complete this lesson.

Assessment Strategies

- Developed and organized a table appropriate to task, audience, and purpose
- Used good keyboarding habits
- Completed warm-up, exit ticket
- Joined classroom conversations
- [tried to] solve own problems
- Decisions followed class rules
- Left room as s/he found it
- Higher order thinking: analysis, evaluation, synthesis
- Habits of mind observed

Steps

Time required: 45 minutes in one sitting or spread throughout the week with a block of 30 minutes for table project
Class warm-up: Keyboarding lower row

_____Continue Problem-solving Board presentations. If something consistently occurs (say, students don't speak loudly or look classmates in the eye), review guidelines. Get a thorough list from Common Core's 4th grade speaking/listening standards.
_____Any evidence of learning to post on Evidence Board?
_____Today: Start a two-week project using tables to recount data using appropriate facts and details that support the theme. Tables do that well.

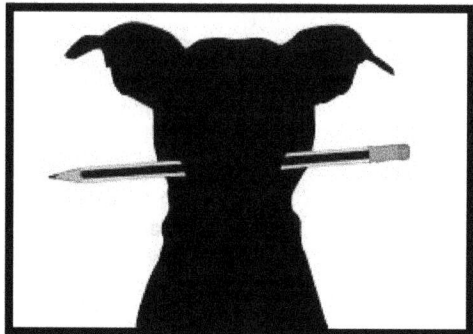

_____Do you remember tables in 2nd grade (*Figure 63a*—the Number Square)? 3rd grade (*Figure 63b*—vocabulary or *Figure 63c*—Landforms)--if you've been using the SL tech curriculum:

Figure 63a—Table in 2nd grade; 63b—3rd grade; 63c—3rd grade

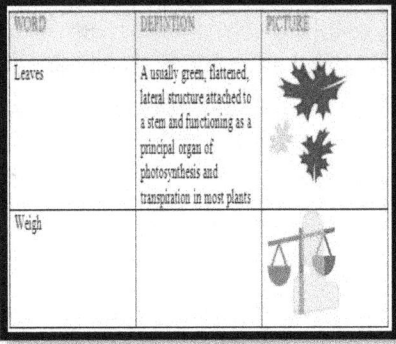
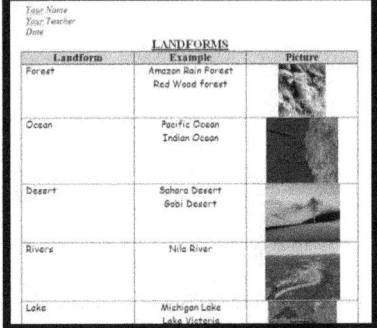

_____Show students the difference between information arranged in a table (*Figure 64a*) and arranged with tabs, columns, and/or returns (*Figure 64b*). Which is easier to understand? Which takes longer to create? Model both methods for students on the class screen:

Figure 64a—Organize data in table; 64b—in columns

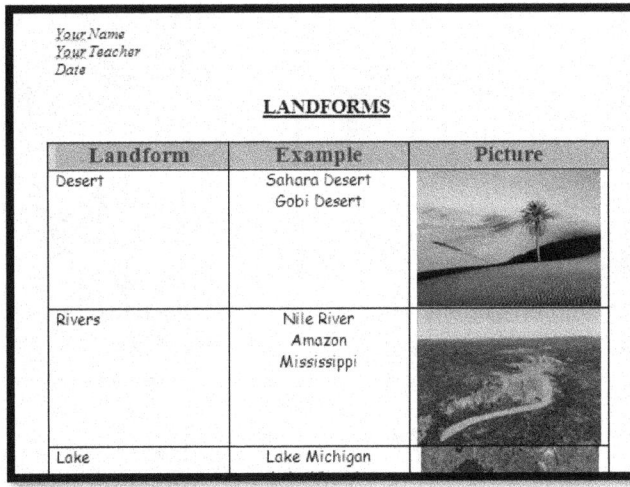
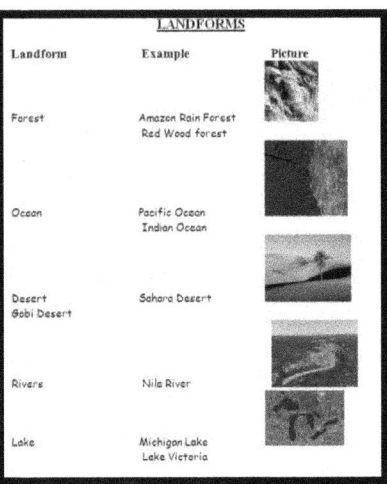

_____Where have students seen tables outside of school (maybe a sports roster)? Where have they seen them in school (*Figures 65a-b*—spreadsheet tables):

Figure 65a-b—Tables in Spreadsheets

_____Open a word processing program on the class screen (MS Word, Notes, Google Docs, or another) and model table creation as the class works along with you. Start by adding a 4x5 table with column headings (such as *Ecosystems, Example, Definition, Picture*) and row categories (such as *Mountains, Coast, Desert*). Figures 66a-b is an example using word processing:

Figure 66a-b—How to build a table

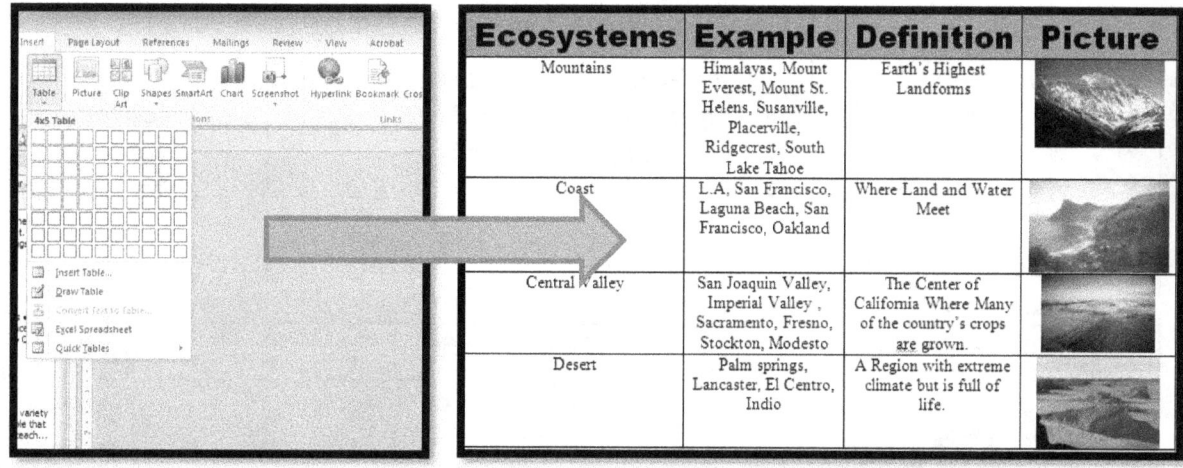

_____Discuss meaning and purpose of column 'headings' and row 'categories'.
_____Center column headings; use #22 font, caps lock, bold.
_____Optional: Shade heading row so it stands out.
_____Discuss each ecosystem included in the row categories. Fill cells based on the class input. Notice how cell enlarges to accommodate more information.
_____Basic table skills from 3rd grade:

- *tab moves right*
- *shift+tab moves left*
- *enter adds another line in the cell*
- *tab in the last cell adds a new row*

_____Finish table by filling in the rest of column one-three (skip 'Picture' column until next week).
_____Check grammar and spelling with red and green squiggly lines.
_____Throughout class, check for understanding.
_____Save to digital portfolio. What's the difference between 'save' and 'save as'?

Class exit ticket: **Students check each other's digital portfolio to be sure table is saved correctly. It will be used next week.**

Differentiation

- *Early finishers: visit class internet start page for websites that tie into classwork.*
- *Add table project to class calendar.*

4th Grade Technology Curriculum: Teacher Manual

Lesson #13—Word Processing Tables II

Vocabulary	Problem solving	Skills
• Cell • Clipboard • Copyright • Crop • Fair use • Format picture • Public domain • Table • Tool • Wrap	• Can't move image? Change 'Wrap'. • Digital device doesn't work (help students solve the problems) • My computer crashed (did you save early save often?) • Project takes two pages (resize images) • There's a word across internet picture (it's copyrighted)	**New** Legalities of using online images **Scaffolded** Table skills Digital citizenship Keyboarding
Academic Applications Any topic that requires organizing—research, report, writing	**Materials Required** word processing program with table facility, image websites, presentation board rubrics, Evidence Board badges	**Standards** CCSS.ELA-Literacy.SL.4.8 NETS: 4b, 5b

Essential Question

How do tables present information in an organized fashion?

Big Idea

Tables organize information neatly and effectively

Teacher Preparation

- Talk with grade-level team so you tie into conversations.
- Know which tasks weren't completed last week.
- Know if you need extra time to complete this lesson.
- Integrate domain-specific tech vocabulary.
- Collect words for Speak Like a Geek Board.
- Have images available OR set Google to Safe Search. Need ideas? Check Ask a Tech Teacher resource page.

Assessment Strategies

- Transferred knowledge from last week
- Organized info appropriately
- Submitted project
- Worked independently
- Used good keyboarding habits
- Completed warm-up, exit ticket
- [tried to] solve own problems
- Decisions followed class rules
- Left room as s/he found it
- Higher order thinking: analysis, evaluation, synthesis
- Habits of mind observed

Steps

Time required: 45 minutes in one sitting or spread throughout the week with a block of 20 minutes to finish table project

Class warm-up: Keyboard all keys on class typing tool

_____Any evidence of learning to post on Evidence Board?
_____Finish Problem-solving Board presentations.
_____If you are the tech teacher, remind students to bring an example of something they are currently writing in class next week—a story, a narrative, a report will work fine.
_____Open table started last week. If student can't find project, try these ideas (*Figure 67*):

- *Did you save it to the local drive—never save there.*
- *If you saved it with **your name in the file name**, search for it. Go to **Start>Search**. Type your last name in the 'Search' field.*
- *Can't find it? **Where were you sitting**? Search can only find files on the network. Did you save on the local drive where you were sitting? Check last week's seat.*

Figure 67—I can't find my file

_____Finish entering data into three columns.

_____Done? Add pictures to the fourth column. Search the internet for an image of each Ecosystem (or whatever topic you are writing about) and copy-paste it into table.

_____Before beginning, discuss the use of internet images. Can you use any you find? Review inset below. What is '**public domain**', '**works of art, copyright, 'fixed', tangible medium, single copy,** and **scholarly research**? Why does **Fair Use** allow you to use images (a single use) but your mother can't use them for a flier she's creating for your soccer team? Does 'scholarly research' include using internet images for a birthday card for dad?

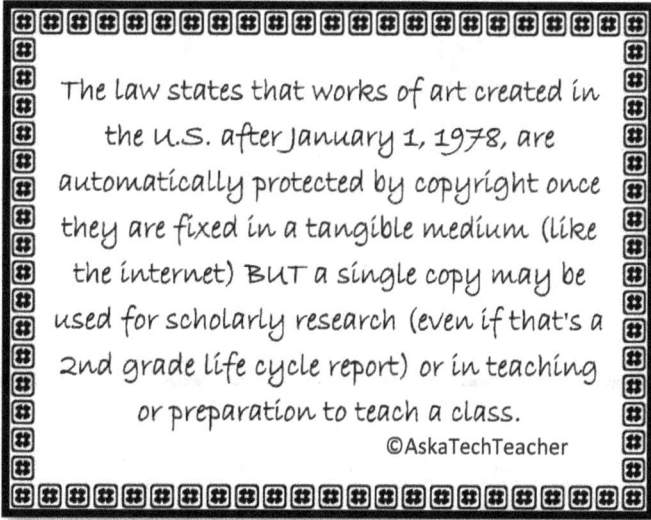

_____Using appropriate websites (find public domain pictures on Ask a Tech Teacher's resource pages for Images) and safe search methods (*Figure 68* shows how to turn on Google SafeSearch), find *ecosystem* images. Copy with a right-click.

Figure 68—How to turn on SafeSearch

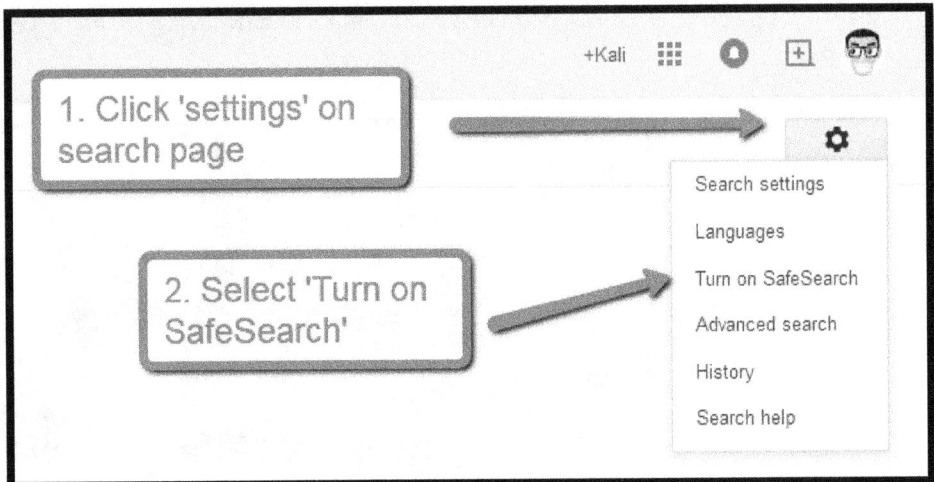

_____If students don't understand 'copy with a right click', explain. Ask where right-click copies to:

Figure 69—How to use clipboard

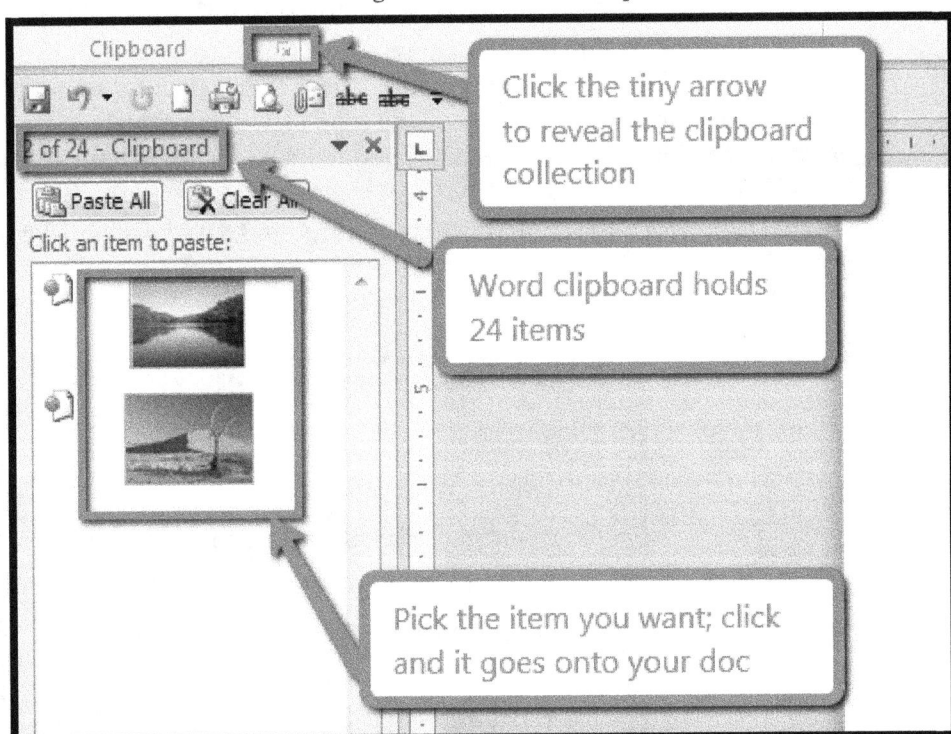

_____Paste image into correct cell; resize as needed to fit. Repeat for each ecosystem.
_____Use crop tool to remove any unneeded part of picture.
_____Review table with neighbor:

ECOSYSTEMS			
Ecosystems	Example	Definition	Picture
Mountains	Himalayas, Mount Everest, Mount St. Helens, Susanville, Ridgecrest, South Lake Tahoe	Earth's Highest Landforms	
Coast	L.A, San Francisco, Laguna Beach, San Francisco, Oakland	Where Land and Water Meet	
Central Valley	San Joaquin Valley, Imperial Valley, Sacramento, Fresno, Stockton, Modesto	The Center of California Where Many of the country's crops are grown.	
Desert	Palm springs, Lancaster, El Centro, Indio	A Region with extreme climate but is full of life.	

- *Is related information grouped together?*
- *Is appearance pleasing?*
- *Is information accurate?*
- *Is spelling accurate?*

_____Check print preview. Is everything on one page? Save to digital portfolio; save-as to a back-up location if you do that in your school. What's the difference between 'save' and 'save as'?

_____Throughout class, remind students to 'save early save often'. What does this mean?

_____Print/save/share/publish as appropriate in your class. Mulligan Rule in effect.

Class exit ticket: **Students check each other's digital portfolio to be sure table is saved correctly. It will be used next week.**

Differentiation

- Show students how to create and activate a table link to additional information.
- Save as a PDF or .jpg and publish to class website or wiki.
- Show students how clipboard item can be pasted into, say, a spreadsheet tool.
- Students who finish visit the class internet start page for websites that go with class inquiry.

Compaq is considering changing the command "Press Any Key" to "Press Return Key" because of the many calls asking where the "Any" key is.

Lesson #14—Word Processing Editing

Vocabulary	Problem solving	Skills
• Dialogue • Dialogue box • Format • Modal auxiliaries • Prepositions • Prepositional phrases • Red/green squiggles • Right click • Spell check • Tense	• Can't exit program (Alt+F4) • My document disappeared • There's a red squiggle under my word (right click and correct) • What's a green squiggle? Blue? • I think green squiggle is wrong (why? Maybe you're right) • What's the difference between backspace and delete? • How do 'edit' and 'format' differ?	**New** **Scaffolded** Editing digitally Keyboarding Using word processing tools
Academic Applications Writing, grammar, language	**Materials Required** Speak Like a Geek signup, Evidence Board badges, word processing, writing sample with mistakes, grammar sites, workbooks (if using)	**Standards** CCSS.ELA-Literacy.CCRA.W.5 NETS: 1d, 3b

Essential Question

How do I use technology to make writing easier?

Big Idea

Word processing programs make it easier to write well

Teacher Preparation

- Have Speak Like a Geek Board sign-up sheets.
- Talk with grade-level team so you tie into conversations.
- Have examples of student writing to use for editing.
- Ensure that all required links are on student computers.
- Know which tasks weren't completed last week.
- Integrate domain-specific tech vocabulary.
- Know if you need extra time to complete this lesson.

Assessment Strategies

- Had writing sample available
- Signed up for Board
- Used good keyboarding habits
- Used proper language conventions in presentation
- Finished project
- Completed warm-up, exit ticket
- Worked well with partner
- [tried to] solve own problems
- Decisions followed class rules
- Left room as s/he found it
- Higher order thinking: analysis, evaluation, synthesis
- Habits of mind observed

Steps

Time required: 45 minutes in one sitting or spread throughout the week with a block of 25 minutes to edit/revise an authentic document
Class warm-up: Sign up for Speak Like a Geek board

_____Do students have tech problems to share? Any evidence of learning for Evidence Board?
_____Sign up for Speak Like a Geek Board. This is second of three Presentation Boards.

- *Post sign-up sheets by the class door where they're easily found. Include slips of paper (Figure 70) that students can track important information:*

Figure 70—Speak Like a Geek required info

My name: _____

My word: _____

My presentation date: _____

- *Alternatively, have sign-ups online. You might do that by one of these methods:*
    - *Google Calendar or spreadsheet (Figure 71a)*
    - *Padlet's calendar template (Figure 71b)*
    - *SignUp Genius*

Figure 71a—Sign ups with Google Apps; 71b—Padlet; 71c—Calendar

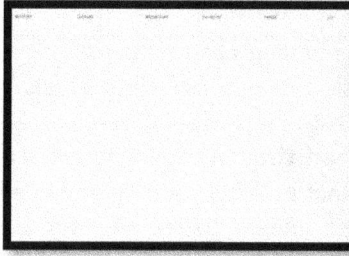

- *Each student signs up for a date to present.*
- *Each student selects a problem they will teach classmates to solve.*
- *Student gets solution from family, friends, or even teacher as a last resort.*
- *Presentation date: Student tells classmates problem, how to solve it, takes questions.*
- *Entire presentation takes about three minutes.*

_____Students may sign up in groups, as long as there is one problem solution per group member.

Assessment 13—Speak Like a Geek presentation rubric

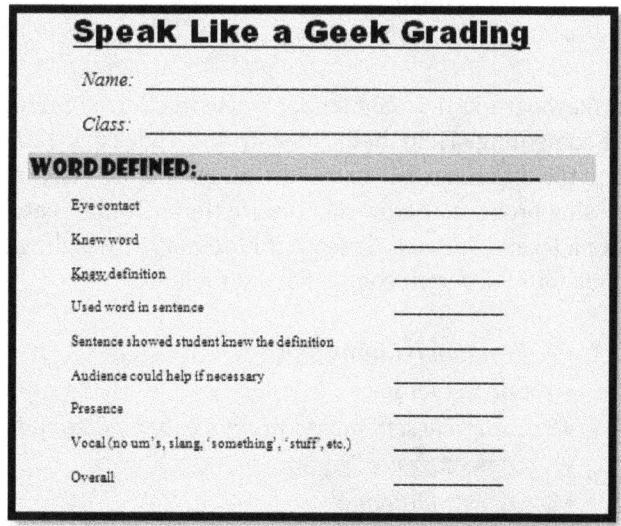

_____In Speak Like a Geek, students define a tech word and use it in a sentence that shows meaning (i.e., *I like formatting* is not good; *I format a letter by adding borders* is).

_____*Assessment 13* is an example of the Board assessment to share with students. Load digital copies for each student to your iPad or other digital device; use an annotation tool like iAnnotate to assess students; save and file as needed.

_____Today, discuss editing a draft, an important concept in Common Core and 4th grade writing:

> ***Develop and strengthen writing as needed by planning, revising, editing, rewriting, or trying a new approach.***
> —CCSS.ELA-Literacy.CCRA.W.5

_____No one writes perfectly the first time. Everyone must edit/revise/rewrite to get their words to match the ideas in their head. This project provides students with skills to accomplish this task.

_____Discuss with students the difference between **revising** and **editing**. Review Project #1-3 and select the one that best fits your writing needs. You can even adapt one to better fit your need for 'revise' or 'edit' skills.

_____Select one of these three projects for your student group.

Project #1

_____Bring up a paragraph on class screen written by an anonymous student. What mistakes do students see? Include (from Common Core CCSS.ELA-Literacy.L.4.1):

- *Pronoun relationships*
- *Correct tenses*
- *Modal auxiliaries*
- *Correct capitalization*
- *Correct dialogue*
- *Correct form and use of prepositional phrases*
- *Complete sentences—noun, verb, no fragment*
- *Correct order of adjectives in sentences*

_____What keyboard keys would students use to edit the middle of the paragraph—add a phrase? Or delete something? Help them come up with 'backspace' and 'delete'.

_____What's the difference between 'edit' and 'format'? What are the red and green squiggles in word processing programs? How reliable are they? Do they catch everything?

_____Create a legend (discuss 'legend' if necessary) by highlighting the editing conventions students will look for in different colors. For example:

- *Pronoun relationships*
- *Correct tenses*
- *Complete sentences—noun, verb, no fragment*
- *Correct capitalization*
- *Correct dialogue*

_____Figure 72_ shows mistakes color coded to match the categories above:

Figure 72—Highlighting writing conventions

> One way wildfires can occur is by campers cooking. They are started by accident. Another way a wildfire occurred by a spark of fire. A recent wildfire in the Angeles National Forest. It was on Labor Day Weekend 2012.
>
> I was curious about this fire; so asked my Uncle. His answer: 'Why do you need to know'?

_____Have students work in pairs for about ten minutes on the writing sample they brought to class or have available from a class project. Highlight different writing skills. They will be the same skills you are discussing in class.

Project #2

_____Go to Dr. Jerrold Zar's famous Candidate for a Pullet Surprise. Type his parody of spell check into a word processing document.
_____Use this to practice typing skills—elbows at sides, no flying hands, fingers on home row.
_____Before beginning, do mental math with students. How long will it take to type this selection?

224 words / 20 wpm = 12 minutes

_____When done, students replace their wpm speed to get the correct estimate.
_____When done typing, highlight Zar's errors. By his count, 127 of the 224 words in the poem are incorrect (although all words are correctly spelled). How many did students find?

Project #3

_____Can students fix these sentences using familiar writing conventions?

Figure 73—Confusing sentence

- Toilet out of order. Please use floor below. Would whoever took the step ladder please bring it back or further steps will be taken
- After tea break staff should empty the teapot and stand upside down on the draining board
- We exchange anything. Why not bring your wife along and get a wonderful bargain?
- The farmer allows walkers to cross the field for free, but the bull charges.

- Help! I am stranded on a dessert island!
- Would you like those eggs over easy or over easily?
- Let's eat Grandpa
- Your welcome.

_____Done? Have grammar websites where students can easily access them.

Class exit ticket: **Student signed up for Speak Like a Geek presentation board.**

Differentiation
• Show how to use Google's **define:[the word]** for definition.

Titanic Virus
Your computer goes down

Alzheimer Virus
It makes your computer forget where it put your files

Child Virus
It does annoying things, but is too cute to get rid of

Disney Virus
Everything in your computer goes Goofy

Lesson #15—Holiday Flier, Cover Page, Greeting

Vocabulary	Problem solving	Skills
• Backup • Border • Cover page • Ctrl+P • Double-space • DTP • Font • Layout • Placeholder • QWERTY • Schemes • Sidebar • Template • Text box • Text box • Title page • Watermark	• Can't find 'save' (use Ctrl+S) • Clicked file-print—nothing (Is there a clue on screen?) • How do I back up my work? • How do I fold this card? (top down, side-to-side) • I can't find my file folder (are you logged in as correct user?) • I can't type on page (did you add a text box?) • Not prepared for presentation (take a deep breath. You know more than you think) • Printer didn't work (where'd you print?) • What's 'A' mean at end of text box (text overflowed text box)	**New** Cover page Title page Compare-contrast productivity tools **Scaffolded** One-page greeting Compare-contrast skills Tables Online research Greeting cards Keyboarding skills Problem solving
Academic Applications Reports, greeting cards, community service	**Materials Required** DTP, Speak Like a Geek rubric, keyboarding program, word processing tool, Evidence Board badges, workbooks (if using)	**Standards** CCSS.ELA-Literacy.W.4.4 NETS: 4a-b, 6a-d

Essential Question

How do I use technology to create a quick one-page document?

Big Idea

Tech can create sophisticated materials for home and school

Teacher Preparation

- Know what event students can make fliers for.
- Have grading rubrics for Speak Like a Geek.
- Talk with grade-level team so you tie into conversations.
- Ensure that all required links are on student computers.
- Know which tasks weren't completed last week.
- Integrate domain-specific tech vocabulary.
- Know whether you need extra time to complete lesson.

Assessment Strategies

- Completed project
- Followed CCSS writing guidelines
- Properly used images
- Worked independently
- Used good keyboarding habits
- Completed warm-up, exit ticket
- Joined classroom conversations
- [tried to] solve own problems
- Decisions followed class rules
- Left room as s/he found it
- Higher order thinking: analysis, evaluation, synthesis
- Habits of mind observed

Steps

Time required: 45 minutes in one sitting or spread throughout the week with a block of 30 minutes for project
Class warm-up: Keyboarding on school typing tool

_____Speak like a Geek board starts today (or right after holidays). Students present information, take audience questions. Grade is based on knowledge and confidence. If necessary, review
_____Remember: Homework due end of each month (practicing all keys by now).
_____Any evidence of learning to post on Evidence Board?
_____Students start desktop publishing unit. What is 'desktop publishing'? What's different between the way DTP shares information and word processors? Prompt students to consider the importance of color, layout, and design elements in creating a project. Show students *Figure 74* and ask them as a group to fill in the blank cells.

Figure 74—Compare/contrast tools—A

Element	Presentation	Word processing	Spreadsheets	DTP
Purpose	Share a presentation	Share words		
Basics		Text, design second to content		
Sentences		Full sentences, proper conventions		
Content	Slides are like a bullet list			
Use		As complete resource		
Presentation		Speaker reads from document		
What else				

_____When they're done, it'll look something like *Figure 75*:

Figure 75—Compare/contrast B

Element	Presentation	Word processing	Spread--sheets	DTP
Purpose	Share a presentation	Share words	Turn numbers into information	Share information using a variety of media
Basics	Graphics-based Design is important to content Layout communicates Few words, lots of images	Text-based Design is secondary to content Layout may detract from words Primarily words communicate	Number-based Focus on tables, graphs Little text; lots of statistics and date Almost no words	Mix of media—equal emphasis on text, images, layout, color
Sentences	Bulleted, phrases	Full sentences with proper conventions	None	Full sentences, bullets,
Content	Slides cover basics, to remind presenter what to say	Thorough discussion of a topic. Meant to be complete document	Statistics, data, charts, graphs	To draw an audience in;
Use	As a back-up to presentation	As complete resource	To support other presentation methods	Good way to group information for easy consumption
Presentation	Speaker presents with their back to the slideshow	Speaker reads from document	Speakers uses it in a presentation or 1:1	Speaker passes out as a handout or take-way
What else				

_____Students have made fliers, cards, magazine covers with DPT if you used this curriculum in K-5:

135

Figure 76a—Fliers from 1st grade; 76b—2nd grade; 76c—3rd grade

_____Select one of the following three projects for your student group:

- *Fliers*
- *Cover pages*
- *Greeting cards*

Project #1: Fliers

_____Characteristics of a desktop publishing flier include:

- *clear, coherent, concise writing*
- *text, images, design engages the audience*

_____Discuss purpose of flier. Is there a holiday concert coming up? A play? A classroom event they'd like fliers to post around school? Pick one.

_____Review desktop publishing program used at your school (*Figure 77a* is from Publisher; *Figure 77b* is from Canva). *Figure 77a* includes steps to create a flier:

Figure 77a—DTP flier projects in Publisher; 77b—Canva

- *select template*
- *select themed picture*
- *add a title (i.e., Class Concert)*
- *add details*

_____If students get pictures from internet, discuss virtual neighborhood. How can they stay safe?
_____Save to digital portfolio; print/publish/share, as appropriate to your student group.
_____When finished, students work on the timeline for next week's trifold (called *My Life Events*).

- *Create a 3x10 table in a word processing program.*
- *Organize as 'Year', 'World Event', and 'My Event'.*
  - *'Year' is the nine years of the student's life, sequentially.*
  - *'World Event' is something big that happened around the world during that year of the student's life. The goal: Provide perspective on what the student experiences compared to what the world does.*
  - *'My Event' is a big event in the student's life. This isn't 'I had a birthday', rather 'I got a baby brother'.*

- *Fill in all required information. Provide resources for researching these events, such as Info Please's Year by Year.*
- *Figure 78 is an example:*

Figure 78—My Life Events timeline table

Year	World Event	My Event
2015	ISIS is considered by some the world's greatest threat	I changed schools
2014	Russia took Crimea from the Ukraine	My essay won a prize
2013	Beijing air pollution levels declared hazardous to human health	I received an award
2012	Kateri Tekakwitha became first native American saint	I won my first violin competition
2011	Osama bin Laden died	My brother joined the Army
2010	The Winter Olympics took place	We got a new dog
2009	Johanna Sigurdardottir took office as Iceland's first female prime minister.	My brother started college!
2008	Bobby Fischer died	My sister graduated from USNA
2007	Barry Bonds passed Hank Aaron as all-time American home run hitter	My dog got cancer

_____Students use their knowledge of creating tables in this project. Include:

- *one event per year in your life (column three—My Event)*
- *one event per year from around the world (column two—World Event)*

_____Students use their online research knowledge to select web-based information for their table.

Project #2: Cover Pages

_____Today, we create cover pages for a class project. What is the purpose of a cover page? Encourage students to come up with these:

- *Draw reader in.*
- *Provide information for categorizing work.*
- *Provide contact information.*

_____We'll use a word processing program (*Figure 79a*), but you can also use Publisher, Google Apps (*Figure 79b*), or an online free tool like Canva (*Figure 79c*).

_____Open program used in your school. Type in title page info (any font, size 36, Bold). Center vertically/ horizontally on page, double-spaced.

_____Add picture (i.e., mission) as watermark; add same picture at bottom as decoration; add border—no art borders. Why not?

_____Discuss why students can use internet images for this school project. Refer to:

- *copyrights*
- *fair use*
- *public domain*
- *scholarly research*
- *digital rights and responsibilities*

_____Students are familiar with cover page skills; expect them to act independently.

Figure 79a—Cover in Word; 79b—Google Apps; 79c—Canva

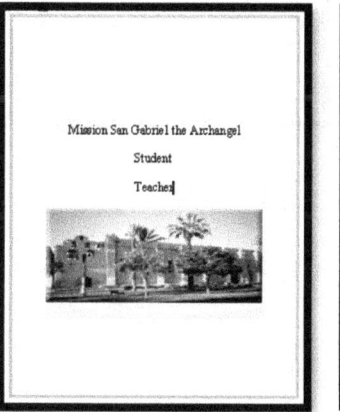

_____Before printing, check 'print preview' for layout.

Project #3: Greeting Cards

_____Remember designing cards in the past (if you've been using the SL tech curriculum):

Figure 80a—Greeting cards in 1st grade; 80b—2nd grade; 80c—3rd grade

_____*Figure 80a* is a one-page card in a drawing program created in 1st grade; *Figure 80b* is a one-page card in a desktop publishing program created in 2nd grade; *Figure 80c* is a folding card (like you might buy in a store) created in either a software or online tool in 3rd grade.

_____Use any desktop publishing program you have available in your school—or even an online tool. *Figure 81a* uses Word; *Figure 81b* uses Open Office; *Figure 81c* uses Google Apps; *Figure 81d* uses an online tool:

Figure 81a-d—Greeting card templates

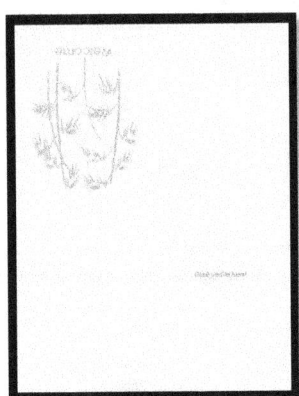   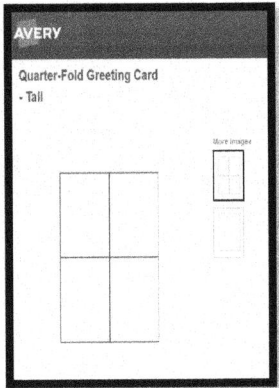

_____Open the desktop publishing program. Find the template for 'greeting cards'. How you do this will vary by digital tool. Preview the program first so you know how to accomplish this.

_____Discuss 'templates' with students, what they are, and their purpose for not only creating greeting cards but lots of other documents.

_____Since fourth graders have used this tool often in the past, let them work independently, adding images, editing text, and tweaking the layout. Help if they get stuck, but give them time to problem solve before you step in.

_____Those new to cards: Minimalize this. Just edit text and add a picture.

_____Greeting cards are excellent projects to practice writing conventions being reviewed in student classes. Consider forming the card's message to include skills being discussed in class, i.e.:

- *Use precise language and domain-specific vocabulary to inform about or explain the topic (CCSS.ELA-Literacy.W.4.2.d).*
- *Use relative pronouns (CCSS.ELA-Literacy.L.4.1.a).*

- *Spell grade-appropriate words correctly, consulting references as needed (CCSS.ELA-Literacy.L.4.2.d).*

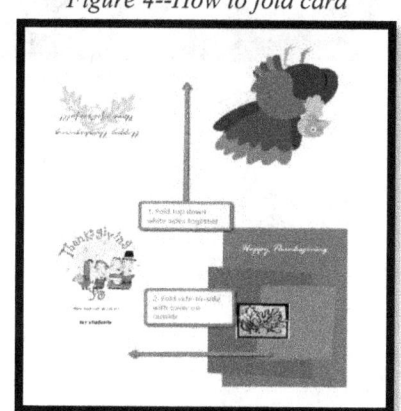

Figure 4--How to fold card

_____Save (Ctrl+S) to your digital portfolio. Print. If you need help folding, see *Figure 82*.
_____Save (Ctrl+S).
_____Throughout class, check for understanding.
_____When students finish, they can work on their My Life Events table in preparation for next week's project.

Class exit ticket: *Students show you how far they are on My Life Events table.*

Differentiation

- Add My Life Events table due date to class calendar.
- Add homework due date to class calendar
- Use cover page as a title page, with adjustments.
- Students go to Ask a Tech Teacher's holiday themed websites (on the resource pages).
- Anytime you can inject tech into class, do it! Students love seeing gadgets in action. For example—take a video of students working and upload to class website/blog/wiki.

Error, no keyboard. Press F1 to continue.

Lesson #16—Timeline Trifold I

Vocabulary	Problem solving	Skills
• Brochures • Color block • Graphic • Layers • Overflow • Panel • Perspective • Text tool • Trifold	• Takes too long to delete data? Drag a box around everything; delete. • Can't write on trifold (insert text box) • Writing doesn't show (Is there an 'A...'? Enlarge text box) • Can't get 1st and 3rd panel to match (copy-paste from one to other ; edit) • Color block doesn't show (layer) • Cover is on page 2 instead of 1 (doesn't matter)	**New** Trifold **Scaffolded** DTP Keyboarding Digital citizenship
Academic Applications History, literacy	**Materials Required** Speak Like a Geek rubrics, Evidence Board badges, DTP, extra completed timelines	**Standards** CCSS.CCRA.W.6 NETS: 3a-d, 4b, 6c

Essential Question

What audiences, tasks, purposes are perfect for DTP?

Big Idea

Different software/widgets are suited to different audiences, task, and purposes

Teacher Preparation

- Remind students to bring their timelines to class.
- Have spare timelines for students who forget.
- Talk with grade-level team so you tie into conversations.
- Ensure that all required links are on student computers.
- Integrate domain-specific tech vocabulary into lesson.
- Know whether you need extra time to complete lesson.
- Know which tasks weren't completed last week and whether they are necessary to move forward.

Assessment Strategies

- Anecdotal
- Completed list of timeline events
- Completed trifold page 1
- Worked independently
- Used good keyboarding habits
- Completed exit ticket
- Joined classroom conversations
- [tried to] solve own problems
- Decisions followed class rules
- Left room as s/he found it
- Higher order thinking: analysis, evaluation, synthesis
- Habits of mind observed

Steps

Time required: 45 minutes in one sitting or spread throughout the week with a block of 30 minutes for project

Class warm-up: None

_____Continue Speak Like a Geek presentations.

_____Do students have tech problems to share? Any evidence of learning to post on Evidence Board?

_____What is a 'trifold'? Share examples. How does a trifold communicate information more clearly than other methods?

_____This trifold can be for any topic that ties into class inquiry and requires a timeline. Our sample is 'This Day in History'. *Figure 83a* is the outside (page 1) of the trifold—the side that shows when it's folded. *Figure 83b* is the inside (page 2) of the trifold.

Figure 83a—Timeline trifold front; 83b—inside

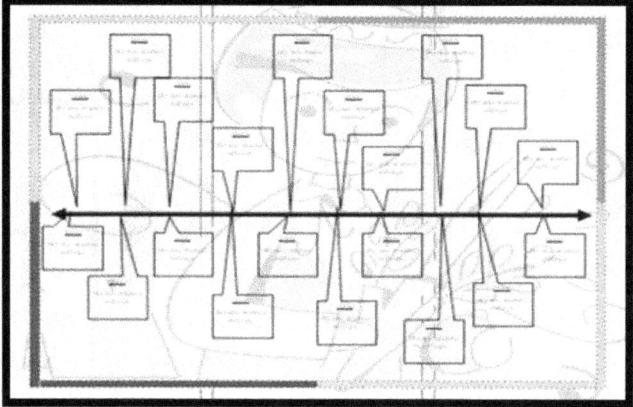

_____It uses the table students created—with important events in student's life and around the world. Students should have that table with them today:

Year	World Event	My Event
2015	ISIS is considered by some the world's greatest threat	I changed schools
2014	Russia took Crimea from the Ukraine	My essay won a prize
2013	Beijing air pollution levels declared hazardous to human health	I received an award
2012	Kateri Tekakwitha becomes first native American saint	I won my first violin competition
2011	Osama bin Laden died	My son joined the Army
2010	The Winter Olympics took place	We got a new dog
2009	Johanna Sigurdardottir takes office as Iceland's first female prime minister.	My brother started college!
2008	Bobby Fischer died	My sister graduated from USNA
2007	Barry Bonds surpassed Hank Aaron as the	My dog got cancer

_____This project takes two weeks—one for each side.
_____Instead of personal life events, this can include historic events being discussed in class, or scientific discoveries, even biographies.
_____Discuss **perspective**. How does knowing what happened in the world during a critical event in your life provide 'perspective'?
_____When done, open the DTP program you use in your school on the class screen.
_____When creating a trifold, why not use word processing? Or a slideshow? Or a spreadsheet?
_____Expect students to be familiar with the program, though not the trifold template.
_____Show how to find the project trifold template.
_____If you don't have a desktop publishing program at school (like Publisher), you can create a trifold using a free download from the

Office.Microsoft.com website (*Figure 84a*) or a template from Google Apps (*Figure 84b* and *Figure 84c*). Adapt directions in this lesson to the tools available in these programs:

Figure 84a—Trifold using Word; 84b-c—Google Apps

 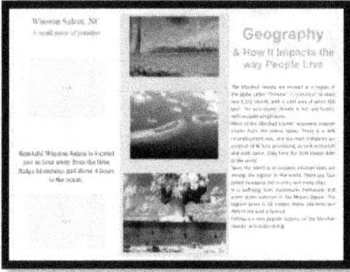 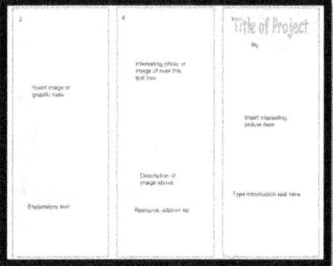

_____As students follow along, delete everything on both sides until all that remains is a blank, scored document. *Figure 85* is an example of page 1 when it's completed:

Figure 85—How to create outside of trifold

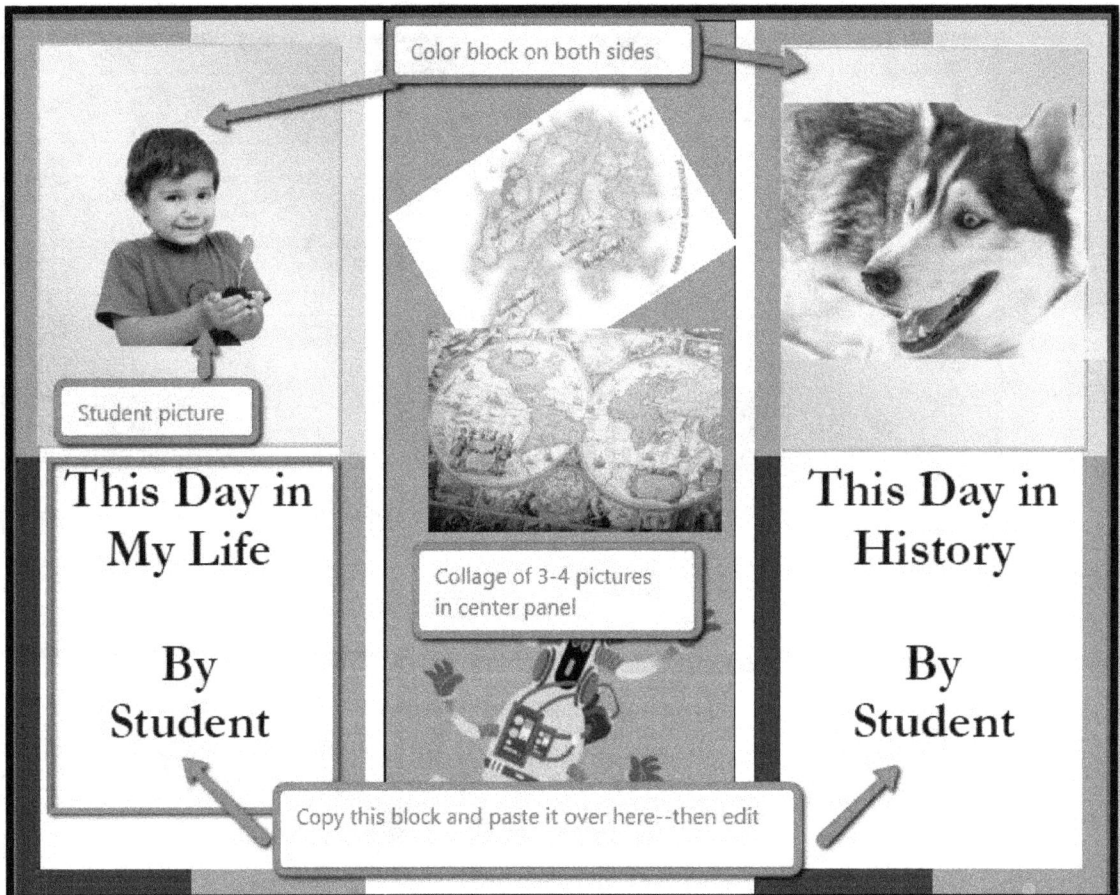

_____Enter a text box to side 1, Panel 1 (the left side of page 1), bottom; type 'This Day in My Life' and student name, font size 36, any font, centered.

_____Copy-paste text box to panel 3 (the right side of page 1) and edit to say, 'This Day in History'. This creates two covers for trifold, depending upon how you fold it.

_____Place a border around panel 1 and copy-paste it to panel 3.

_____ Add color block to top of Panel 1, 3, and entire Panel 2.

_____ Add student picture to top of panel 1, layered over color block. This ties into an event they will include in the Table of Events. For example, the boy holding the plant in his hands in *Figure 85* might be a tree he planted in grandpa's memory.

_____ Add picture of an historic event during student life to the top of panel 3, again layered over the color block. This should be one of the events in the table of events you collected. In the *Figure 85* example, what historic event includes a wolf?

_____ Add collage of three-four pictures to Panel 2 (canted or straight—be creative).

_____ Review print border (*Figure 86*)—it's a line around the document edges that all page parts must be inside of to print correctly. If your digital tool doesn't have one, remind students to keep page parts about one-half inch from page edge.

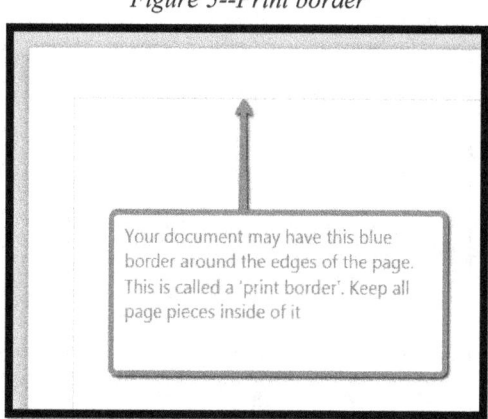

Figure 5--Print border

_____ *Figure 87* shows the assessment factors students will include (full size *Assessment* is at the end of the Lesson 17):

Figure 87—Timeline trifold rubric

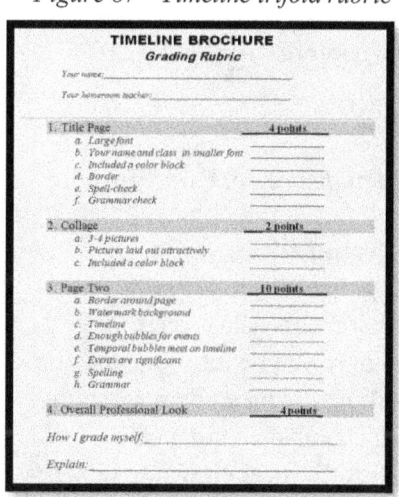

_____ Throughout class, check for understanding.

_____ Save to digital portfolio (Ctrl+S). Be sure file name includes student last name. Why?

Class exit ticket: ***Confirm with neighbor that trifold is saved to student digital portfolio before leaving.***

Differentiation

- *Early finishers: visit class internet start page for websites that tie into classwork.*
- *Add trifold to class calendar.*

4th Grade Technology Curriculum: Teacher Manual

Lesson #17—Timeline Trifold II

Vocabulary	Problem solving	Skills
• Brochure • Bubbles • Grammar-check • Handles • Layering • PDF • Pithy • Plagiarism • Washout • Watermark	• Computer doesn't work (check power, check plug) • Why my last name in file name? • I can't find last week's document (where did you save it?) • Still can't find trifold (try 'search') • What's the difference between 'save' and 'save as'? • I clicked file-print and nothing (look around screen for a clue)	**New** Timelines **Scaffolded** DTP Keyboarding Digital citizenship
Academic Applications History, literacy	**Materials Required** Speak Like a Geek rubrics, Evidence of Learning badges, DTP tool, typing test, extra timelines, student workbooks (if using)	**Standards** CCSS.ELA-Literacy.W.4.2 NETS: 3a-d, 4b, 6c

Essential Question

What audiences, tasks, purposes are perfect for DTP?

Big Idea

Software/widgets fit varied audience, task, and purpose

Teacher Preparation

- Remind students to bring timelines to class.
- Have spare timelines for students who forget.
- Talk with grade-level team so you tie into conversations.
- Ensure that all required links are on student computers.
- Know which tasks weren't completed last week.
- Integrate domain-specific tech vocabulary into lesson.
- Know if you need extra time to complete this lesson.

Assessment Strategies

- Completed speed quiz
- Completed project
- Completed rubric
- Worked independently
- Used good keyboarding habits
- Completed warm-up, exit ticket
- Joined classroom conversations
- [tried to] solve own problems
- Decisions followed class rules
- Left room as s/he found it
- Higher order thinking: analysis, evaluation, synthesis
- Habits of mind observed

Steps

Time required: 45 minutes in one sitting or spread throughout the week with a block of 30 minutes to complete trifold

Class warm-up: Warm-up practice for keyboarding speed and accuracy quiz

_____Keyboarding speed and accuracy quiz today. This is the second of the year. Goal:

- Sufficient command of keyboarding skills to type one page in a single sitting
- Speed of 25 wpm—about as fast as students handwrite

_____Figure 88 is a list of criteria to evaluate student keyboarding technique:

Figure 88—Keyboarding technique checklist

Keyboarding Technique Checklist
(3rd – Middle School Grades)

Student _____

Technique	Date	Date	Date	Date	Date
Feet placed for balance and sits up straight.					
Body centered to the middle of keyboard.					
Eyes on the screen.					
Types with correct fingering.					
Types with a steady, even rhythm.					
Keeps fingers on home row keys.					
Has a good attitude and strives for improvement.					
WPM (words per minute)					
Accuracy percent					

4 pts = Mastery level
3 pts = Near Mastery level
2 pts = Partial Mastery level
1 pt = Minimal Mastery level

_____There is a full-size skills checklist at the end of an earlier lesson. Print it or load a digital copy for each student and then use an annotation tool like iAnnotate or Adobe Reader to assess student.

_____If your students have just started keyboarding, assess only a few of these criteria. If you use iPads for keyboarding, adapt this list to that digital device.

_____The speed quiz can be delivered in several ways:

- *Place a page from a book being read on the class screen. Students copy it.*
- *Print a page from a book being read in class or a sample document for each student. They place it to the side of their keyboard and type from it.*
- *Use an online test like TypingTest.com.*

```
20% improvement:      10/10
10% improvement:       9/10
1-10% improvement:     8/10
No improvement:        7/10
Slowed down:           6/10

K-2                    None
3rd Grade              15 wpm
4th Grade              25 wpm
5th Grade              30 wpm
6th Grade              35 wpm
7th Grade              40 wpm
8th Grade              45 wpm
```

_____Students type for 3-5 minutes, then save/share/print.

_____Grade based on improvement from first quiz. If students do homework and use good keyboarding habits when they sit at the computer, they'll do fine.

_____Inset is the grading scale.

_____While students type, anecdotally assess keyboarding habits by walking around and observing posture, hand position, use of fingers.

_____Done? Spell-check and correct. Find word count; type at bottom of quiz. Save (Ctrl+S) to digital portfolio; print (Ctrl+P) if desired.

_____Let students know your expectations and rewards. I give Free Dress Passes (we wear uniforms) to students who meet the grade level standard of 25 wpm. Prizes are optional.

_____Continue Speak Like a Geek presentations.

_____Did students have any technology problems to share with the class? Any evidence of learning to post on Evidence Board?

_____Continue trifold. Today: Page 2, the timeline (*Figure 89*).

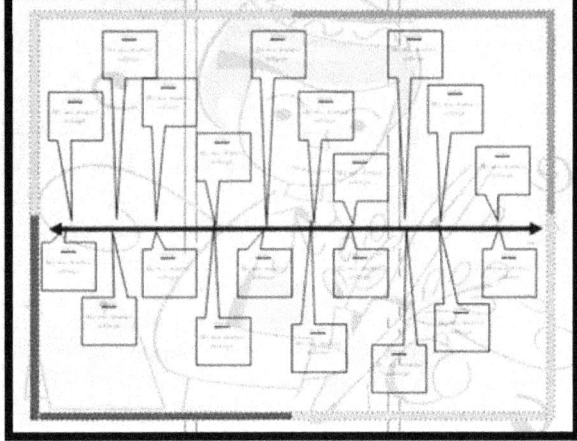

Figure 6--Timeline page of trifold

_____Learning events in chronologic order is a challenge. Common Core addresses this:

> *Write narratives to develop real or imagined experiences or events using effective technique, well-chosen details and well-structured event sequences.*

_____Timelines are graphical representations of a sequence of events over a period of time. Researching and creating timelines appeals to students' visual, mathematic, and kinesthetic intelligences.

_____Rather than using the native DTP tool, you may decide to create the timeline in a digital tool designed for that purpose and then embed a screenshot onto the DTP tool. Here are three suggestions:

- Create a timeline template in a spreadsheet program such as Excel (*Figure 90a*) or Google Spreadsheets (*Figure 90b*). Students will enter their data into this template.

Figure 90a—Timeline in Excel and 90b—Google Spreadsheets

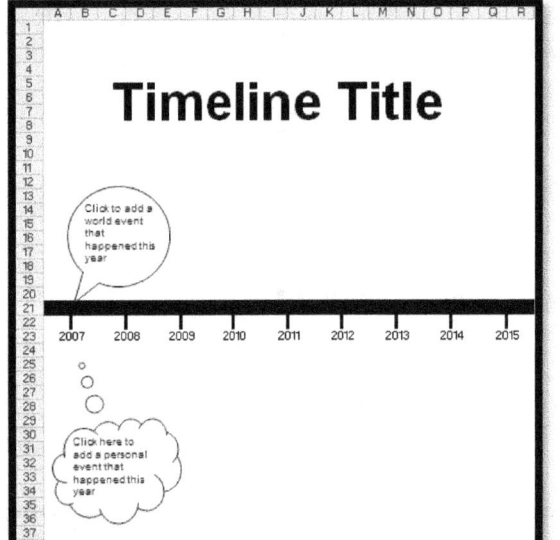
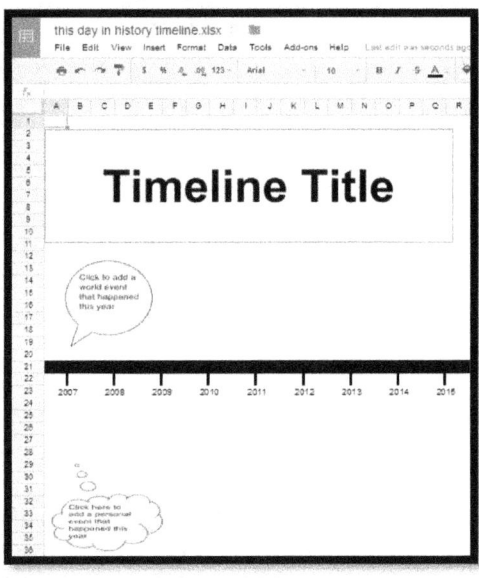

- Use an online timeline creator like TimeToast_(*Figure 91a*), Dipity_(*Figure 91b*), or Tikitoki_(*Figure 91c*) – Google for addresses.

Figure 91a-c—Online timeline tools

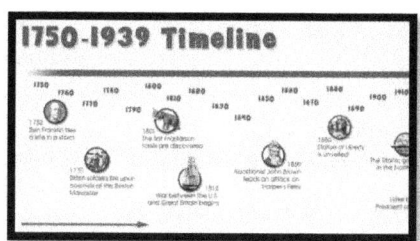 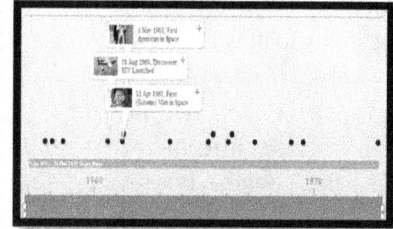 

- Or create your own timeline template in a word processing program like word, Google Docs, or Open Office.

_____Open DTP or Timeline tool. Can't find last week's file--see inset.

- *Think where it was saved.*
- *Check My Documents (common mistake is saving there instead of digital portfolio).*
- *Use 'search' on Start button and search last name.*

_____See *Figure 92* for steps to this sub-project:

Figure 92—How to create timeline

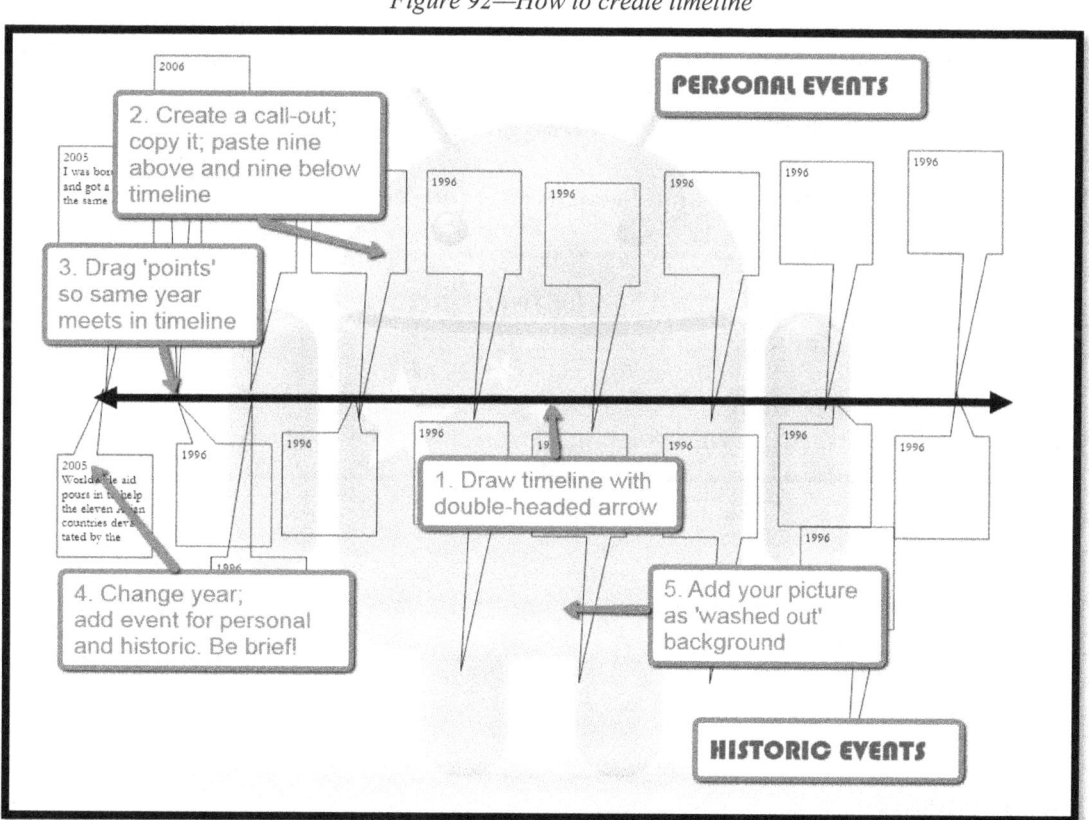

- Add a thick line to bisect Page 2 (*Figure 92—#1*). Use shift key to keep line straight.

- Add a call-out. Size so it fills about 1/3 of one panel. Copy-paste so there are three call-outs per panel, nine above timeline and nine below (see *Figure 92—#2*). Pull the tail of each call-out so it touches timeline (*Figure 92—#3*). Matching dates above and below the timeline should touch each other.
- Fill in the call-out for each year of your life (above line) and historic events (below line). Do not copy-paste from internet—that would be plagiarism. Rephrase in 4th-grade words. Keep bubbles brief, concise, but pithy. (*Figure 92—#4*).
- Add student picture as a watermark (*Figure 92—#5*). Here's how you do it:

  - *paste picture to Page 2*
  - *format to washout*
  - *layer behind the text*

- Add a border (optional).

_____This is a good time to discuss plagiarism with class. Lawful use of text and images is a topic that should be discussed four-five times before students are out of elementary school.

_____When timeline is completed, work with a partner to match your work to *Assessment* at the end of this lesson. Check off completed skills and leave other requirements blank.

_____Throughout class, check for understanding.

_____Save (Ctrl+S) to digital portfolio; save-as to flash drive (if available)

_____Print two-sided if available. If not, print both pages. Place white sides together and fold with covers out.

Class exit ticket: **Students turn in their This Day brochure and rubric**

Differentiation

- *Publish as a PDF and make trifolds available online.*
- *Add pictures to Page 2 that tie into public or personal events.*
- *Early finishers: visit class internet start page for websites that tie into classwork.*

Assessment 14—Timeline trifold rubric

THIS DAY TRIFOLD
Rubric

Your name: _____

Your homeroom teacher: _____

1. Page One	**4 points** _____

    a. Large font _____
    b. Your name and class in smaller font _____
    c. Included a color block _____
    d. Border _____
    e. Spell-check _____
    f. Grammar check _____

2. Collage	**2 points** _____

    a. 3-4 pictures _____
    b. Pictures laid out attractively _____
    c. Color block included _____

3. Page Two	**10 points** _____

    a. Border around page _____
    b. Watermark background _____
    c. Timeline _____
    d. Enough bubbles for events _____
    e. Temporal bubbles meet on timeline _____
    f. Events are significant _____
    g. Spelling _____
    h. Grammar _____

4. Overall Professional Look	**4 points** _____

How I grade myself: _____

Explain: _____

_____

4th Grade Technology Curriculum: Teacher Manual

Lesson #18—Graphic Organizers

Vocabulary	Problem solving	Skills
• Central idea • Diagram • Drill down • Graphic organizer • Infographics • Org chart • Text box • Toggle	• Online widget doesn't allow printing (take a screen shot) • Document disappeared (check taskbar, Ctrl+Z) • Typing doesn't show in bubble (change font size) • Can't type on canvas (add text box)	**New** Target graphic organizer **Scaffolded** Graphic organizers
Academic Applications Science, history, literacy—anything with subtopics	**Materials Required** Graphic organizer template, Speak Like a Geek rubric, Evidence Board badges, keyboarding program	**Standards** CCSS.ELA-Literacy.CCRA.R.2 NETS: 4b, 5b-d, 6a-d

Essential Question

How does visually representing ideas communicate effectively?

Big Idea

Representing ideas visually is a powerful communication tool

Teacher Preparation

- Have samples from last year's students if appropriate.
- Talk with grade-level team so you tie into conversations.
- Ensure that all required links are on student computers.
- Know which tasks weren't completed last week.
- Integrate domain-specific tech vocabulary.
- Know if you need extra time to complete this lesson.

Assessment Strategies

- Completed project
- Correctly identified central ideas and supporting ideas
- Selected background image that supported central ideas
- Transferred knowledge
- Used good keyboarding habits
- Completed warm-up, exit ticket
- Joined classroom conversations
- [tried to] solve own problems
- Left room as s/he found it
- Habits of mind observed

Steps

Time required: 45 minutes in one sitting or spread throughout the week with a block of 30 minutes for project

Class warm-up: Keyboarding

_____Warm up with keyboard practice. Observe habits.
_____Remember: Homework due the end of each month. Any questions?
_____Continue Speak Like a Geek presentations.
_____Any tech problems to share? Any evidence of learning for Evidence Board?
_____Discuss what a graphic organizer is. Share familiar examples i.e., school org chart.

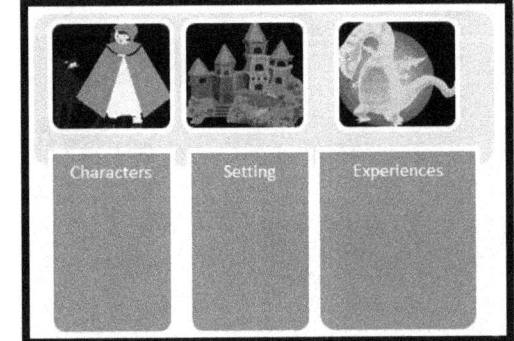

151

_____Remind students of graphic organizers completed in 1st, 2nd, 3rd grade (*Figures 93a-c*) -- if you've been using the SL tech curriculum:

Figure 93a-c—Graphic organizers in 1st, 2nd, 3rd grade

 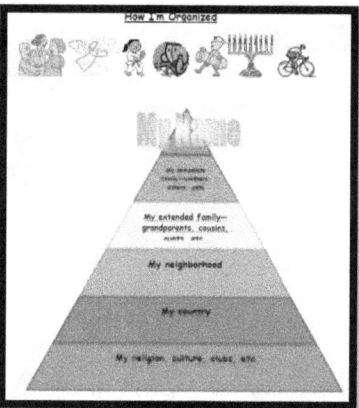 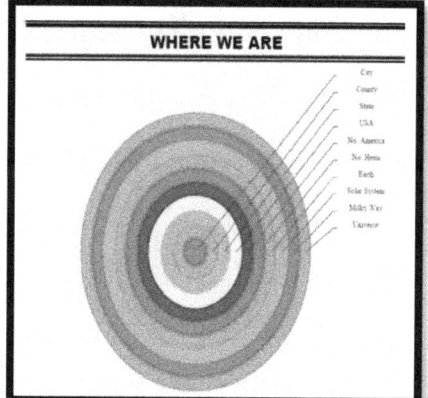

_____How do graphics organize the topic? What task might they be particularly appropriate to? How about what audience?

Figure 94—Graphic organizer

_____From *Figure 94*, you clearly understand:

- *central idea (via wheel)*
- *supporting ideas (via spokes)*
- *details (via background image)*

_____Discuss difference between how a graphic organizer displays information compared to a table such as the one created in Lesson 11. Let's put them side-by-side (*Figures 95a-b*):

Figure 95a-b—Table vs. graphic organizer

_____Which is easier to understand? What are the differences? Which do students prefer?

_____For this project, use any program (Google Apps, MS Office) or webtool (Inspiration_or Enchanted Learning) with graphic organizer templates. Be sure to check their licensing. For example, in *Figure 96*, Holt requires a linkback:

Figure 96—Online graphic organizer templates

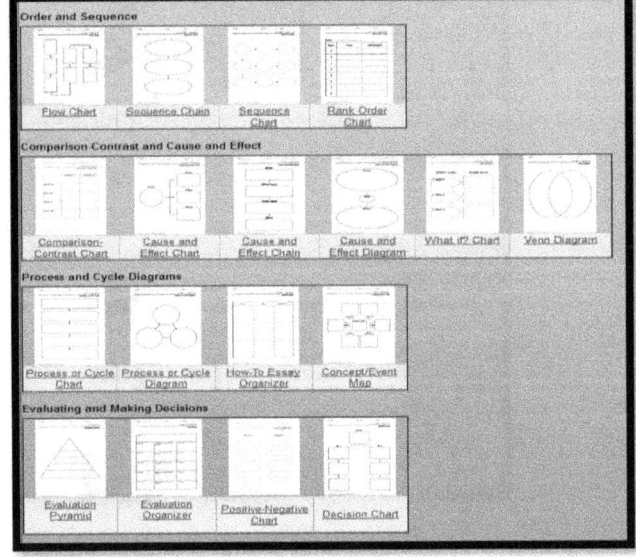

_____Open a new document. Add heading at top of page (your name, teacher name, date).

_____Insert the graphic organizer you are using for this project or let students pick one they believe fits. For this example, we'll use SmartArt in MS Word, the wheel-and-spokes. Topic will support a class project, such as biomes (*Figure 97a*) or California Missions (*Figure 97b*).

Figure 97a—Graphic organizer for science; 97b—history

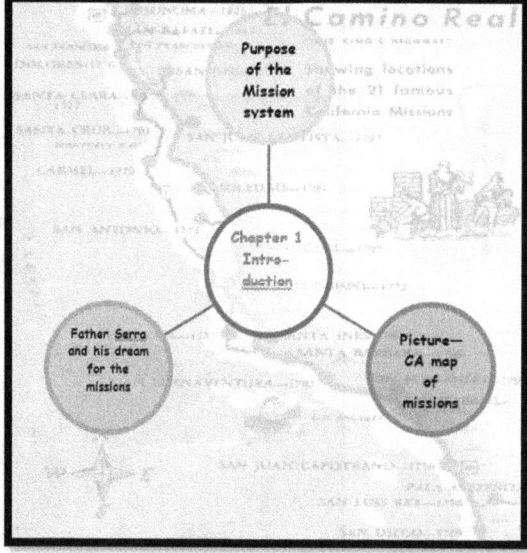

_____Add enough shapes for project; put central theme in middle with supporting details on spokes.

_____Students use knowledge from class inquiry (no research) to add 'five fast facts' to bubbles.

_____Adjust fonts in bubbles as needed to accommodate facts. Format colors and style to fit topic (to the extent allowed by your school graphic organizer tool). Students should do this as independently as possible because they've done it several times in prior years.

_____Use internet to find an image for background that supports central idea. Insert with some assistance. Model this on class screen if necessary.

_____Review legal use of images from the internet. Explain why common facts are rarely considered plagiarized, but other types of information (i.e. creative work) require credit given to author. Why can students use the image without giving credit to creator?

The law states that works of art created in the U.S. after January 1, 1978, are automatically protected by copyright once they are fixed in a tangible medium (like the internet) BUT a single copy may be used for scholarly research (even if that's a 2nd grade life cycle report) or in teaching or preparation to teach a class.

©AskaTechTeacher

_____When a student is done, review their work with a neighbor.

_____Print/publish/share, as required. Save as to a back-up (if available). Ask students difference between 'save' and 'save-as'.

4th Grade Technology Curriculum: Teacher Manual

Class exit ticket: ***Using a Padlet Wall (embedded into class start page as in Figure 98), share a project suited to a graphic organizer.***

Figure 98—Padlet for exit ticket

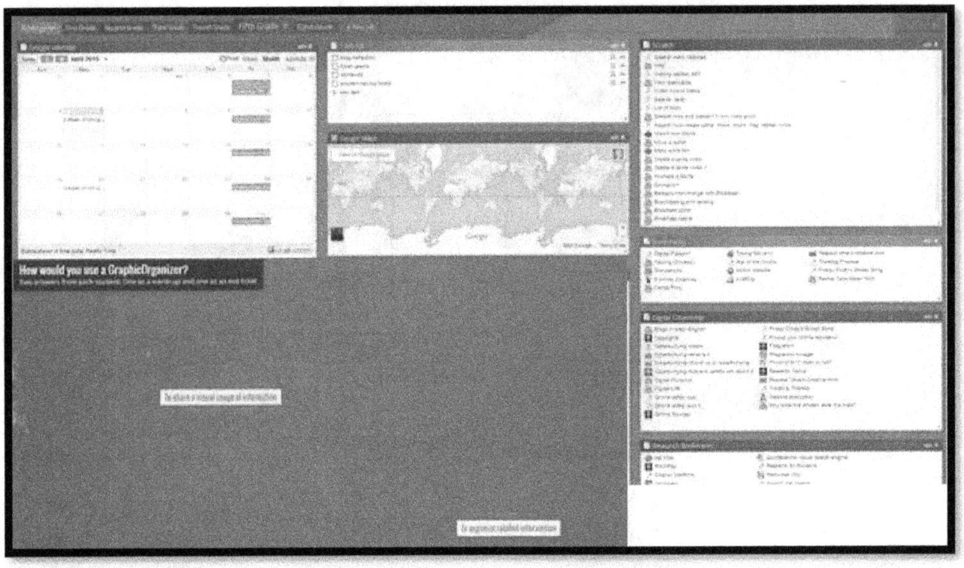

Differentiation

- Early finishers: visit class internet start page for websites that tie into classwork.
- Diagram a chapter in a story being read in class.
- Instead of printing, save as jpg and upload to class website (if available).
- Offer websites that tie into class inquiry for those who finish early.
- Full digital citizenship curriculum for K-8 available from Structured Learning.

"There is no reason anyone would want a computer in their home."

– *Ken Olson, founder of Digital Equipment Corp., 1977*

Lesson #19—Web-based Vocabulary Study

Vocabulary	Problem solving	Skills
• Embed • Format • Roots • Screenshot • Tag cloud • Tagxedo • Visual organizer • Web-based tool • Word cloud	• Can't format colors/fonts in app (adapt instructions to your tool) • Students don't have blogs to embed project (use a screen shot). • How do I add Tagxedo to class blog (with embed code) • Forgot my Presentation Board today (if room, move to later week) • We don't have a screenshot tool	**New** Embed **Scaffolded** Digital citizenship Use of webtools Screenshot
Academic Applications Grammar, writing, language	**Materials Required** keyboarding program, Speak Like a Geek rubric, Evidence Board badges, cloud tools	**Standards** CCSS.ELA-Literacy.L.4.6 NETS: 1b, 3a, 3d

Essential Question

How do I share the joy of words with students?

Big Idea

Words are beautiful

Teacher Preparation

- Have light cloths for keyboarding (to cover hands).
- Integrate domain-specific tech vocabulary.
- Ensure all required links are on student digital devices.
- Know which tasks weren't completed last week.
- Get list of site words or grammar-specific lists for word clouds (prefixes, suffixes, etc.).
- Know whether you need extra time to complete this lesson with your student group.

Assessment Strategies

- Completed presentation
- Completed project
- Shared published project
- Used good keyboarding habits
- Completed warm-up
- [tried to] solve own problems
- Left room as s/he found it
- Higher order thinking: analysis, evaluation, synthesis
- Habits of mind observed

Steps

Time required: 45 minutes in one sitting or spread throughout the week with a block of 20 minutes to complete project

Class warm-up: Keyboarding all keys, hands uncovered or covered as fits your students

_____Warm up with keyboard practice on software or online typing website. Remind students of good keyboarding habits. Consider having students cover their hands at this point in the school year. Every time they warm up with keyboarding (five-ten minutes), they use a light cloth to cover their hands. Provide colorful choices made from remnants (*Figures 99a-b*). When done, they can return to you or take them home. If you don't think they're ready, wait until they are.

_____Continue Speak Like a Geek presentations.

_____What tech problems did students have that they'd like to share? Or can they share 'evidence of learning'—applying what they learned last week to their daily life--for Evidence Board?

Figure 99a-b—Hands covered for keyboarding

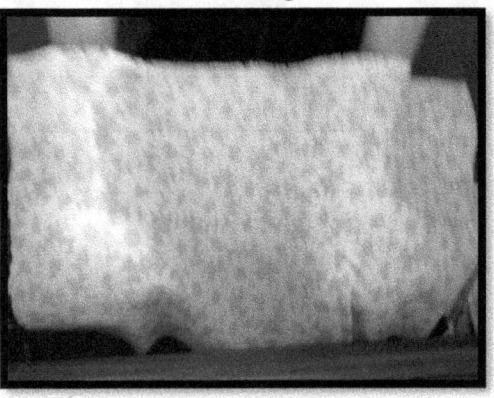
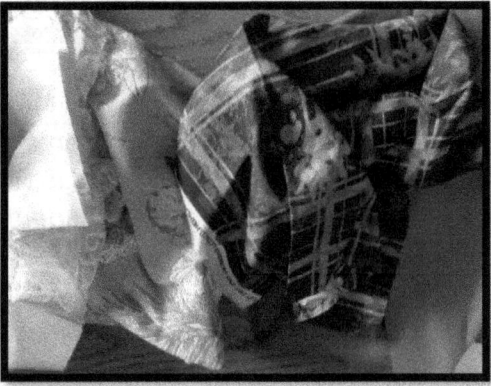

_____Open Word Cloud digital tool on the class screen to demonstrate:

Figure 100a-c—Word clouds with digital tools

_____If you use iPads, choose an iOS app such as (or check Ask a Tech Teacher resource pages for ideas):

- *CloudArt*
- *Word Clouds*
- *Word Salad*

_____If you can't access the internet and DO have Google Apps, use the Google Docs add-on Tag Cloud Generator (free). Here's what you do:

- Add text to Google Docs.
- Click *Add-ons>Tag Cloud Generator.* If you haven't already, add this to student add-on list by going to *Add ons>Get Add ons>Tag Cloud Generator*
- It appears in the right sidebar. You might have to 'refresh' to activate it.
- When the cloud appears, students take a screenshot (using Snipping Tool or whichever tool you use in your school for this activity) and save to their digital portfolio or insert into their blog.

_____*Figure 101* shows typing on the left, the generated cloud on the right, and the steps required to make that happen:

4th Grade Technology Curriculum: Teacher Manual

Figure 101—Word clouds in Google Docs

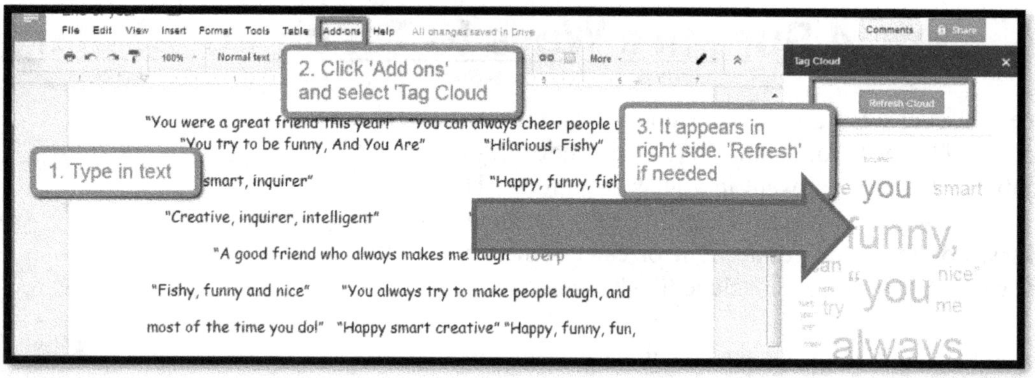

_____Good categories for this activity include (if necessary, clarify terms):

- *site words/spelling words from class*
- *all the synonyms you can think of for one word (i.e., 'boy')*
- *prefixes (brainstorm—how many can you think of?)*
- *suffixes (brainstorm—how many can you think of?)*
- *roots (brainstorm—how many can you think of?)*
- *words related to a book being read in class*
- *domain-specific words related to a topic being discussed*

_____Pick a category. Ask students to call out words that belong to the group (i.e., suffixes would include -*ment, -able, -tion, -est, -ious*). Type student suggestions into tool's dialogue box. When contributions are exhausted, ask students for help creating the cloud.

_____Format with colors, shapes, fonts (if available).

_____Share by embedding into class wikis, blogs, or another online location. Once embedded, hovering over a word makes it pop out (depends upon the tool you're using).

_____Now, working in pairs, students create their own. Have each group select a different topic (for example, only one group can create a word cloud with prefixes).

_____When done, discuss how this is a personal work of art. Creators own the copyright and can share it—no one else.

_____Discuss (or review) legalities of using internet images. Include summarized law in prior lessons and how to use an image not excepted by 'scholarly research'.

_____Print/publish/share, whichever works better for your student group. Make the collection available to support Common Core language skills.

_____Throughout class, check for understanding.

Class exit ticket: **Students tack a post-it to the classroom bulletin board with word parts from a category not included in their word cloud project.**

Differentiation

- *Early finishers: visit class internet start page for websites that tie into classwork.*
- *Use words from Speak Like a Geek as a summative review.*
- *Love words? Have students Adopt a Word at the Adopt a Word website.*

Article 15—4 Sure-fire Ways to teach vocabulary

4 Sure-fire Ways to Teach Vocabulary

Have you ever been around someone who knows exactly the right word? Don't you immediately conclude they're smart? Capable? The one you want in your study group? How about the inverse—an individual struggling with language, maybe picks words that aren't quite right or can't come up with the right word. What do you conclude then?

Figure 7--Common Core Tiered Vocabulary

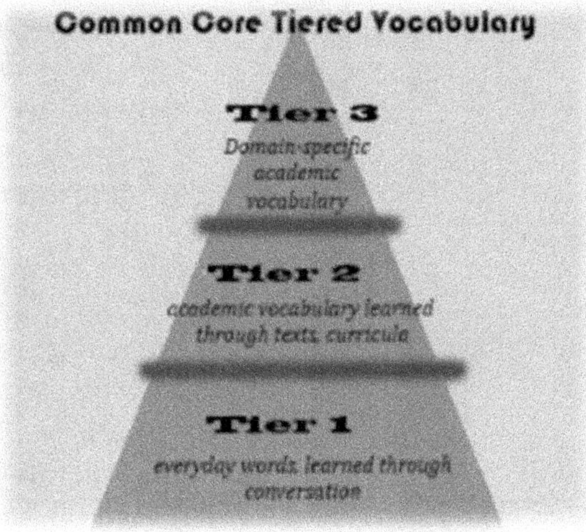

Teachers have always taught 'vocabulary' using names like *word study, site words, Dolch, Hi-Frequency words*. Common Core considers the proper use of words part and parcel to preparing for college and career. They categorize words into three types:

- *Tier 1:* Words acquired through every day speech, usually learned in early grades
- *Tier 2:* Academic words that appear in textbooks, precise words that refine meaning, i.e. 'sprint' instead of 'run'.
- *Tier 3:* Domain specific words tied to content, words included in glossaries, highlighted in textbooks, and considered important to understanding content.

The 'tier' you focus on in your teaching depends upon the age of your students and the material being taught. Here are five ways technology will make your Vocabulary Teaching more effective, fun, differentiated, and authentic:

- *Context clues*
- *SpellingCity*
- *Online graphic dictionaries*
- *Word clouds*
- *Vocabulary websites*

Before we begin, let's lay some groundwork. Teaching vocabulary (or word study) isn't done in a vacuum. You don't pass out word lists and tell students to memorize words and definitions (you don't do that, do you?). Maybe you used to, but that's all changed with Common Core. Now, you take time to integrate vocabulary into learning rather than spotlight it as a stand-alone subject. Every time students run into a word they don't get, pause, and help them decode it. It may be obvious from context, its parts (roots and affixes), but always—always—pay attention so that students know word meanings are important. Unfamiliar words are not skipped, hoping no one will notice.

Make this approach to vocabulary part of your teaching. Don't treat 'word study' like something you get to if there's time, or relegate it to homework.

The shift for you is in 'attention'—nothing else. Once you've trained yourself to use the right words and expect students to do the same, to pause every time confusion on their faces tells you they don't understand, it will become as important to your teaching as differentiation. Like breathing.

Use these five strategies to let students experience the Wow of using exactly the right word. BTW, they can be used across all tiers.

Context Clues

The first step to understanding word meaning is context. 'Context' is not only surrounding words, but construction of the word itself. What is its root? Prefixes and suffixes? What clues do these parts provide to meaning?

Have students read something for class—any subject is fine—and find at least five new vocabulary words. Don't research. Jot down each with its meaning based solely on context clues. Share via Google Docs (or a method of your choice) with a defense of their analysis.

Spelling City

This is ever-popular with 1st grade and up. Use it three ways:

- *one of the themed word lists included on the site*
- *a teacher-created list (through a fee-based account)*
- *student's own words from class*

Once a list is selected/created, the site provides word-oriented activities (a test, a teach-me, games, flash cards) that the student uses to learn words. Youngers love the games. This is great for classtime or homework, is easy to understand, intuitive to use, and never gets boring.

Graphic Dictionaries

Sure, students can use Dictionary.com or Thesaurus.com, but those won't excite students about word study. Those are online resources, but they aren't graphic dictionaries. They don't **share information visually**.
A great option for visually representing words and their meanings is VisuWords or Lexipedia. These are free. Students type in a word and the site populates a mind-mapped image of the word, its definition and related words. This image makes it easy to find connections and relationships that assist with the meaning, determine the perfect synonym, and better understand the shades of meaning inherent to our rich vocabulary.

Vocabulary websites

Finally, there is a massive grouping of sites that gamify the teaching of words, grammar, writing conventions and the like. Go through a list of sites like this from Ask a Tech Teacher and list five-ten of them so students can use them in those snippets of time that would otherwise be wasted—right before lunch, for early-finishers of a project, while you're finishing up with another student.

There you are—five ways to add automaticity to word study and scaffold vocabulary learning. One characteristic all of them have is they make words beautiful.

Article 16—3 Grammar Apps

2 Apps to Combat Grammar Faux Pas

Grammar has often been a subject students resisted learning, were bored by, or flat out didn't understand. That's changed, thanks to the popularity of iPads and their multimedia, multi-sensory apps. Here are three apps that will turn your classroom grammar program around.

Grammaropolis

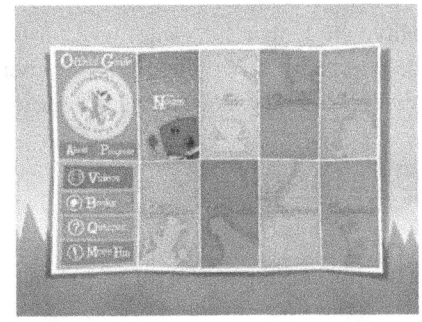

Called the Schoolhouse Rock of the 21st Century, Grammaropolis gamifies a subject that has traditionally been about laboriously conjugating verbs and diagramming sentences. Its eight cheery cartoon characters star in 9 books, 9 music videos, 20 animated shorts, 26 quiz categories, and a multitude of games which—when blended together—teach grammar. Through the vehicle of a map, catchy music and fast-paced lessons, students learn the parts of speech and win seals. Content is thorough, useful, and accurate, the app intuitive to use with a minimal learning curve. There is no software to download, no maintenance, no fuss. Students can sign up as an individual or through a class account where the teacher can track their progress. It's available on iPads, smartphones, and the web. The iPad app opens immediately to the student account (only one user per iPad account) while the web interface requires a log-in.

Developed by a teacher, this app does an excellent job of differentiating for varied learning styles. It has big, bold buttons, an easy-to-understand interface, and a dashboard to allow parents, teachers, even children to track progress. It is aligned with both Common Core standards and Texas Expected Knowledge and Skills Objectives for grades K-6.

Grammaropolis is aligned with both national Common Core standards and Texas Expected Knowledge and Skills Objectives for grades K-6.

Pros

The app opens quickly. Its enticing layout will keep student attention while they learn about nouns, verbs, conjunctions, and five other parts of speech. It also provides short assessments in the form of three- or ten-question multiple choice quizzes.

Cons

The Free app includes only nouns. The other seven parts of speech (verbs, adjectives, adverbs, pronouns, conjunctions, prepositions, and interjections) require a purchase that costs $1.99 for each section or $12.99 for the group.

Quizlet

Quizlet does for grammar what SpellingCity.com does for spelling. Despite heavyweight competitors like StudyBlue, Quizlet had over 13 million flashcard sets created in one year. The reasons are its easy-to-use interface, its quick start, and its focus on accomplishing exactly what learners require without unnecessary clicks, questions, and the insidious creep of marketing. It's free and requires no log-in to use the teacher-created community resources. When I searched 'grammar', I found 102 options!

Once you register, you can build class flashcards in the amount of time it takes you to type in the information. You make 'index cards' which include a question and an answer, then share them with students in your classes and other teachers in your network. Users can study via flashcards, short answer, or a matching game. Collections are accessible from an iPad or the web.

Pros

The learning curve is almost horizontal. The app is intuitive, easy to read, pokes you for information at all the right times. I had no problems, even the first time through.

No ads on the app (they are on the web version)! In an internet world where free apps usually include endless marketing, Quizlet is refreshing.

Cons

Not visual—no color variation beyond what you see in the pictures here. No images (though pictures are available in the Plus upgrade, which right now is $15 a year).

The app is limited compared to the web version. You can't create data sets from it. It offers only three learning options instead of the six+ available on the web. This limits teacher ability to differentiate for student learning styles.

Probably the most negative aspect of the app is that students can search the online database of users. There is no filter.

Insider tips

Take time to search the community offerings. When you find a teacher you like, keep track of them. Their flashcards will save you time.

Use the embed function (available only on the web) to focus students on your flashcards and prevent browsing in the Quizlet online community.

Lesson #20—Storybook in DTP I

Vocabulary	Problem solving	Skills
• Canvas • Ctrl+F • Export • Jpg • PDF • Taskbar • Text box • Toggle	• I can't find my file (are you logged in correctly?) • My picture looks weird (did you resize using side handles?) • How do I save as a PDF? (file-save-PDF) • Can't find my DTP (Start button>search) • Computer crashed (save early save often) • How do I search a website (Ctrl+F)	**New** Digital storytelling in DTP **Scaffolded** Digital storytelling
Academic Applications Writing, language, art	**Materials Required** DTP, Speak Like a Geek grading, Evidence Board badges, drawing program, stories from class, workbooks (if using)	**Standards** CCSS.ELA-Literacy.W.4.3 NETS: 4a-b, 6b-d

Essential Question

Can a story plot, scenery, and characters be developed effectively with pictures as well as words?

Big Idea

To engage readers requires plot development, effective scenery, and strong characters

Teacher Preparation

- What class writing conventions can you reinforce?
- Remind students to bring stories.
- Know which tasks weren't completed last week.
- Integrate domain-specific tech vocabulary into lesson.
- Know whether you need extra time to complete lesson.

Assessment Strategies

- Made progress with DTP
- Anecdotal observations
- Used prior knowledge
- Used writing conventions
- Worked independently
- Used good keyboarding habits
- Completed warm-up, exit ticket
- Joined class conversations
- [tried to] solve own problems
- Decisions followed class rules
- Left room as s/he found it
- Habits of mind observed

Steps

Time required: 45 minutes in one sitting or spread throughout the week with a block of 40 minutes to start storybook
Class warm-up: Keyboarding

_____Finish Speak Like a Geek presentations. Any evidence of learning for Evidence Board?

_____Today, students brought a story written in class. It is ten-twenty sentences long—no more—yet incorporates writing elements like plot, characterization, setting, action, climax, and other pieces discussed in class. For the next four weeks, students will create a digital storybook that uses text, pictures, and design to reinforce writing skills.

_____If story is not in digital format, type it using a word processing program. Let students do the math on how long it will take to type:

4th Grade Technology Curriculum: Teacher Manual

20 sentences = 200 words (or less)
Student WPM = 25 wpm
200/25 = 8 minutes

_____When done typing, pair up and review each other's stories for (from Common Core):

- *establishment of a situation*
- *introduction of characters and lay out an event sequence*
- *use of dialogue and description*
- *use of transitional words and phrases*
- *conveyance of events with concrete words and sensory details*

_____Use highlighter tool to mark elements. Add a legend to clarify. *Figure 103a* is a similar exercise from Lesson 8 and *Figure 103b* is a project you may have done to reinforce grammar.

Figure 103a-b—Highlighted stories

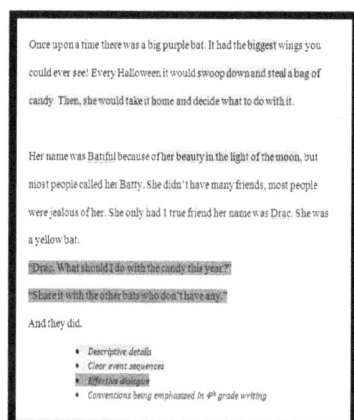 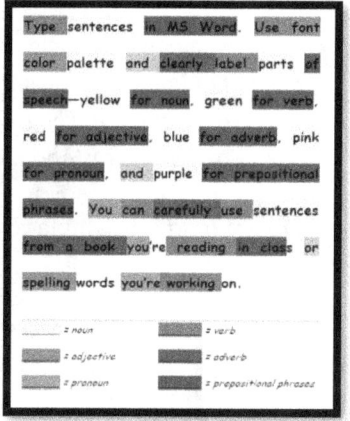

_____When done, students review neighbor's notes and make necessary changes.
_____Save the edited copy to digital portfolio. Then, remove highlights and save another copy called 'Draft II'. Students will use 'save-as' for Draft II. Why?
_____Open a drawing program (like KidPix, Paint, TuxPaint, Pixie, ABCYa). Take five minutes to discuss with the neighbor who edited story what image best represents each other's stories and then draw a cover. Show it to neighbor and get their input. *Figures 104a-b* are examples of what the cover might look like:

Figure 104a-b—Sample covers

_____ When done, export as jpg to student digital portfolio and close drawing program. If the program doesn't allow saving or exporting, take a screen shot.

_____ Open the desktop publishing program or online tool used to create a storybook. You might use Storybird or Storyjumper. If you have iPads, try these apps:

- *Adobe Slate*
- *Adobe Voice*

_____ We use Publisher for this example.

_____ From what you can see so far, why is a desktop publishing tool (instead of word processing, a spreadsheet or a presentation program) a good choice for this project. Consider:

- *laying out storybook pieces*
- *telling story with pictures and text*
- *layout and design elements that are fundamental to desktop publishing*

_____ The story will be thirteen pages long:

- *one page for the cover*
- *ten pages for the story*
- *one page for The End*
- *one page for 'About the Author'*

_____ *Figure 105a* is a sample cover, *105b* a story page, and *105c* 'About the Author':

Figure 105a-c—Sample pages from digital storybook

_____ Select a blank page to use as a cover and do these steps:

- *Insert the picture you drew in the drawing program.*
- *Add title—font size 48, any font, any color.*
- *Add text box underneath with student name and optionally, teacher's name.*

_____ You may need to resize the image with corner handles to fit space available. Why use corner handles rather than side? You also may need to layer the text or image.

_____ Save storybook to digital portfolio and close the program. Be sure to include your last name in the file name. Why?

4th Grade Technology Curriculum: Teacher Manual

Class exit ticket: *Students submit a copy of the edited story created by their partner.*

Differentiation

- *Early finishers: visit class internet start page for websites that tie into classwork.*
- *If you have a class Twitter account, have students practice pithy writing by adding their sentences to the stream and tightening them up.*
- *Add Storybook project to class calendar.*

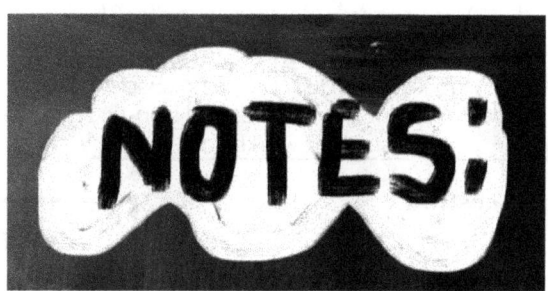

_____

_____

_____

_____

_____

_____

Lesson #21—Storybook in DTP II

Vocabulary	Problem solving	Skills
• Border • Export • Flash drive • Footer • Graphic • Greyed-out • Handles • Jpg • Layout • Page parts • Text box	• I can't find my project (where did you save it?) • Can't find drawing (did you save as jpg?) • Can't type on page (insert textbox) • I can't edit text (is it greyed out—in the footer?) • My footer doesn't show (is border covering it?) • My picture looks weird (did you resize with side handles?)	**New** Digital storytelling with DTP **Scaffolded** Keyboarding Digital citizenship Research skills Google Earth DTP
Academic Applications Writing, language, research skills	**Materials Required** DTP, keyboarding program, Evidence Board badges, Google Earth Board sign-ups and rubric, student workbooks (if using)	**Standards** CCSS.ELA-Literacy.W.4.3 NETS: 4a-b, 6b-d

Essential Question

Can a story be developed with pictures as well as words?

Big Idea

Stories require plot development, effective scenery, and strong characters to engage the reader

Teacher Preparation

- Know writing rules taught by grade-level team.
- Know which tasks weren't completed last week.
- Integrate domain-specific tech vocabulary into lesson.
- Know if you need extra time to complete this lesson.

Assessment Strategies

- Followed CCSS writing guidelines
- Worked well with partner
- Used good keyboarding habits
- Completed warm-up, exit ticket
- Joined class conversations
- [tried to] solve own problems
- Decisions followed class rules
- Left room as s/he found it
- Higher order thinking: analysis, evaluation, synthesis
- Habits of mind observed

Steps

Time required: 45 minutes in one sitting or spread throughout the week with a block 25 minutes for project

Class warm-up: sign up for Google Earth Board

_____ Do students have technology problems to share with class? Or evidence of learning for Evidence Board?

_____ Today, students sign up for Google Earth Board. This is the third of three Presentation Boards.

_____ Each student selects a location from 1) list of places visited in fourth grade, 2) places to be visited in fifth grade, 3) Wonders of the World, or 4) another list. *Figure 106* is an example of the type of locations you might select:

Figure 106—Sample GE locations

Sample Google Earth Locations	
Egyptian Pyramids	Tierra del Fuego
Great Wall of China	Straits of Gibraltar
Stonehenge	The Red Sea
Hagia Sophia, Istanbul	Mt. St. Helens
Leaning Tower of Pisa	San Andreas Fault
The Eiffel Tower	Great African Rift
Panama Canal	Madagascar
Taj Mahal	Istanbul
Victoria Falls	Siberia
Ngorongoro Crater	Death Valley
Mt. Everest	Suez Canal
Ayers Rock	Vatican City
The Ross Ice Shelf	The Chunnel

_____They use research skills to find one Fascinating Fact about location to share. During their one-three minute presentation, they share that with classmates and take questions.
_____Here's how it works:

- *Post sign-up sheets by the class door where they're easily found. Include slips of paper (Figure 107) that students can track important information:*

Figure 107—Info for GE Board

> My name: _____
> My Google Earth location: _____
> My presentation date: _____

- *Alternatively, have sign-ups online through:*
  - *Google Calendar or Spreadsheets*
  - *Office 365*
  - *Padlet (using calendar template)*
  - *SignUp Genius*
  - *Appointment Slots in Google Calendar that you have shared with students.*

- *Each student signs up for a date to present.*
- *Grading based on criteria listed on Figure 108 (full-size template at end of lesson):*

Figure 108—GE Board grading

GOOGLE EARTH BOARD GRADING	
Name:	_____
Class:	_____
You were prepared with filled-out project sheet	_____
Your project sheet had a picture of your location	_____
You shared an interested fact with the class	_____
You spoke loudly enough for all to hear	_____
You seemed knowledgeable	_____
You had a calm, confident presence	_____
You didn't use vocal cues that showed nervousness	_____
You didn't use visual cues that showed nervousness	_____
You looked your audience in the eye as you talked	_____
Overall impression	_____

- *If desired, allow students to skip a homework and use that time to research Fascinating Fact and complete study guide.*

_____Open DTP project. Go to pg. 1 (the only page so far). Add picture created last week; resize with corner handles to fit space available; layer under titles (see sample last lesson).

_____Add twelve pages—10 for sentences, one for 'the end'; one for 'About the Author'.

_____Insert footer with student name and page number (recall how this was done in 3rd grade); remember to close footer when done (see *Figure 109*).

Figure 109—Border and footer

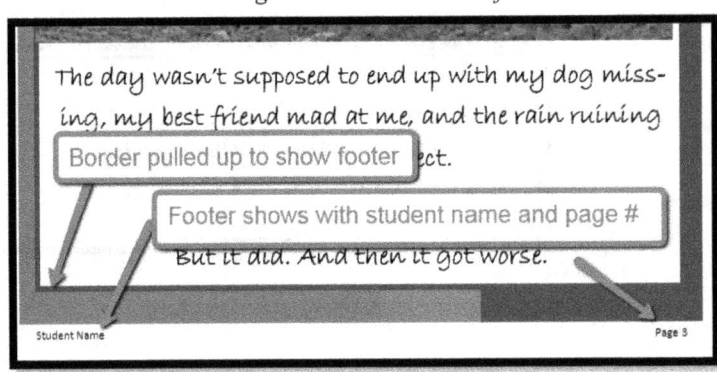

_____Page 2: Insert a border; size to fit around footer. Insert a text box at bottom third of page. Leave top for picture. Copy border to pages 2-13. Copy text box to pages 2-11.

_____Page 2-11: Insert a text box at bottom third of page. Leave top for picture. Copy border to pages 2-13. Copy text box to pages 2-11.

_____Page 2-11: Copy-paste one-two sentences from the typed story to the text box at the bottom of each page—no more than that. It must fit on ten pages. Show students how to use Alt+Tab to toggle back-and-forth between the digital story and the DTP storybook. *Figure 110a* is what each of the ten pages might look like before image is added (space at top for image; one-two typed sentences at bottom) and *Figure 110b* is after:

Figure 110a—Story page without image; 110b—with image

_____Remind students: Every time they use a digital device, practice good keyboarding skills.

Class exit ticket: Students have a neighbor check their page set-up before leaving to make sure it looks like *Figure 110b*.

Differentiation

- Add due date for story to class calendar.
- Early finishers: visit class internet start page for websites that tie into classwork.

If screen freezes:

- "Smash forehead on keyboard to continue..."
- "Enter any 11-digit prime number..."

Assessment 15—Google Earth Board grading

GOOGLE EARTH BOARD GRADING

Name: _____

Class: _____

You were prepared   _____

You shared an interested fact with the class   _____

You spoke loudly enough for all to hear   _____

You were knowledgeable   _____

You had a calm, confident presence   _____

You didn't use vocal cues that showed nervousness   _____

You didn't use visual cues that showed nervousness   _____

You looked your audience in the eye as you talked   _____

Overall impression   _____

4th Grade Technology Curriculum: Teacher Manual

Lesson #22—Storybook in DTP III

Vocabulary	Problem solving	Skills
• Alt+Tab • Google Earth • Layer • Print border • Toggle • Washout • Watermark	• Image has a watermark (don't use) • How do I toggle between my word processing and DTP without losing my place (Alt+Tab) • Page edges didn't print (you are outside blue print border) • I can't see 'The End' (layer)	**New** **Scaffolded** DTP Digital storytelling Digital citizenship Online images
Academic Applications Writing, language	**Materials Required** DTP, Google Earth Board grading, Evidence Board badges, storybook rubric, student wkbks (if using)	**Standards** CCSS.ELA-Literacy.W.4.3 NETS: 4a-b, 6b-d

Essential Question

Can a story—plot, scenery, characters—be effectively developed with pictures as well as words?

Big Idea

Stories require plot development, effective scenery, and strong characters to engage the reader

Teacher Preparation

- Have Google Earth Board assessments
- Know which tasks weren't completed last week.
- Integrate domain-specific tech vocabulary into lesson.
- Know if you need extra time to complete this lesson.
- What class writing skills are reinforced with this project?

Assessment Strategies

- Anecdotal
- Followed writing conventions
- Worked well in a group
- Understood use of online images
- Used good keyboarding habits
- Completed warm-up, exit ticket
- [tried to] solve own problems
- Decisions followed class rules
- Left room as s/he found it
- Higher order thinking: analysis, evaluation, synthesis
- Habits of mind observed

Steps

Time required: 45 minutes in one sitting or spread throughout the week with a block of 30 minutes for project
Class warm-up: Added sentences to story

_____Any tech problems students want to share? Evidence of learning for Evidence Board?
_____Keyboarding homework due at end of month.
_____Google Earth Board presentations start today.
_____Open DTP tool to continue storybook. Finish adding one or more sentences to pages 2-11 (in text box at bottom of page). Use Alt+Tab to toggle between word processing tool and digital storytelling if necessary.

_____When completed, with or without a partner, confirm that story (*Figure 111*):

- *has good grammar and spelling*
- *establishes a situation*
- *introduces characters*
- *unfolds event sequence naturally*
- *uses dialogue and description to develop events*
- *uses transitional words to manage the sequence of events*
- *uses sensory details*
- *concludes based on narrated events*

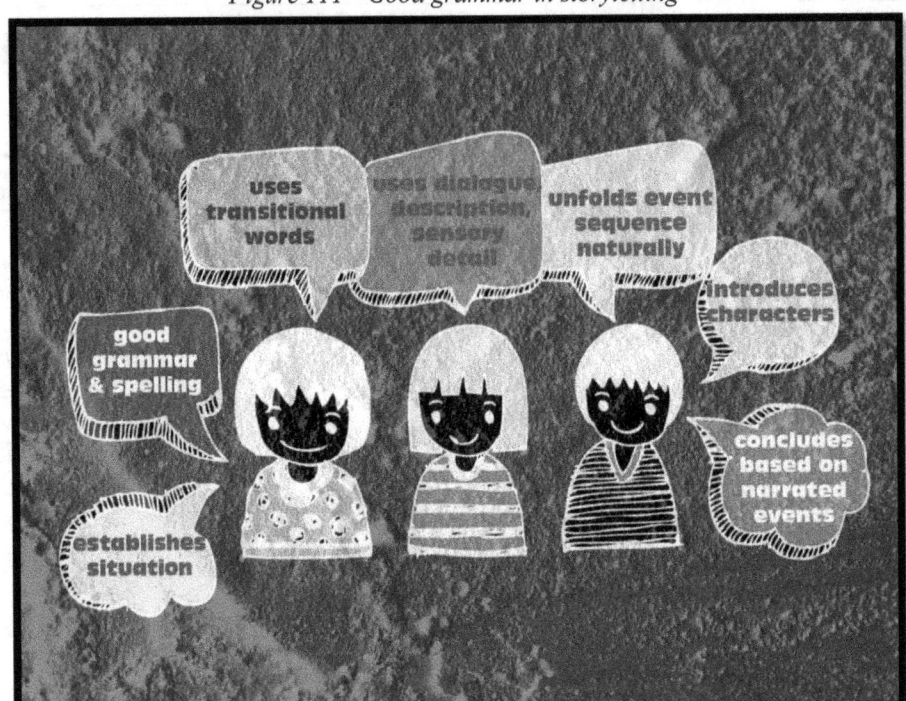

Figure 111—Good grammar in storytelling

_____**Pages 2-11:** Add a picture to each page from clip art, Google images, or created in school drawing program. It should communicate the same information as the text, but deeper, more detailed, and more passionately. Readers should know what is happening in the story by this image—even without words.

_____If using Google images, discuss the legality of using online pictures. Why is it OK to use them for this project? Why is it NOT OK if you publish the story?

_____Resize pictures to fit space; stay inside print border. *Figures 112a-d* are examples:

- *layout*
- *font variety*
- *colored text*
- *use of images to communicate the same message as text*

_____Which picture among *Figures 112a-d* DOESN'T communicate the same message with the picture as with text? How could this be fixed?

Figure 112a-d—Storybook interior pages

_____**Page 12 (*Figures 113a-c*):**

- *Insert drawing program picture (same one as on front cover)*
- *Format as washout (or watermark)*
- *Add 'The End' using WordArt; layer over picture*
- *This page may or may not have a border—you decide*

_____What's wrong with *Figures 113a-b*? (Hint: Footer is covered by border or picture):

Figure 113a-c—The End page in storybook

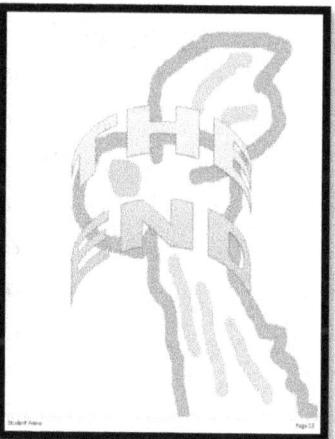

_____Throughout class, check for understanding.

_____Save storybook to digital portfolio. Students will finish next week. Full-size assessment is found at the end of the lesson.

Class exit ticket: ***Students have neighbor verify that all page elements are within print border (or about half an inch from paper's edge)***

Differentiation

- *Those who finish can complete rubric and submit project.*

Assessment 16—Storybook assessment

Storybook Assessment

Creator: _____

Teacher: _____

Date: _____

1. Title Page includes
   a. Story title in large font
   b. Your name in smaller font
   c. Drawing related to topic

2. Each Story Page includes
   a. Border
   b. Picture appropriate for story
   c. Spell-check
   d. Page filled (text/pictures)

3. Provide evidence that you
   a. Established a situation
   b. Introduced characters
   c. Organized event to unfold naturally
   d. Used dialogue to develop events
   e. Used description to develop events
   f. Used transitional words to manage sequence
   g. Used concrete words to convey events
   h. Used sensory details to convey events
   i. Concluded story based on narrated events.

4. About the Author includes
   a. A few points about yourself
   b. Border

5. The End Page has
   a. The End
   b. Watermark of cover

6. Overall Professional Look

Lesson #23—Storybook in DTP IV

Vocabulary	Problem solving	Skills
• Brainstorm • Color block • Mulligan Rule • PDF • Print preview • Rubric • Text box • White space	• Project disappeared (use search) • Project isn't in my folder (where did you save it?) • How do I add a color block behind pictures? • How do I 'Print Preview'? (check print dialogue box) • Can I use images I selected?	**New** **Scaffolded** DTP Digital storytelling Keyboarding Digital citizenship Online images
Academic Applications Writing, language	**Materials Required** DTP, keyboard program, Google Earth Board rubric, Evidence Board badges, storybook rubrics, student workbooks (if using)	**Standards** CCSS.ELA-Literacy.W.4.3 NETS: 4a-b, 6b-d

Essential Question

Can story—plot, scenery, and characters—be effectively developed with pictures as well as words?

Big Idea

Stories require plot development, effective scenery, and strong characters to engage the reader

Teacher Preparation

- Understand legality of using online images.
- Have grading rubrics for story.
- Know which tasks weren't completed last week.
- Integrate domain-specific tech vocabulary into lesson.
- Know if you need extra time to complete this lesson.

Assessment Strategies

- Completed presentation
- Completed DTP project
- Completed rubric
- Worked well in a group
- Used good keyboarding habit.
- Completed warm-up, exit ticket
- Joined classroom conversations
- [tried to] solve own problems
- Decisions followed class rules
- Left room as s/he found it
- Higher order thinking: analysis, evaluation, synthesis
- Habits of mind observed

Steps

Time required: 45 minutes in one sitting or spread throughout the week with a block of 30 minutes for project
Class warm-up: Keyboarding

_____Warm up with keyboarding tool. Remind students to follow good typing habits.
_____Did students have any technology problems they'd like to get solutions to, ask about?
_____Any evidence of learning to post on Evidence Board?
_____Keyboarding homework due at end of month.
_____Continue Google Earth presentations.
_____Finish adding pictures. Resize images or add a color block to eliminate white space.
_____Trouble coming up with a picture? Think about the sentence. Read it aloud. What

comes to mind? Nothing? Brainstorm with neighbors.
_____Here are samples of storybook pages (*Figures 114a-d*):

Figure 114a-d—Sample storybook pages

_____**Page 13:** Add text box 'About the Author'. See *Figures 115a-b* for examples:

Figure 115a-b—About the author

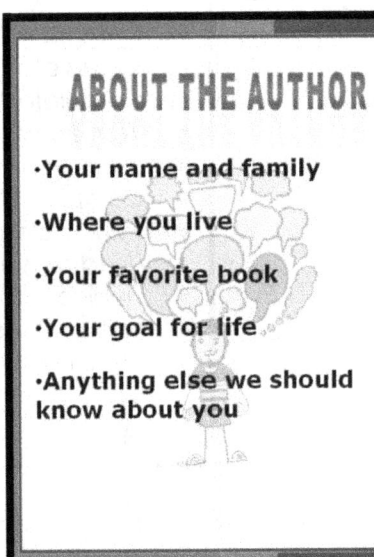

_____What should readers know about you? How about:

- *Where do you live?*
- *Who's in your family?*
- *What's your favorite book?*
- *What inspired you to write this story?*
- *What's your goal/What do you want to do when you grow up?*

_____Add school picture if available by copy-pasting from school website.
_____Students should review checklist with a neighbor (*Assessment 16*) for all story elements.

4th Grade Technology Curriculum: Teacher Manual

Figure 116—Storybook assessment

Storybook Grading Rubric

Creator: _____

Teacher: _____

Date: _____

1. Title Page includes
   a. Story title in large font
   b. Your name in smaller font
   c. KidPix Picture related to topic

2. Each Story Page includes
   a. Border
   b. Picture appropriate for story
   c. Spell-check
   d. Page filled (text/pictures)

3. Provide evidence that you
   a. Established a situation
   b. Introduced characters
   c. Organized event to unfold naturally
   d. Used dialogue to develop events
   e. Used description to develop events
   f. Used transitional words to manage sequence
   g. Used concrete words to convey events
   h. Used sensory details to convey events
   i. Concluded story based on narrated events.

4. About the Author includes
   a. A few points about yourself
   b. Border

5. The End Page has
   a. The End in WordArt
   b. Watermark of cover

6. Overall Professional Look

_____ Print preview before printing. Publish/share, as required by your school.

_____ For grading: **Mulligan Rule** in effect.

_____ Now that students are finished, discuss whether this could have been done in a word processing program, or a slideshow tool. The goal: Understand the use of technology in authentic projects.

Class exit ticket: ***Students submit the grading rubric as they leave class***

Differentiation

- Early finishers: visit class internet start page for websites that tie into classwork.
- Read stories with kindergarten/first grade by displaying them on class screen.
- Save as PDF and import to iBooks or other iPad reader. Share during Reading Hour, DEAR, or Sustained Silent Reading.
- Embed stories in class website, wiki, or blog.

4th Grade Technology Curriculum: Teacher Manual

Lesson #24—Analyze Data and Excel Games

Vocabulary	Problem solving	Skills
• Columns • Data • Format • Formula • Sort • Spreadsheet • Tab • Workbook	• My formula doesn't work (did you start with =?) • I used shortkey, but it didn't work (does it work in spreadsheet tool?) • Text doesn't fit in cell (double click line between column letters) • My computer crashed (did you save early save often?)	**New** Data analysis Spreadsheet games New spreadsheet skills **Scaffolded** Spreadsheet basics Digital citizenship Keyboarding skills
Academic Applications Research skills, math, history, Genius Hour	**Materials Required** keyboard program, Google Earth Board rubrics, Evidence Board badges, spreadsheet program, game links	**Standards** CCSS.Math.Practice.MP4 NETS: 3a-d, 5a-d

Essential Question

How can I use available data to determine the best way to evaluate a project??

Big Idea

Data analysis helps determine success and/or failure

Teacher Preparation

- Talk with grade-level team so you tie into project that requires data analysis.
- Integrate domain-specific tech vocabulary into lesson.
- Know whether you need extra time to complete lesson.
- Ensure that links to spreadsheet games are available.
- Know which tasks weren't completed last week.

Assessment Strategies

- Transferred knowledge from prior lessons
- Followed directions
- Completed project
- Used good keyboarding habits
- Completed warm-up
- Joined class conversations
- [tried to] solve own problems
- Decisions followed class rules
- Left room as s/he found it
- Higher order thinking: analysis, evaluation, synthesis
- Habits of mind observed

Steps

Time required: 45 minutes in one sitting or spread throughout the week with a block of 30 minutes for project
Class warm-up: Keyboarding

_____Practice keyboarding with installed software or online typing site. Remember: correct hand position, correct posture. Both speed and accuracy count in fourth grade.
_____Continue with Google Earth presentations.
_____Did students have any problems with technology they'd like to share?
_____Any evidence of learning to post on Evidence Board?
_____Students completed spreadsheet projects in K-3rd grade. See if they remember *Figures 117a-d*:

Figure 117a-d—Spreadsheet projects in Kindergarten-3rd grade

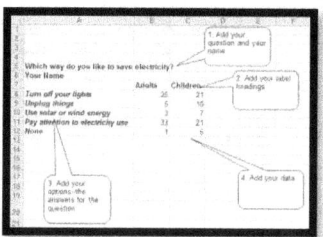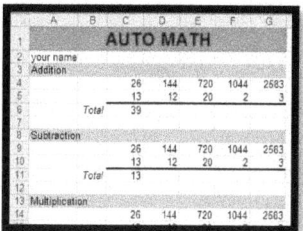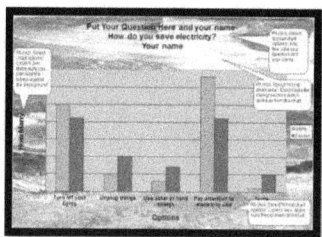

_____What is a spreadsheet? When is it better to use this than word processing, a slideshow, DTP? Show students a partially-completed version. See if they can fill in the blanks:

Element	Presentation	Word processing	Spread-- sheets	DTP
Purpose	Share a presentation	Share words	Turn numbers into information	Share information using a variety of media
Basics	Graphics-based Design is important to content Layout communicates Few words, lots of images	Text-based Design is secondary to content Layout may detract from words Primarily words communicate	Number-based Focus on tables, graphs Little text; lots of statistics and date Almost no words	Mix of media—equal emphasis on text, images, layout, color
Sentences	Bulleted, phrases	Full sentences with proper conventions	None	Full sentences, bullets,
Content	Slides cover basics, to remind presenter what to say	Thorough discussion of a topic. Meant to be complete document	Statistics, data, charts, graphs	To draw an audience in;
Use	As a back-up to presentation	As complete resource	To support other presentation methods	Good way to group information for easy consumption
Presentation	Speaker presents with their back to the slideshow	Speaker reads from document	Speakers uses it in a presentation or 1:1	Speaker passes out as a handout or take-way
What else				

_____Select one of the following two projects for your student group.

Project #1

_____Use spreadsheet skills to analyze classroom inquiry. This can tie into Genius Hour if you follow that project in your school. Whatever project you select, it must require spreadsheets to collect and evaluate data.

_____Here, we use the popular Invention Convention. Before beginning data analysis, students will:

- *research and select a topic for several weeks*
- *build invention for several weeks*
- *collect data on research and invention construction*
- *set up a spreadsheet for the invention*
- *using collected data, evaluate costs associated with building and marketing invention*

_____Because students have several years of spreadsheet practice behind them (if you've been using the SL tech curriculum), expect as much independence as possible on their part in analyzing data. Be there to guide, remind, not teach.

_____To brush up on spreadsheet skills, ask for a student volunteer to review skills that will be required for the Invention Convention spreadsheet, listed in *Figure 118*. Put the list on the class screen. If the student volunteer doesn't know how to do one, s/he can ask for help from classmates. This list should include only skills already learned in 2nd and 3rd grade:

- *rename tab 'Skills'*
- *add a title*
- *add an image*
- *add data to cells*
- *create a formula*
- *find an average*
- *identify cells*
- *move around a worksheet*

_____Required new skills include:

- *a hyperlink*
- *date and time*
- *two-line heading*
- *sort alphabetically*

Figure 8--Spreadsheet skills for project

Do as many of the following skills as there is time for:
1 Make a two-line heading
2 Insert a WordArt title
3 Widen rows/columns
4 Sort a list alphabetically
5 Autosum a list of numbers
6 Find average of a list of numbers
7 Chart data
8 Format the numbers as money
9 Shade cells
10 Enter a hyperlink
11 Add a call-out to worksheet
12 Enter the date
13 Enter the time
14 Add an image

Figure 119—Invention Convention spreadsheet

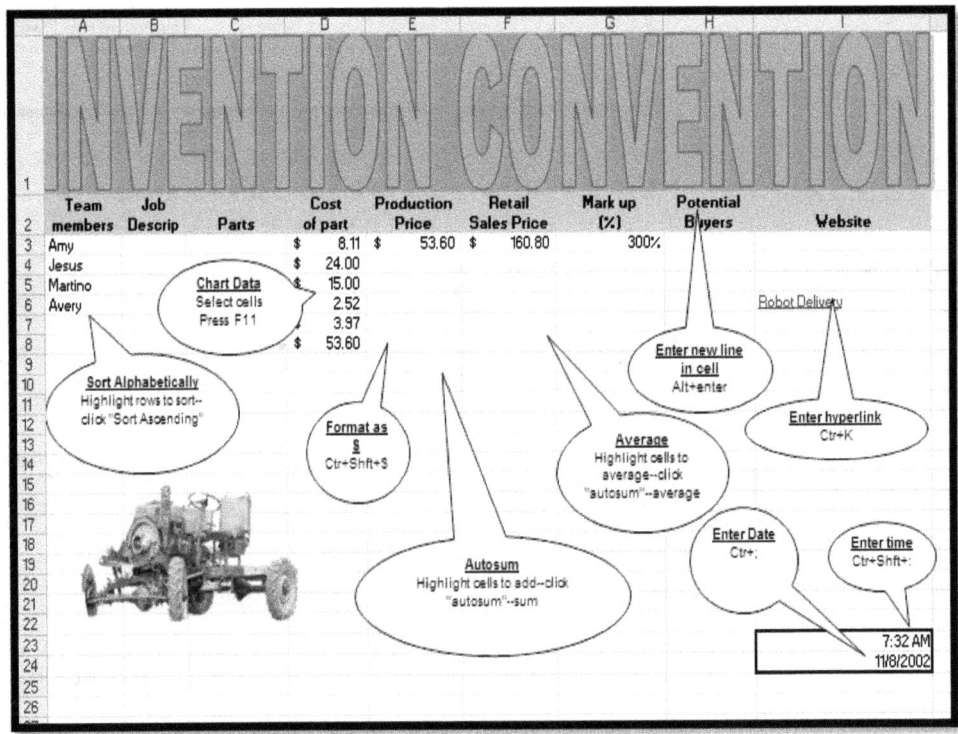

_____Discuss as a group what types of data you'll track over the weeks it takes to complete this project. Collect it in a spreadsheet, separate it into categories (see the column headings in *Figure 119*), and include at least one picture of your project.

_____There are two types of data in this spreadsheet:

- *Input*—type data into the cell and it appears as typed
- *Formula*—enter a formula that calculates what appears in cell. These start with =

_____Look through this list and decide which calculations are right for your group. Here's a breakdown of each column in *Figure 119*. A column is **a category of information which you are collecting**. Yours may not include all these columns, but it will include sufficient data to analyze your project. Input cells are blue. **Formula cells are red.** *Formula cells* change as the data they read change (you did this last year with the 'Auto Math' sheet):

- Cost of part—what does each item in 'Parts' cost? Are they donated (parent drives you for free) or purchased? How do you create *Figure 120* chart?

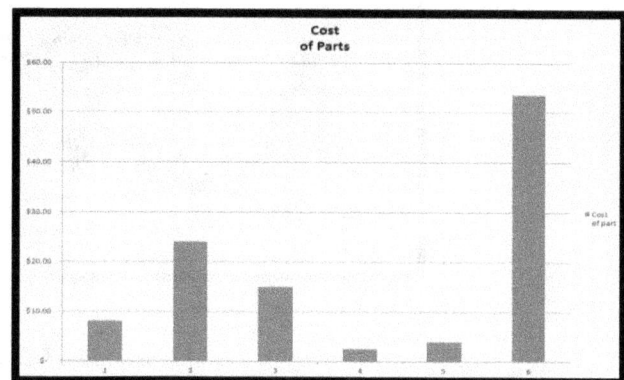

Figure 120—Chart

- Job description—what does each team member do for the project? Use only one-two words; for example: *'researcher', 'builder', 'writer'*. If necessary, widen the column.
- Mark up (%)—divide 'Retail Sales Price' by 'Production Price'. Since you want it a percent, format the cell with % tool. No surprise in *Figure 121* that it's 300%—you multiplied by 3:

Figure 121—How to find mark-up

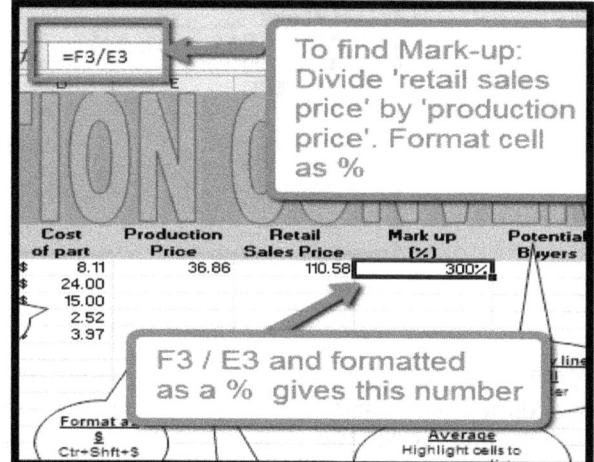

- Parts—what is required to complete project? This includes materials such as a computer, a car to get to the store, and parent help. Think this through as you list materials.
- Potential Buyers—who are the customers for your new product?
- Production price—how much does it cost to create this product? Autosum the 'Cost of parts' column, then program the 'Production Price' cell to read the sum. Format the cell as money. See *Figure 122* and *Figure 123*:

Figure 122—Production price

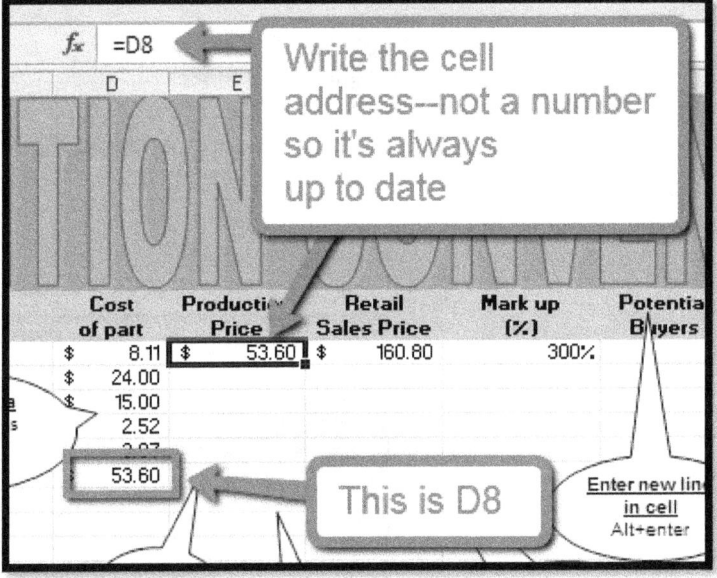

Figure 123—Detail in cell

- Retail sales price—what price will you sell the invention for? To figure this out, multiply production price by a mark-up number that will cover all other costs (i.e., labor, utilities, marketing, staff—that sort of stuff). Review this concept with students or provide a number to use. If you use *3* as the multiplier, it will look like *Figure 124*:

Figure 124—Retail sales price

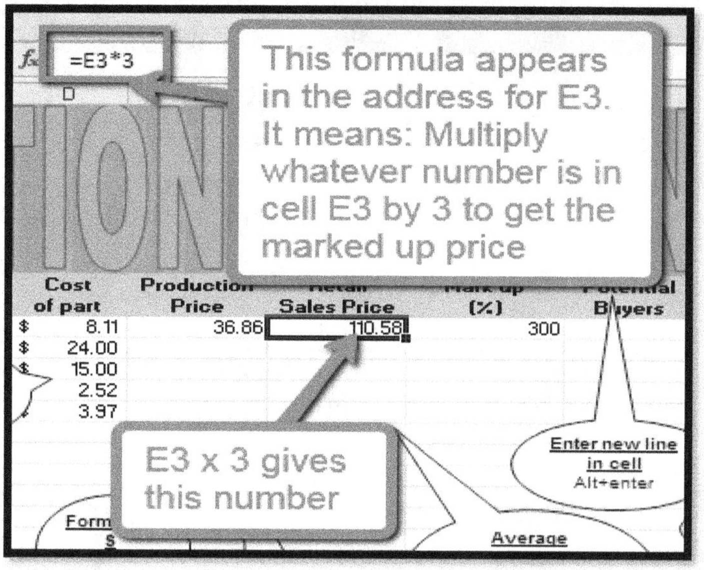

- **Team members**—what are the names of classmates working on this project with you? Use spreadsheet AZ tool to alphabetize names.
- **Website**—what are the websites of potential buyers?

_____Take the rest of class to work on the analysis of your invention (or similar).

Project #2

Figure 9--Game spreadsheet

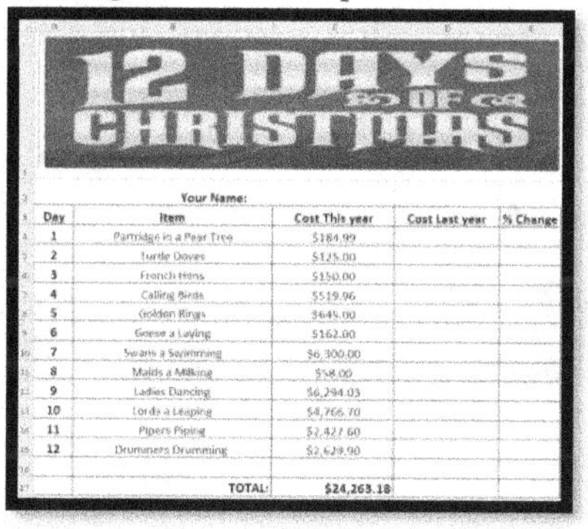

_____A great way to learn how to use spreadsheets is with specially-adapted games. Have students **play an Excel game** with a partner. Turning a spreadsheet into a game makes that daunting six-syllable phrase (data analysis) just one syllable–fun. These are popular and tie in well with the 'gamification of education':

- *Coolmath Games'* **Lemonade Stand** —*a strategy game for building a business*
- *Visit Ask a Tech Teacher's Spreadsheets resource page for more Excel games.*

Class exit ticket: None.

Differentiation

- *Early finishers: Play some of the games in Project #2.*

Lesson #25—Internet Research III

Vocabulary	Problem solving	Skills
• Background • Bullets • Extensions • Slide • Slideshow • Storyboard	• How do I research ("", +, look for qualified websites) • Got off the main website (use the back arrow) • I can't find 'difficulties' for my inventor (use critical thinking)	**New** Storyboard **Scaffolded** Online research
Academic Applications Any academic class that requires presentation of research	**Materials Required** keyboarding program, Google Earth Board rubric, Evidence Board badges, student workbooks (if using)	**Standards** CCSS.ELA-Literacy.W.4.7 NETS: 1c, 3a-d

Essential Question

How do I explain a research topic so friends understand?

Big Idea

The hard part of research is paraphrasing in fourth-grade words. That means I really have to understand it

Teacher Preparation

- Have Google Earth Board grading rubrics.
- Talk with grade-level team so you tie into inquiry.
- Ensure all required links are on student digital devices.
- Know which tasks weren't completed last week.
- Integrate domain-specific tech vocabulary into lesson.
- Know whether you need extra time to complete lesson.

Assessment Strategies

- *Completed storyboard*
- *Engaged in critical thinking*
- *Worked independently*
- *Used good keyboarding habits*
- *Completed warm-up, exit ticket*
- *Joined classroom conversations*
- *[tried to] solve own problems*
- *Decisions followed class rules*
- *Left room as s/he found it*
- *Higher order thinking: analysis, evaluation, synthesis*
- *Habits of mind observed*

Steps

Time required: 45 minutes in one sitting or spread throughout the week with a block of 30 minutes for project

Class warm-up: Keyboarding

_____Warm up with keyboard practice.
_____Continue Google Earth presentations.
_____This week, students start a seven-week summative assessment on a topic that ties in with class inquiry. We'll use inventors. Students may work in groups. They will:

- *research—one week*
- *create a slideshow (PowerPoint, Google Slides, or similar)—four weeks*
- *present to classmates—two weeks*

_____Students did slideshows in 2nd (*Figure 126a*) and 3rd grade (*Figure 126b*):

Figure 126a-b—Previous slideshow projects

 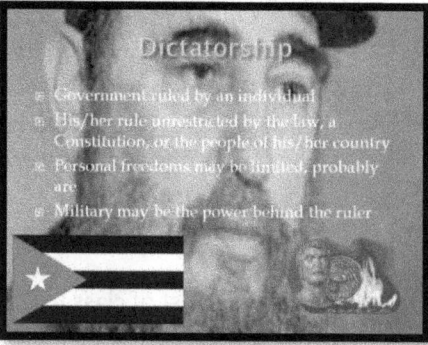

_____Show samples of slideshows completed by last year's fourth graders.

_____Today, students will complete a storyboard to organize ideas. This can be filled out as a hard copy or a digital document using a word processing or annotation tool.

_____What is a storyboard?

_____Have students follow along as you go over the storyboard template on class screen (*Figures 127a* and *127b*—full-size *Assessment* at the end of the lesson). This example coordinates with last lesson's theme of 'Invention Convention'. You will have a different topic:

Figure 127a-b—Storyboard for Inventors

PRESENTATION PROJECT—INVENTORS

Your name: _____

Your teacher: _____

Slide 1: Cover
Slide 2: Table of Contents
Slide 3: Why do people invent stuff:
  1. _____
  2. _____
  3. _____

Slide 4: First of 3 inventors:
  1. _____ (their name)
  2. _____ (What they invented)
  3. _____ (Why was it needed)
  4. _____ (Difficulties inventing it)

Slide 5: Second of 3 inventors
  1. _____ (their name)
  2. _____ (What they invented)
  3. _____ (Why was it needed)
  4. _____ (Difficulties inventing it)

Slide 6: Third of 3 inventors
  1. _____ (their name)
  2. _____ (What they invented)
  3. _____ (Why was it needed)
  4. _____ (Difficulties inventing it)

Slide 7: Three things invented by accident:
  1. _____
  2. _____
  3. _____

Slide 8: What would you invent—steps inventing it:
  1. _____
  2. _____
  3. _____

Slide 9: About the Author
  • Who do you live with
  • What are your favorite books
  • What is your favorite song
  • What is your favorite activity
  • What's your dream when you grow up

- *Slides 1 and 2—fill in later, during slideshow preparation.*
- *Slide 3—fill out as a group. Why do people invent? Money? Power? Bored? Record three reasons that resonate for you.*

- *Slides 4-7—pick three inventors and find out 1) what they invented, 2) why, and 3) what difficulties they faced.*
- *Discuss what 'difficulties' means. Lack of money? Naysayers? Seemed impossible? If you want to invent something, discuss the reasons you aren't.*
- *Slide 8—if 4th graders are doing the Invention Convention. Record three fascinating facts about that process, for example: why you selected it, what was difficult/easy, did it work?*
- *Slide 9—fill out during slideshow preparation.*

_____You have the rest of class to fill in slides 3-8 on the storyboard, but no more classtime than that. This is part of the challenge: **To work quickly and efficiently, to stay on task, to complete the project in prescribed amount of time**.

_____Remind students to use the vocabulary decoding tools you've provided on their digital devices, i.e., Dictionary.com.

_____Information can come from class conversations, textbooks, library books, videos, and personal knowledge. When using the internet, follow good digital citizenship (*Figure 128*). When recording information to storyboard, paraphrase in 4th-grade words.

Figure 128—Internet safety

_____Before beginning, discuss safe/effective internet searches. If necessary, review earlier lessons.

_____On class internet start page, post a list of websites on this topic.

Class exit ticket: ***Students show you their completed storyboard before leaving class.***

Differentiation

- *Early finishers: visit class internet start page for websites that tie into classwork.*
- *Have students edit the 'reasons' slide after they create their invention. At that point, they will have personal knowledge of difficulties.*
- *Add slideshow project to class calendar.*

Assessment 17—Inventor storyboard

PRESENTATION PROJECT—INVENTORS

Your name: _____

Your teacher: _____

Slide 1:   Cover

Slide 2:   Table of Contents

Slide 3:   Why do people invent stuff:

   1. _____
   2. _____
   3. _____

Slide 4:   First of 3 inventors:

   1. _____(their name)
   2. _____(What they invented)
   3. _____(Why was it needed)
   4. _____(Difficulties inventing it)

Slide 5:   Second of 3 inventors

   1. _____(their name)
   2. _____(What they invented)
   3. _____(Why was it needed)
   4. _____(Difficulties inventing it)

Slide 6:   **Third of 3 inventors**

1. _____(their name)

2. _____What they invented)

3. _____(Why was it needed)

4. _____(Difficulties inventing it)

Slide 7:   **Three things invented by accident:**

1. _____

2. _____

3. _____

Slide 8:   **What would you invent—steps inventing it:**

1. _____

2. _____

3. _____

Slide 9:   **About the Author**

- *Who do you live with*
- *What are your favorite books*
- *What is your favorite song*
- *What is your favorite activity*
- *What's your dream when you grow up*

4th Grade Technology Curriculum: Teacher Manual

Lesson #26—Slideshow Project I

Vocabulary	Problem solving	Skills
• Background • Design • Evidence • Subtopics • Text box • Wrap	• Save rather than 'save as' to keep project where it opened. • I'm not ready for my presentation (can you move to later date?) • Why do I have to put my name in file name? (easier to find)	**New** Storyboard **Scaffolded** Slideshow presentation Keyboarding skills
Academic Applications Language, topic requiring research presentation	**Materials Required** slideshow program, storyboards, Evidence Board badges, Google Earth Board rubrics, student workbooks (if using)	**Standards** CCSS.ELA-Literacy.W.4.2a NETS: 1d, 3c-d, 6a-d

Essential Question

How do I use technology to communicate details visually?

Big Idea

Use technology to produce and publish writing as well as to interact and collaborate with others

Teacher Preparation

- Talk with grade-level team so you tie into conversations.
- Remind students to bring storyboards today.
- Know which tasks weren't completed last week.
- Integrate domain-specific tech vocabulary into lesson.
- Know if you need extra time to complete this lesson.

Assessment Strategies

- Anecdotal observation of work
- Transferred knowledge of slideshows from prior years
- Worked independently
- Used good keyboarding habits
- Completed warm-up
- [tried to] solve own problems
- Decisions followed class rules
- Left room as s/he found it
- Higher order thinking: analysis, evaluation, synthesis
- Habits of mind observed

Steps

Time required: 45 minutes in one sitting or spread throughout the week with a block of 30 minutes for project

Class warm-up: Storyboards are placed next to digital devices, in preparation for typing. Or, have students begin the transcription process.

_____Continue with Google Earth presentations. If you notice that lots of presenters are making the same mistake, review that before today's presentations.

_____Any evidence of learning to post on Evidence Board? Which class has the most badges by this point in the school year?

_____Did students have any technology problems they'd like to share with the class?

_____Open a presentation tool that uses slideshows:

- o computers: PowerPoint (Figure 129a), Google Slides (Figure 129b)
- o online tools: Kizoa, Haiku Deck (Figure 129c)
- o iPads: Haiku Deck

Figure 129a—Presentation tools: PowerPoint; 129b—Google Slides; 129c—Kizoa

  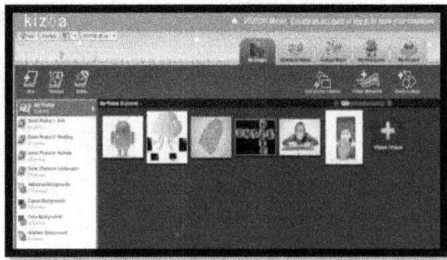

_____As you follow instructions, adapt them to the program you use as follows:

- *Review all instructions before beginning.*
- *Read the instructions.*
- *Figure out how to accomplish the steps called out in your program.*
- *Adapt instructions to suit your program.*

_____Before beginning, discuss the difference between writing with a presentation tool and a word processing program. *Figure 130* provides a few ideas. What else would you add?

Figure 130—Presentation tool vs. word processing

Element	Presentation program	Word processing
Purpose	Share a presentation	Share words
Basics	Graphics-based	Text-based
	Design is important to content	Design is secondary to content
	Layout communicates	Layout may detract from words
	Few words, lots of images	Primarily words communicate
Sentences	Bulleted, phrases	Full grammatical sentences
Content	Slides cover basics, to remind presenter what to say	Thorough discussion of a topic. Meant to be complete document
Use	As a back-up to presentation	As complete resource
Presentation	Speaker looks at audience	Speaker reads from document
What else		

_____Open storyboard either as a hard copy or on the student digital device. Remind them to use Alt+Tab to toggle between digital tools as they copy from storyboard to slideshow. Demonstrate how much easier it is.

_____Add nine slides. One will look like a cover (*Figure 131a*); the rest like *Figure 131b*:

Figure 131a—Cover slide; 131b—interior slide

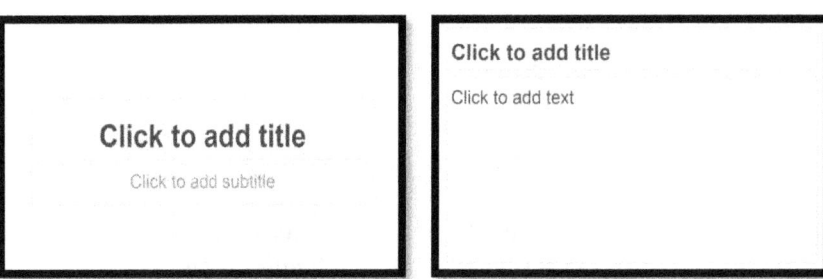

_____Each slide will correspond to storyboard research.

4th Grade Technology Curriculum: Teacher Manual

_____While typing, don't worry about selecting font, sizes, color, or look. The theme you select (after typing) will adjust those for you.

_____If using Google Presentations or an online tool, you may pick a theme before you start.

_____**Slide #1**—add slideshow title (i.e., *Inventors*) and your name (*Figures 132a-c*). No need to adjust font size, color or look. That'll be done later based on the theme you select:

Figure 132a-b—Cover slides in PowerPoint; 132c—Slides

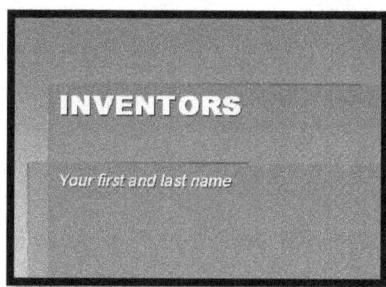  

_____**Slide #2**—Title is 'Table of Contents' (in 'Click to add title'). In 'Click to add text', add topics from storyboard. See *Figures 133a-c*:

Figure 133a—Slide 2 sample in PowerPoint; 133b—Slides; 133c—Haiku

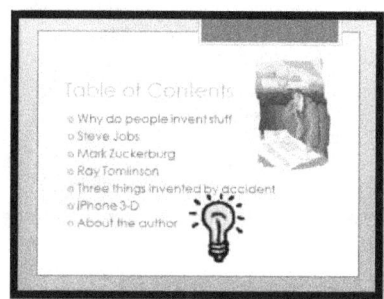 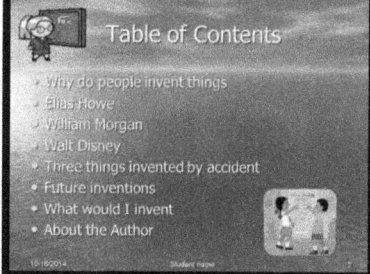 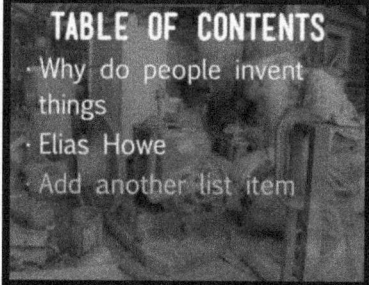

_____**Slide #3**— Title is 'Why Do People Invent [Stuff]?' Type reasons why in the textbox below the title (*Figures 134a-c*). These come from group discussion last week:

Figure 134a—Slide 3 sample in PowerPoint; 134b—Slides; 134c—Haiku

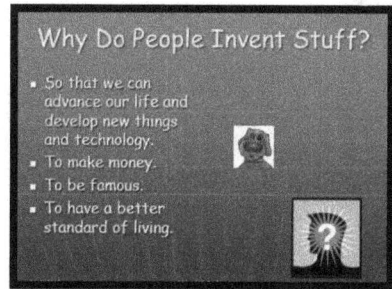 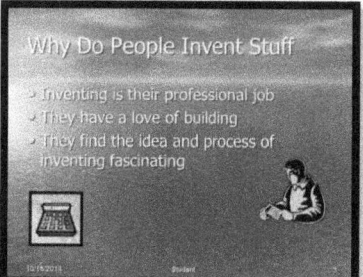 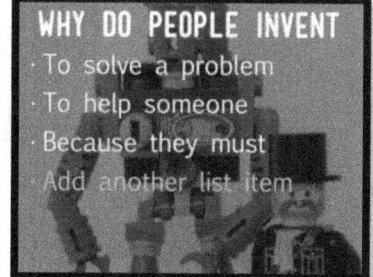

_____**Slide #4-6**—These slides cover the three inventors you selected. The title of each is one of the inventors. Underneath the person's name, add the three details you collected. See *Figures 135a-b* for examples in different digital devices:

Figure 135a-b—Slide 4-6 samples

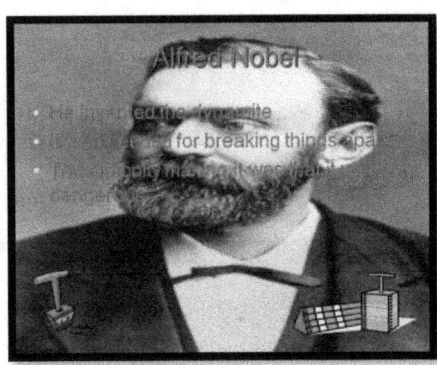

_____Note: Inventor's picture is added to the background in a few weeks.
_____**Slide #7**—*Title* is 'Three Things Invented by Accident'. Copy these from your storyboard. See *Figures 136a-b* for examples:

Figure 136a-b—Slide 7 samples

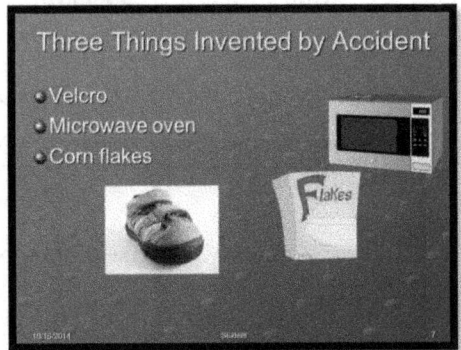

_____**Slide #8**—*Title* is your invention if you're participating in Invention Convention. If not, this slide will cover your dream. Bullet three steps required to create it or three points viewers should know about it. See *Figures 137a-b*:

Figure 137a-b—Slide 8 samples

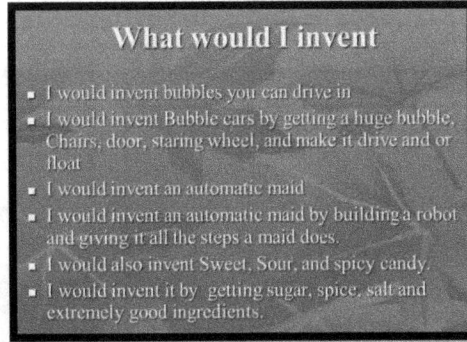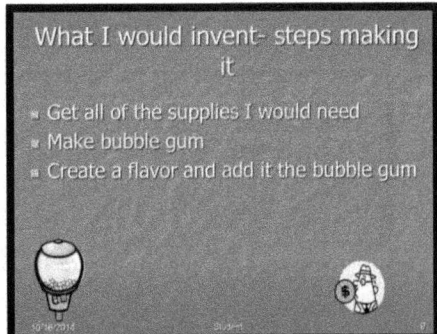

_____**Slide #9**—*About the Author*—tell your viewers five things about yourself. They may be the topics included in *Figures 138a-b*:

Figure 138a-b—Slide 9 samples

_____As students type, consider the following:

- *Does the title introduce the topic?*
- *Is related information grouped (as bullets)?*
- *Is the topic well developed?*

_____Use this slideshow to practice typing. Remember good habits. By 4th grade, students should be able to type 300+ words in a single sitting. How many words are on your storyboard?
_____Ctrl+S every ten minutes to save; save early, save often.
_____Watch grammar and spelling, punctuation and capitals as you type. Don't change fonts, sizes, colors—these are tied into the theme.
_____The tool you select will have different approaches to adding text, formatting, and more. Test the tool out before using it with students, and then adapt these instructions.
_____Save to digital portfolio; back up to flash drive.

Class exit ticket: None

Differentiation

- *Early finishers: visit class internet start page for websites that tie into classwork.*
- *If students analyzed inventions during spreadsheet lesson, add a slide on that research.*
- *If you have a VoiceThread account, consider using this instead of a slideshow.*
- *You might also use Animoto, Photostory (free Windows download), Prezi, Glogster, or GoAnimate to create an interactive exploration of inquiry.*

"A computer is like an Old Testament God, with a lot of rules and no mercy."

Assessment 18—Slideshow presentation rubric

SLIDESHOW RUBRIC

Name_____ Teacher_____

Here's a list of required skills. Check off those included. Add those missed. Turn rubric in with storyboard after presentation

1. Title slide introduces topic   _____
2. About the Author slide   _____
3. Table of Contents   _____
4. Each slide has title to introduce topic   _____
5. Each slide has bullets from storyboard   _____
6. Bullets group related facts, definitions, details _____
7. Each slide has picture that aids comprehension _____
8. Each slide has movie (GIF)—may be optional _____
9. Spelling is correct   _____
10. Grammar follows conventions discussed in class _____
11. No slang used   _____
12. 5 animations—may be optional   _____
13. 5 transitions—may be optional   _____
14. 5 sounds—may be optional   _____
15. Slides auto-advance   _____
16. Enough time on each slide to cover material _____
17. High level of professionalism   _____
18. (Custom background)   _____
19. (Custom animation)   _____
20. (Custom sound)   _____
21. **Class presentation**   _____
    a. **Face audience**   _____
    b. **Talk to audience**   _____
    c. **Introduce yourself and topic** _____
    d. **Speak loud enough**   _____
    e. **No 'umms' or stuttering**   _____

Assessment 19—Slideshow presentation rubric

PRESENTATION RUBRIC

Name _____

Teacher _____

Date _____

Face audience   _____

Talk to audience   _____

Introduce yourself   _____

Introduce your topic   _____

Speak loudly and clearly   _____

No 'umms', slang, stuttering   _____

Answer questions   _____

Slideshow progresses smoothly   _____

Understand your topic   _____

4th Grade Technology Curriculum: Teacher Manual

Lesson #27—Slideshow II

Vocabulary	Problem solving	Skills
• Animation • Background • Bullet list • Drop-down menu • Edit • Format • GIFs • Image • Scheme • Transitions • Visual	• Student digital device doesn't work? Help them solve problems—don't do for them. • I can't find my project (Did you save it with your last name?) • Computer didn't save my project (Try back-up) • What's the difference between edit and format? • My computer crashed (did you save early, save often?)	**New** Quick research of topics **Scaffolded** Keyboarding, slideshows
Academic Applications Language, academic topic, quick research	**Materials Required** slideshow program, storyboards, Evidence Board badges, Google Earth Board rubrics	**Standards** CCSS.ELA-Literacy.W.4.2a NETS: 1d, 3c-d, 6a-d

Essential Question

How do I use technology to communicate visually?

Big Idea

Use technology to produce and publish writing as well as to interact and collaborate with others

Teacher Preparation

- Talk with grade-level team so you tie into conversations.
- Know which tasks weren't completed last week.
- Integrate domain-specific tech vocabulary into lesson.
- Know if you need extra time to complete this lesson.

Assessment Strategies

- Anecdotal observation
- Progress on slideshow
- Applied past knowledge to project
- Used good keyboarding habits
- Completed exit ticket
- [tried to] solve own problems
- Left room as s/he found it
- Higher order thinking: analysis, evaluation, synthesis
- Habits of mind observed

Steps

Time required: 45 minutes in one sitting or spread throughout the week
Class warm-up: None

_____Continue with Google Earth presentations.

_____Any evidence of learning for Evidence Board?

_____Open slideshow project saved last week. Continue filling in text. Watch spelling and grammar. Don't use paragraphs or full sentences—use bullets and phrases.

_____Take this opportunity to develop and strengthen writing by planning, revising, and editing each slide before moving on.

_____Ctrl+S every ten minutes to save; save early, save often.

_____Don't change fonts, sizes, colors—these are tied into the theme.

_____Use the internet only to verify information learned in class to support the topic—don't guess. Remember search skills covered earlier in the year.

_____ When done with each slide, edit and revise before moving on.
_____ Use this as typing practice. Remember good habits. By the end of 4th grade, you should be able to type 300+ words in a single sitting. How many words are on a storyboard?
_____ Continually throughout class, check for understanding.
_____ Save; save-as to flash drive as back up. Include last name in the file name (why?). Close to the desktop. Tuck chairs under desk, headphones over the tower; leave station as it was.

Class exit ticket: *Have a neighbor check to be sure all topics are covered and on the correct slide.*

Differentiation

- *Early finishers: visit class internet start page for websites that tie into classroom inquiry.*
- *If students analyzed inventions during spreadsheet lesson, add a slide to cover that.*
- *Instead of a slideshow, use Animoto, Photostory (free Windows download), Prezi, Glogster, or GoAnimate (Google for addresses).*

There are 10 types of people in the world; those who understand Binary and those who don't.

— *Author Unknown*

NOTES:

Lesson #28—Slideshow III

Vocabulary	Problem solving	Skills
• Animation • Auto-advance • GIF • Greyed out • Looped • Multimedia • Shift+F5 • Transition • WPM	• Slideshow doesn't auto-advance (check 'animation'). • Can't read webpage (Ctrl+ zooms in) • What's the difference between 'save' and 'save as'? • Menu command is greyed out (push escape four times) • Can't find project (where did you save?) • I type slower with all fingers (practice)	**New** **Scaffolded** Keyboarding Slideshows
Academic Applications Language, research, speaking/listening	**Materials Required** slideshow program, storyboards, Evidence Board badges, Google Earth Board rubrics	**Standards** CCSS.ELA-Literacy.W.4.2a NETS: 1d, 3c-d, 6a-d

Essential Question

How do I communicate facts and details to different audiences?

Big Idea

Use technology to produce and publish writing as well as to interact and collaborate with others

Teacher Preparation

- Talk with grade-level team so you tie into conversations.
- Ensure all required links are on student digital devices.
- Know which tasks weren't completed last week.
- Integrate domain-specific tech vocabulary into lesson.
- Know if you need extra time to complete this lesson.

Assessment Strategies

- Anecdotal observation
- No problem opening slideshow
- Progressed on slideshow
- Worked independently
- Used good keyboarding habits
- Completed warm-up, exit ticket
- [tried to] solve own problems
- Decisions followed class rules
- Left room as s/he found it
- Higher order thinking: analysis, evaluation, synthesis
- Habits of mind observed

Steps

Time required: 45 minutes in one sitting or spread through week with a block of 30 minutes for project
Class warm-up: Keyboarding

_____Warm up for speed quiz. Remind students:

- *correct posture; hands curled over the home row*
- *eyes on the screen as much as possible*
- *paper to the right/left of keyboard (not over screen)*

_____Today's keyboarding goal:

- *25 wpm*
- *Type a page without difficulty at one sitting, with good habits—about three hundred words. You should do fine typing for five minutes without a break.*

_____Review how student hands should look (*Figures 139a-b*):

Figure 139a-b—Hand position

_____The speed quiz can be delivered in several ways:

- *Place a page from a book being read in class on the class screen. Students will copy it for the quiz. This method forces their heads up rather than on their hands.*
- *Print a page from a book being read in class or a sample document for each student. They place it to the side of their keyboard and type from it.*
- *Use an online typing test like TypingTest.com.*

_____Students type for 3-5 minutes, paying attention to posture:

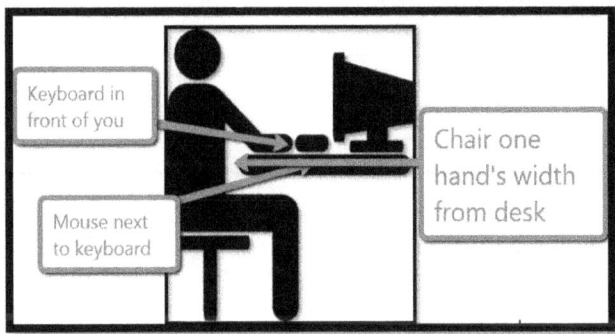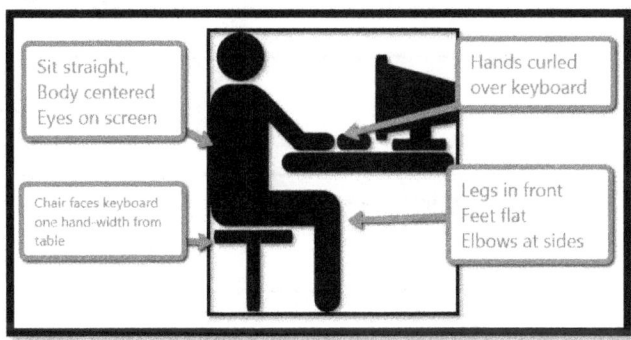

_____Add word count to the bottom of the page. Take one minute to spell/grammar check.
_____Save (does it matter if student 'saves' or 'save-as'?); print/publish/share, as required.
_____Continue with Google Earth presentations.
_____Any evidence of learning for Evidence Board? Any technology problems to share?
_____Open slideshow saved last week.
_____**Slide #1-9**—add Transition (if available in your slideshow tool). Discuss what 'transition' means. What's the prefix 'trans-' mean? What are other *trans-* words? Select a transition for each slide. Once it's selected, it is on the slide until changed.
_____Repeat for each slide, with a different transition.
_____To have slideshow automatically move forward, select 'auto-advance' in Transition screen and bump time to eight seconds. Now slideshow will advance after eight seconds with no hands.
_____Repeat for each slide, with a different transition.
_____Ctrl+S every ten minutes—save early save often.
_____**Slide #1-9**—click title. Select 'Animation' (if available in your slideshow tool). Select an appealing animation. Only animate title. Once added, it's there until changed.
_____Push F5 to test slideshow. Does each slide auto-advance?

4th Grade Technology Curriculum: Teacher Manual

Class exit ticket: ***Students show their slideshow to a neighbor.***

Differentiation

- *Early finishers: visit class internet start page for websites that tie into classwork.*

"Computers in the future may weigh no more than 1.5 tons."

– *Popular Mechanics*, 1949 forecasting the march of science

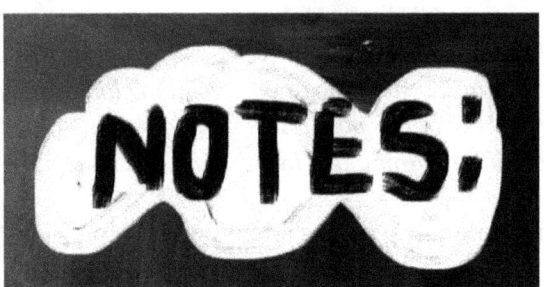

_____

_____

_____

_____

_____

_____

4th Grade Technology Curriculum: Teacher Manual

Lesson #29—Slideshow IV

Vocabulary	Problem solving	Skills
• 'Greyed out' • Auto-play • Background • Copyright • Ctrl+Enter • Custom animation • Custom path • Drill down • GIF • Public domain • Task pane	• My picture got weird (resize with corner handles) • Slides go too fast (slow speed) • I can't find my project (where did you save it?) • I still can't find my project (go to start button>search) • Background went on all slides (Did you add to selected slide?) • I'm not ready to present (next week is last week)	**New** Slideshow presentations Copying pictures from school website **Scaffolded** Keyboarding Slideshows Speaking and listening Using online images
Academic Applications Language, research, speaking/listening	**Materials Required** storyboards, Evidence Board badges, Google Earth Board grading, workbooks (if using)	**Standards** CCSS.ELA-Literacy.W.4.2a NETS: 1d, 3c-d, 6a-d

Essential Question

How do I communicate facts and details to different audiences?

Big Idea

Use technology to produce and publish writing as well as to interact and collaborate with others

Teacher Preparation

- Know 'keyboard speedsters' and fastest class.
- Know which tasks weren't completed last week.
- Integrate domain-specific tech vocabulary into lesson.
- Know if you need extra time to complete this lesson.

Assessment Strategies

- Completed slideshow, rubric
- Used slideshow prior knowledge
- Used good keyboarding habits
- Completed warm-up, exit ticket
- Joined classroom conversations
- [tried to] solve own problems
- Decisions followed class rules
- Left room as s/he found it
- Higher order thinking: analysis, evaluation, synthesis
- Habits of mind observed

Steps

Time required: 45 minutes in one sitting or spread throughout the week with a 30-minute block for project

Class warm-up: Keyboarding

_____Continue with Google Earth presentations.

_____Announce 'Keyboard Speedsters' and Fastest Class. 'Keyboard Speedsters' (*Figure 140a*) are students who meet grade level speed requirement (25wpm) while maintaining good keyboarding habits. I award them a prize and post the list on the bulletin board. Choose a method of recognition that works for your students (such as *Figure 140c*).

_____'Fastest Class' (*Figure 140b*) has fastest average speed. Discuss what 'average' means and how it is calculated. Discuss how far class is behind/ahead and what that means—i.e., each student must improve/slow down .2 wpm. What's *that* mean? Top class gets a prize suited to your student group.

Figure 140a—Keyboard speedsters; 140b—Fastest class; 140c—keyboard certificate

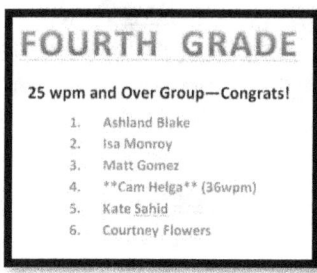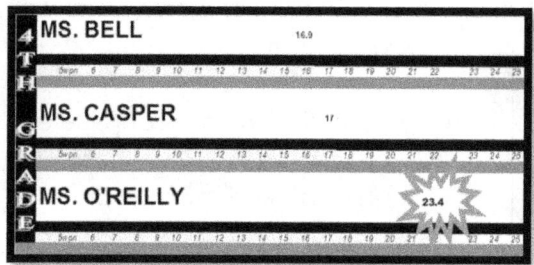

_____Did students have any problems with technology they'd like to share?

_____Any evidence for Evidence Board?

_____Open project saved last week.

_____**Slides 4-6**: Add inventor picture to background (*Figures 141a-b*). This is the same procedure students followed to add their picture to 'About the Author' slide (*Figures 141c-d*):

Figure 141a-d—Custom slideshow backgrounds

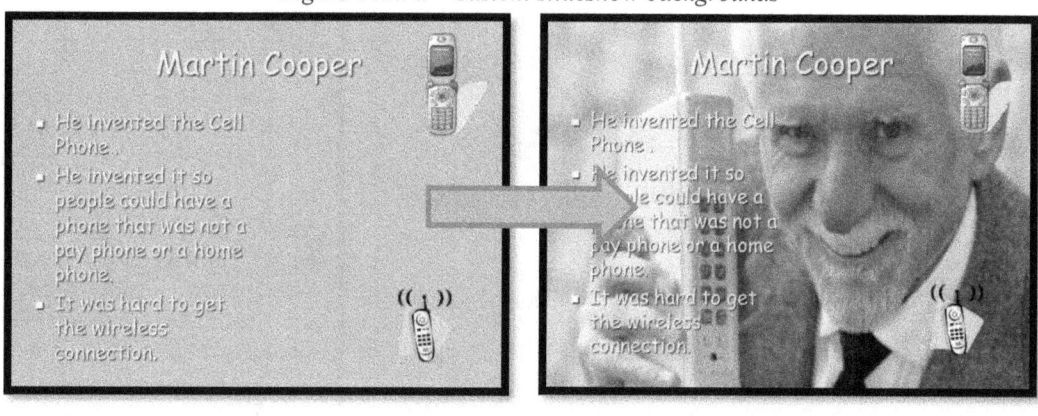

_____Here's how you do that if you're using PowerPoint (*Figure 142*):

- *Find a picture on the internet or another place pictures are available; save to digital portfolio. Be sure the image is in the public domain. Discuss how to ensure this is true.*

- *Right click on slide background; select Format background; go to **Fill>Image**.*
- *Browse your digital device until you find the image you saved. Select it.*
- *Do NOT apply to all slides—just this one.*
- *Close dialogue box.*

Figure 142—How to create custom background

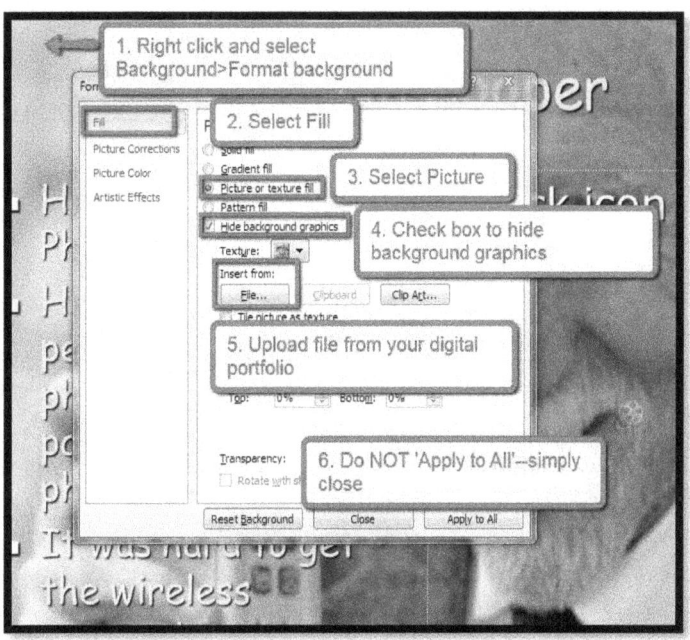

_____Add a customized background to remaining slides. Make each relevant to slide topic.
_____Here's the variety you'll see in backgrounds when you're done (*Figures 143a-b*):

Figure 143a-b—Variety of slide backgrounds in PowerPoint, Haiku

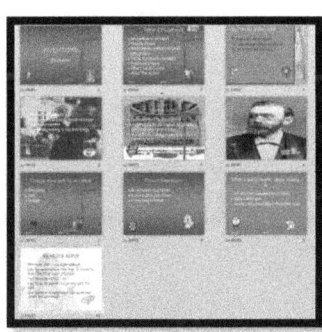 

_____Add an image to each slide to enhance the message.
_____Add a GIF (movie, moving picture) to each slide to enhance the message. See if students can figure out how to do this. There's a collection of GIFs on Ask a Tech Teacher's resource pages. Students copy-paste to their slideshows.
_____Play slideshow from beginning. Does it stall? Does it look the way you want? Is there enough time on each slide for the information shared? Use problem-solving solutions to fix.
_____Play sideshow with the assessment rubric. Check to be sure everything required is included:

4th Grade Technology Curriculum: Teacher Manual

SLIDESHOW PRESENTATION RUBRIC

Name_____ Teacher_____

Here's a list of required skills. Check off those included. Add those missed.
Turn rubric in with storyboard after presentation

1. Title slide introduces topic
2. About the Author slide
3. Table of Contents
4. Each slide has title to introduce topic
5. Each slide has bullets from storyboard
6. Bullets group related facts, definitions, details
7. Each slide has picture that aids comprehension
8. Each slide has movie (GIF)
9. Spelling is correct
10. Grammar follows conventions discussed in class
11. No slang used
12. 5 animations
13. 5 transitions
14. 5 sounds
15. Slides auto-advance
16. Enough time on each slide to cover material
17. High level of professionalism
18. (Custom background)
19. (Custom animation)
20. (Sound)
21. Class presentation
    a. Face audience
    b. Talk to audience
    c. Introduce yourself and topic
    d. Speak loud enough
    e. No 'umms' or stuttering

PRESENTATION RUBRIC

Name _____
Teacher _____
Date _____

Face audience _____
Talk to audience _____
Introduce yourself _____
Introduce your topic _____
Speak loudly and clearly _____
No 'umms', slang, stuttering _____
Answer questions _____
Slide show progresses smoothly _____
Understand your topic _____

_____ Done? Swap slideshows with classmate who is done and complete checklist on his/her project, and then make corrections s/he found.

_____ Now, student presents their slideshow to neighbor. Compare this against the Presentation Rubric (*Assessment 19*).

_____ Ctrl+S every ten minutes.

Class exit ticket: **Submit rubrics. This tells you the student is ready to present next week.**

Differentiation

- *Early finishers: visit class internet start page for websites that tie into classwork.*
- *Add sound and custom animation to slideshow (if available).*
- *Publish slideshows to class website, blog, or via an online program like Slideshare, Slideboom. Google for addresses.*
- *Add musical track that plays throughout slideshow (if available). Have a folder of music available that students can pick from.*

Lesson #30—Slideshow Presentations I

Vocabulary	Problem solving	Skills
• Animation • Auto-advance • Mouse click • Net • Rubric • Transition	• Slide moves too fast (change transition speed) • Can't see my slideshow (did you practice with back to slideshow?) • Slideshow doesn't advance (push spacebar for student)	**New** **Scaffolded** Speaking and listening Presenting with a slideshow
Academic Applications Speaking and listening, presentations	**Materials Required** Class screen, student slideshows	**Standards** CCSS.ELA-Literacy.SL.4.4 NETS: 6d

Essential Question

How do I communicate facts and details to different audiences?

Big Idea

Use technology to interact with others

Teacher Preparation

- Know which tasks weren't completed last week and whether they are necessary to move forward.
- Integrate domain-specific tech vocabulary into lesson.
- Know whether you need extra time to complete this lesson with your student group.

Assessment Strategies

- Followed class guidelines for speaking and listening
- Used good keyboarding habits
- Completed (optional) warm-up
- Joined classroom conversations
- [tried to] solve own problems
- Left room as s/he found it
- Higher order thinking: analysis, evaluation, synthesis
- Habits of mind observed

Steps

Time required: 45 minutes in one sitting or a block of 10 minutes and 35 minutes
Class warm-up: Keyboarding (optional)

_____Finish Google Earth Board presentations.

_____If there's time (meaning: if student presentations won't take the entire class), go to TypingTest.com or a similar online tool to check speed and accuracy:

- Select a test; select '3 minutes' and start.
- Don't stop for corrections; type until time runs out.
- Test gives a gross and net speed. 'Gross' shows speed with no mistakes. 'Net' deducts for mistakes.

_____Students start slideshow presentations today. The only option that reliably includes all animations and transitions is the native software (i.e., PowerPoint)—*Figure 144a*. Other options available to collate presentations or share an uploaded version might not (which may work fine for you). For example, if you embed a Google slideshow into your class website or blog, it may not show all the detail

students have added (*Figure 144b*). The same is true if you upload to an online tool like *Figure 144c*:

Figure 144a—Slideshow in PowerPoint; 144b—in Google Slides; 144c—Slideshare

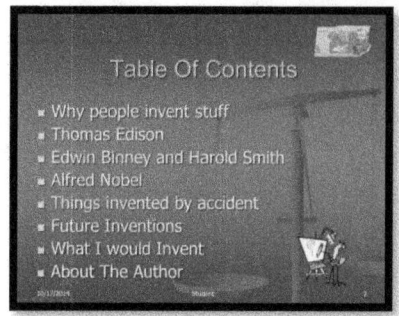 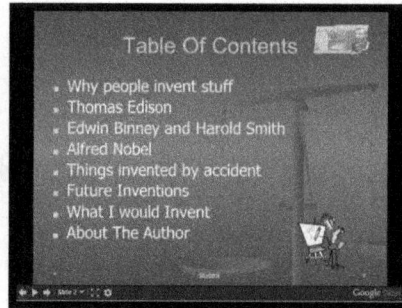 

_____Explain grading (according to rubric on prior pages).
_____Begin presentations. What do students remember from last year?

- *Students should come prepared, having practiced required material.*
- *Keep eyes on audience, glancing at screen only when necessary.*
- *Summarize information where necessary and use the bullet item to remind them of additional information.*
- *Speak loudly so whole room can hear.*
- *Be prepared to respond to specific questions to clarify or follow up on information.*
- *Presenter always should sound interested and knowledgeable about topic.*

_____Audience should:

- *pay attention, not fidget*
- *be polite*
- *make comments that contribute to discussion and link to both presentation and remarks of others*

_____Presenter grade is based in part on how good s/he is as an audience
_____Be prepared to push spacebar to move slideshow forward if it gets 'stuck'.
_____Students can have parents or classroom teacher present.
_____If an audience question speculates why presenter made a mistake, remind audience that feedback is positive, upbeat—everyone makes mistakes so not to focus on those.

Class exit ticket: None

Differentiation

- *Finished early: Organize for End-of-Year Challenge.*
- *Take a video of presentations and upload to school website or blog.*

4th Grade Technology Curriculum: Teacher Manual

Lesson #31—Slideshow Presentations II

Vocabulary	Problem solving	Skills
• Animation • Auto-advance • Rubric • Transition	• Slide moves too fast (change transition speed) • Student slideshow doesn't advance (push spacebar for them)	**Scaffolded** *Speaking and listening* *Presenting with slideshow*
Academic Applications *Speaking and listening, presentations*	**Materials Required** *Class screen, student slideshows*	**Standards** *CCSS.ELA-Literacy.SL.4.4* *NETS: 6d*

Essential Question

How do I communicate effectively to different audiences?

Big Idea

Use technology to produce and publish writing as well as to interact and collaborate with others

Teacher Preparation

- Integrate domain-specific tech vocabulary into lesson.
- Know if you need extra time to complete this lesson.

Assessment Strategies

- *Followed class guidelines for speaking and listening*
- *Joined class conversations*
- *[tried to] solve own problems*
- *Left room as s/he found it*
- *Higher order thinking: analysis, evaluation, synthesis*
- *Habits of mind observed*

Steps

Time required: 45 minutes in one sitting
Class warm-up: None

_____Presentations finish today. Open student slideshow on classroom monitor or class screen. Review rules with presenter and audience.

_____Allow students to sit in comfortable groups with friends as long as they remain respectful and quiet during presentations.

_____Before class ends, divide students into teams for next week's Challenge. Pass out questions and let students take balance of class to prepare. Some teams assign specialists. Others, everyone is a generalist.

Class exit ticket: None

Differentiation

- *Early finishers: visit class internet start page for websites that tie into classwork.*

Lesson #32—End-of-Year Challenge

Vocabulary	Problem solving	Skills
• Generalist • Specialist	• I can't remember Challenge answer (you're part of a team)	**Scaffolded** Tech skills
Academic Applications Test-taking, speaking and listening	**Materials Required** challenge questions, clock with a second hand, prizes for winners	**Standards** CCSS: Anchor standards NETS: 1d, 3a-c

Essential Question

What did I learn this year?

Big Idea

I know more than I think I do

Assessment Strategies

- Decisions followed class rules
- Left room as s/he found it
- Higher order thinking: analysis, evaluation, synthesis
- Habits of mind observed

Teacher Preparation

- Integrate domain-specific tech vocabulary into lesson.
- Know whether you need extra time to complete this lesson with your student group.

Steps

Time required: 45 minutes in one sitting
Class warm-up: None

_____End of Year Challenge—students play a Jeopardy-style game to see who knows the most about different categories of technology. Adapt questions to material you covered between kindergarten and fourth grade. *Assessment 20* is a sample.

_____Ask students to go into their teams. One member on each Team is Speaker—and the only one who can answer questions. S/he will confer with colleagues before answering.

_____Speaker selects a category (*Word Processing Skills, Keyboard Shortcuts, and Vocabulary*. Teacher then asks a question from that group. Team has ten seconds to confer and answer. If they are wrong or don't answer, next team gets a chance. Do not repeat questions. Teams must listen to your question and other Team answers.

_____Repeat with new Team and new question, but they must select a different category. No category can be repeated.

_____When time runs out, count points (one per correct answer), announce winner, and award prize.

_____Students love this game. If I had time, I'd play it at mid-year also.

Class exit ticket: None

Differentiation

- For more excitement, put this into a Jeopardy template

Assessment 20—End-of-year challenge

END-OF-YEAR TEAM CHALLENGE

Review the following concepts. These are the questions that will be asked during the Team Challenge—to find the year's most tech-savvy team of students!

Basics
- How do you 'Print screen'
- How do you print
- How do you save
- Name 5 parts of digital device
- Name four ways to save a file (.jpg, .PDF...)
- What is a local disk
- What is the network file

Classroom Tech Rules
- Name two speaking/listening skills
- Name three tech use rules
- How often should you save
- How do you print from the internet
- What does "Respect everyone's work" mean
- When can you eat in the lab
- What internet site can you go on
- What is proper posture at the computer
- When can you plagiarize
- When do you not have to credit info from internet
- Who is to blame if you miss homework
- If you don't know a rule, do you have to follow it
- When is it OK to go into someone else's file folder
- What if you miss a class
- When can you touch someone else's equipment

Coding/Programming
- How do you create a macro
- How do you learn sequencing from coding
- How do you learn problem solving from coding
- How do you create a shortkey
- Name three tools for coding
- Why learn coding/programming

Digital Citizenship
- Name three netiquette rules
- Name three rules to make online search easier
- What are your digital responsibilities
- What are your digital rights
- What is a good digital citizen
- What is fair use online
- What is social media
- What is your digital footprint
- What is the digital neighborhood
- When do you share online
- What is a cyberbully
- Why use an avatar
- Why use UN and PW

Digital tools—for the classroom
- Name 5 parts of an iPad (or Chromebook)
- What digital tool takes a screenshot
- What digital tool tapes audio
- What are digital portfolios
- What is a blog
- Why use a blog
- What are Google Apps
- What is the class digital calendar
- What is the class internet start page
- Where does the class collect weblinks
- Why use a class website
- Why use a student dropbox
- Why use Discussion Boards
- Why use email

DTP
- How do you add a border
- How do you add text
- How do you insert a page
- How do you move material to another page
- How do you add a footer
- How do you add the page number to the footer
- How do you insert a picture
- Name four projects we did in DTP
- Why use DTP instead of WP?
- What project did you use DTP in this year

4th Grade Technology Curriculum: Teacher Manual

Graphics
- How do you change a picture background
- How do you crop a picture
- How do you move an image around page
- How do you resize a picture
- How do you wrap text around a picture
- List three examples of graphic organizers
- Name two image editors you used this year
- When can you use an online image
- Why use a mindmap

Internet
- How do you attach a document to an email
- How do you copy-paste from the internet
- How do you select the best site from a search engine
- Name 3 website extensions and what they are
- Name one address we have visited on the internet
- Name three ways you know a site is trust-worthy
- What are the four pieces of a web address
- What is a search engine
- What is the 'Back' button
- What is the 'Forward' button
- What is the 'Home' button
- What is the 'Refresh' button
- What is the Address Bar
- What's the 'History' tool
- When can you go on the internet at school

Keyboarding
- An A in keyboarding requires 20% of what
- Describe good keyboarding posture
- How fast should you keyboard in 4th grade
- How fast should you keyboard in 4th grade
- When do you use proper keyboarding habits
- Why learn to keyboard properly

Keyboard Shortkeys
- Add a hyperlink (Ctrl+K)
- Bold (Ctrl+B)
- Bring back internet toolbar (F11)
- Copy (Ctrl+C)
- Exdent in an outline (Shift+tab)
- Exit a program (Alt+F4)
- Find (Ctrl+F)
- Help (F1)
- Indent in an outline (tab)
- Name 5 shortkeys on an iPad/Chromebook/Mac
- Italics (Ctrl+I)
- Make a graph in spreadsheet (F11)
- New page (Ctrl+Enter)
- Paste (Ctrl+V)
- Print (Ctrl+P)
- Save (Ctrl+S)
- Toggle between tasks (Alt+Tab)
- Underline (Ctrl+U)
- Undo (Ctrl+Z)
- Zoom in on a webpage (Ctrl++)
- Zoom out of a webpage (Ctrl+-)

Presentation Tools
- Why use a presentation tool
- How do you add slides
- How do you delete slides
- How do you add animations
- How do you add transitions
- How do you add moving pictures
- How do you add GIF's
- How do you add sounds
- How do you change background
- How do you use pictures for backgrounds
- How do you insert hyperlinks
- How do you auto-advance slides

Problem Solving
- How do you find the date on a digital device
- How do you fix a weird looking resized image
- How do you search for a file
- How do you take a screenshot on digital device
- If double-click doesn't work, what do you do
- Name 4 reasons you can't find your file
- Name five problem-solving strategies
- Name two things you do if your screen is frozen
- What do you do if desktop icons are messed up
- What do you do if monitor is black
- What if you accidentally delete words/pictures
- What if your capitals are stuck on
- What if your digital device doesn't work
- What if your mouse doesn't work
- What if your Start button disappears
- What if your volume doesn't work
- What is the name of the classroom printer
- What is the next thing you do if monitor is black

- What is the password to log-on the digital device
- What is the user name to log-on the digital device
- What keyboard shortcut auto-inserts current date
- What's the right mouse button for
- Why use a brainstorming tool

Spreadsheet
- Why use a spreadsheet?
- Name three spreadsheet projects you've done
- How do you build arrays in spreadsheets
- Decode spreadsheet formulas
- What must be at the start of every formula
- How do you enter data
- How do you graph data
- How do you alphabetize names
- How do you auto-sum
- How do you average numbers
- How do you add numbers
- How do you subtract numbers
- How do you multiply numbers
- How do you divide numbers
- How do you widen columns
- How to widen rows
- How do you format text
- How do you insert a picture
- How do you add the date
- How do you add the time
- How do you change the worksheet name
- How do you change the tab color
- How do you add a worksheet

Vocabulary
- .com
- .edu
- .net
- .org
- Active window
- Address bar
- Animation
- Auto-advance
- Auto-play
- Back button
- Back-up
- Browser
- Bullets
- Caps lock
- Cc
- Class exit ticket
- Class warm-up
- Clip art
- Clone
- Crop
- Cursor
- Data
- Default
- Desktop
- Dialogue box
- Digital locker
- Drill down
- Drop down menu
- Export
- F4
- Flash drive
- Folder
- Font
- Footer
- Format
- Forward button
- GIF
- Google (verb)
- Handles
- Hits
- Hue
- Hyperlink
- I-beam
- Icon
- Import
- Initialize
- Internet address
- JPG
- Jump drive
- Kilobyte
- Landscape
- Log-on
- Monitor
- Mouse over
- Multimedia
- Netiquette
- Network
- Numbered list
- Page Break
- PC
- Photoshopped
- Pixel
- Place saver
- Portrait
- Print preview
- Printkey
- Protocol
- Queue
- Recycle bin
- Right-click menu
- Scrollbar
- Search bar
- Search engine
- Select-do
- Shortcut
- Synonym
- Taskbar
- Thesaurus
- Thumbnail
- Toolbar
- Transition
- Upload
- USB port
- Washout
- Watermark
- Wizard
- Worksheet
- Wrap

Word Processing
- Why use word processing
- Compare/contrast WP and DTP
- What are three examples of projects you did
- How are grammar and formatting different
- What does the red squiggly line mean
- How do you clear a red squiggly line
- What does green squiggly line mean
- How do you clear a green squiggly line
- How do you change image background?
- How do you insert a page border
- How do you resize a picture
- How do you add a text box
- How do you spell-check a document?
- How do you add a watermark?
- How do you add a footer
- How do you double-space
- How do you share a Google Doc
- How do you collaborate on a Google Doc
- How do you include citations in a Google Doc

CLASSROOM POSTERS

1. Backspace and Delete
2. Digital Neighborhood
3. Email Etiquette
4. Fair Use
5. Here's What We've Done
6. How I Learn
7. How to Save—4 Ways
8. I Can't Find My File
9. Internet Research
10. K-5 Keyboarding Stages
11. Keyboarding Hints
12. Landscape
13. Netiquette Rules
14. Portrait
15. Save or Save-as
16. Save Early Save Often
17. Select-Do
18. Troubleshooting Computer Problems
19. What's a Mulligan
20. Why Learn to Keyboard?

Difference Between 'Save' and 'Save-as'

WHAT'S THE DIFFERENCE BETWEEN SAVE AND SAVE AS?

SAVE
- Save the first time
- Resave changes to the same location

SAVE AS
- Resave under a new name
- Resave to a new location

Difference Between 'Backspace' and 'Delete'

TWO WAYS TO DELETE

BACKSPACE

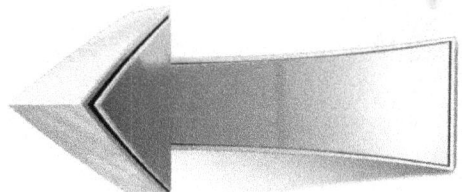

Deletes to the left, one character at a time

DELETE

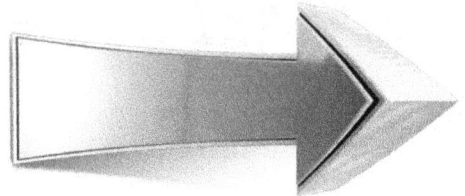

Deletes to the right, one character at a time

LANDSCAPE

4th Grade Technology Curriculum: Teacher Manual

PORTRAIT

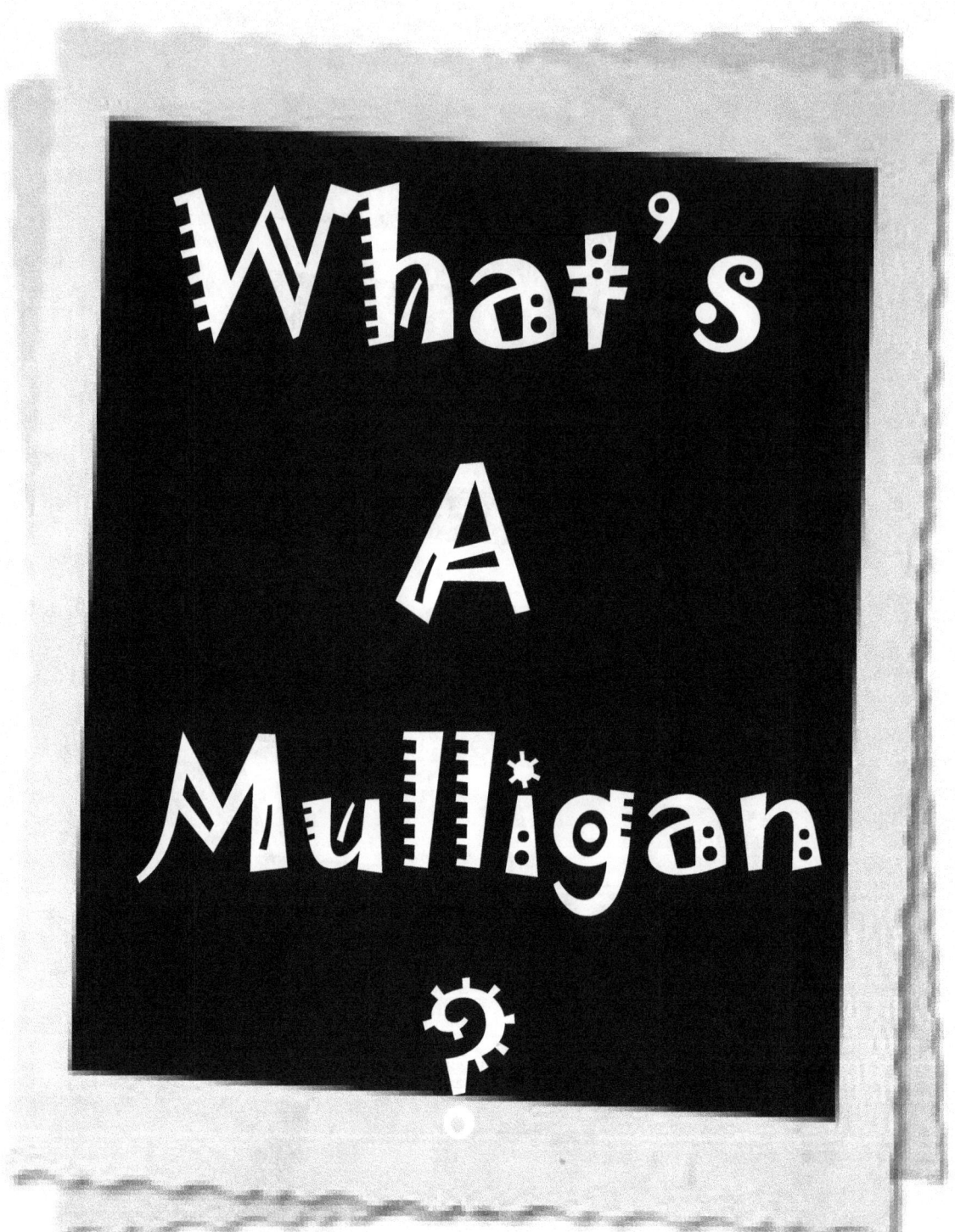

K-5 Keyboarding Stages

- **K-1st:** Introduce mouse skills, keyboarding, key placement, posture
- **2nd:** Work on keyboarding, key placement, posture, two-hand position
- **3rd:** Reinforce basics, work on accuracy and technique
- **4th-5th:** Continue accuracy, technique. Begin work on speed

©AskATechTeacher

4th Grade Technology Curriculum: Teacher Manual

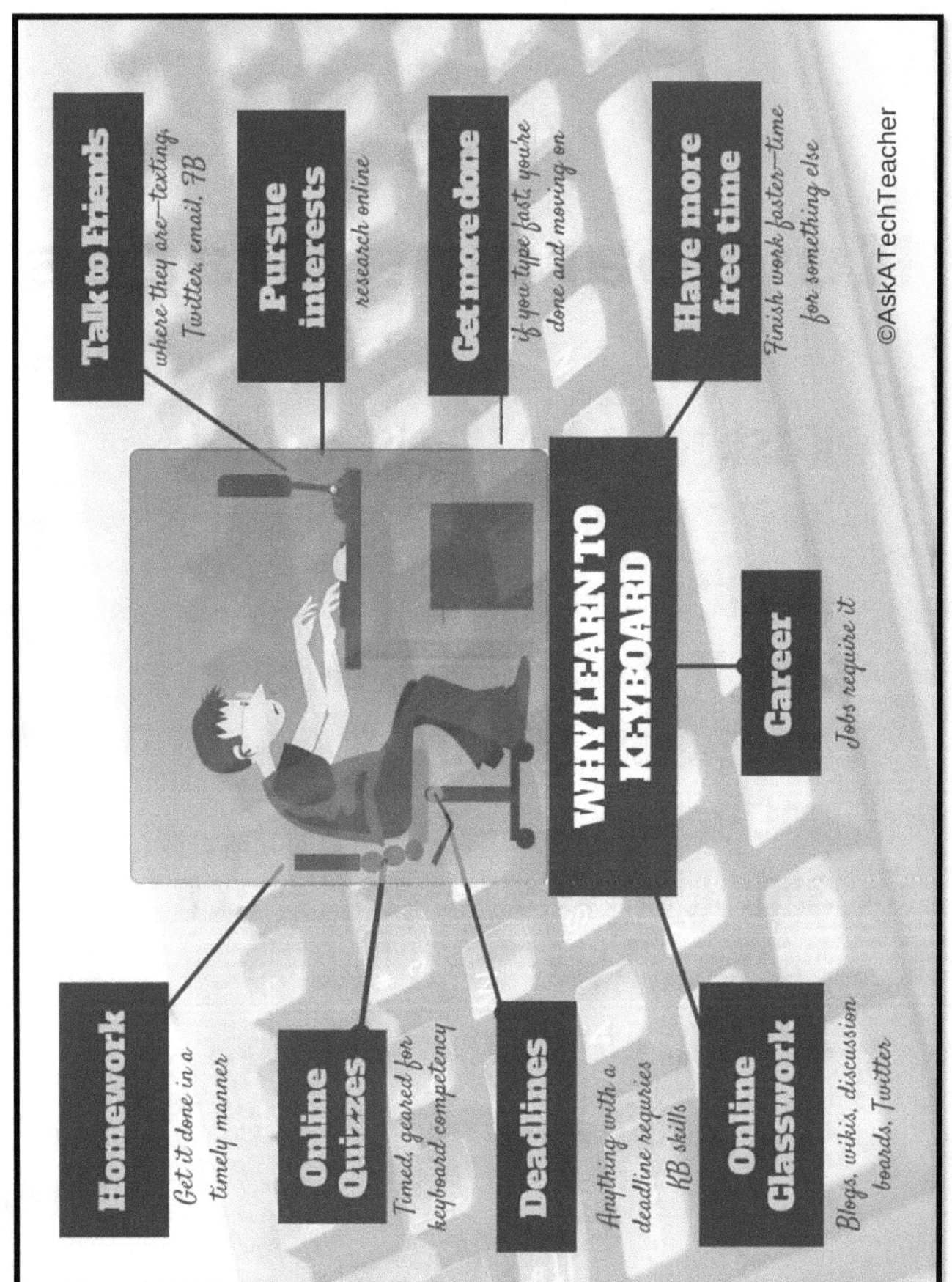

TROUBLESHOOTING COMPUTER PROBLEMS

	Problem	Why	Solution
1.	Deleted a file	Deleted by accident	Open Recycle Bin—right-click-restore
2.	Can't exit a program	Can't find X or Quit	Alt+F4
3.	Can't find a program	Shortcut moved	Type 'Word' (or program name) into Search bar
4.	Keyboard doesn't work	Unplugged, lost file	Plug cord into back; reboot
5.	Mouse doesn't work	Unplugged, lost file	Plug cord into back, reboot
6.	Start button is gone	Task bar gone	Push Windows button
7.	No sound	Mute on	Unmute
		Volume down	turn volume up
		Unplugged headphones	plug headphones in
		Lost file	Reboot
8.	Can't find a file	Saved wrong, moved	Start button—Search
9.	Menu command grayed out	You're in another command	Push escape 3 times
10.	What's today's date?	You forgot!	Hover over the clock
11.	Taskbar gone	Student interference	Push Windows button
			Drag border up to expose
12.	Taskbar was moved	Student interference	Drag it to the bottom of screen
13.	Desktop icons messed up	Student interference	Right click on screen—arrange icons
			Too small? Highlight and Ctrl+ to enlarge
14.	Computer frozen	Mouse frozen	Reboot
15.	Program frozen	Dialog box open	Clear the dialog box
		Not selected on taskbar	Click program on taskbar
16.	I erased my document/text	Ooops	Ctrl+Z
17.	Screen says "Ctrl-Alt-Del"	You rebooted	Hold down Ctrl-Alt—push Delete
18.	Program closed down	Ooops	Is it open on the taskbar? If so—click on it
			Reopen program—see if it saved a back-up
19.	Tool bar missing on www	Pushing F11 key	Push F11 key
20.	Internet window too small	Hard to read	Ctrl+ to enlarge; Ctrl- to delarge (or Ctrl+mouse wheel)
21.	Double click doesn't work	Who knows?	Push enter
22.	Shift key doesn't work	Caps lock on	Push caps lock to disengage
23.	I can't remember how to…	So many skills…	Try a right click with the mouse
24.	When I type, it types over	I want to insert text	Push the 'insert' key
25.	The document is 'read only'	I didn't do anything	Just 'save-as' under a new name and all is fixed

EMAIL ETIQUETTE

1. Use proper formatting, spelling, grammar
2. CC anyone you mention
3. Subject line is what your email discusses
4. Answer swiftly
5. Re-read email before sending
6. Don't use capitals—THIS IS SHOUTING
7. Don't leave out the subject line
8. Don't attach unnecessary files
9. Don't overuse high priority
10. Don't email confidential information
11. Don't email offensive remarks
12. Don't forward chain letters or spam
13. Don't open attachments from strangers

©AskaTechTeacher

Netiquette Rules

- Be human
- Follow the same rules of behavior you follow in real life
- Be aware of your digital footprint
- Share your knowledge
- Help keep 'flame wars' under control
- Respect other's privacy
- Be forgiving of other's mistakes

4th Grade Technology Curriculum: Teacher Manual

Don't talk to strangers. Look both ways before crossing the (virtual) street. Don't go places you don't know. Play fair. Pick carefully who you trust. Don't get distracted by bling. And sometimes, stop everything and take a nap.

©AskaTechTeacher

The law states that works of art created in the U.S. after January 1, 1978, are automatically protected by copyright once they are fixed in a tangible medium (like the internet) BUT a single copy may be used for scholarly research (even if that's a 2nd grade life cycle report) or in teaching or preparation to teach a class.

These keyboarding hints came directly from the classroom, tested on 400 students a year. These are the most common fixes that help students excel at keyboarding:

1. Tuck elbows against sides of body. This keeps hands in the right spot—home row
2. Use thumb for space bar. That leaves hands on home row
3. Curl fingers over home row—they're cat claws, not dog paws
4. Use inside fingers for inside keys, outside fingers for outside keys
5. Use finger closest to the key required. Sounds simple, but this isn't what usually happens with beginners
6. Keep pointers anchored to f and j
7. Play keyboard like a piano (or violin, or guitar, or recorder). You'd never use pointer for all keys
8. Fingers move, not hands. Hands stay anchored to f and j keys
9. Don't use caps lock for capitals! Use shift
10. Add a barrier between sides of the keyboards. I fashioned one from cover stock. That reminds students to stay on the correct side of keyboard

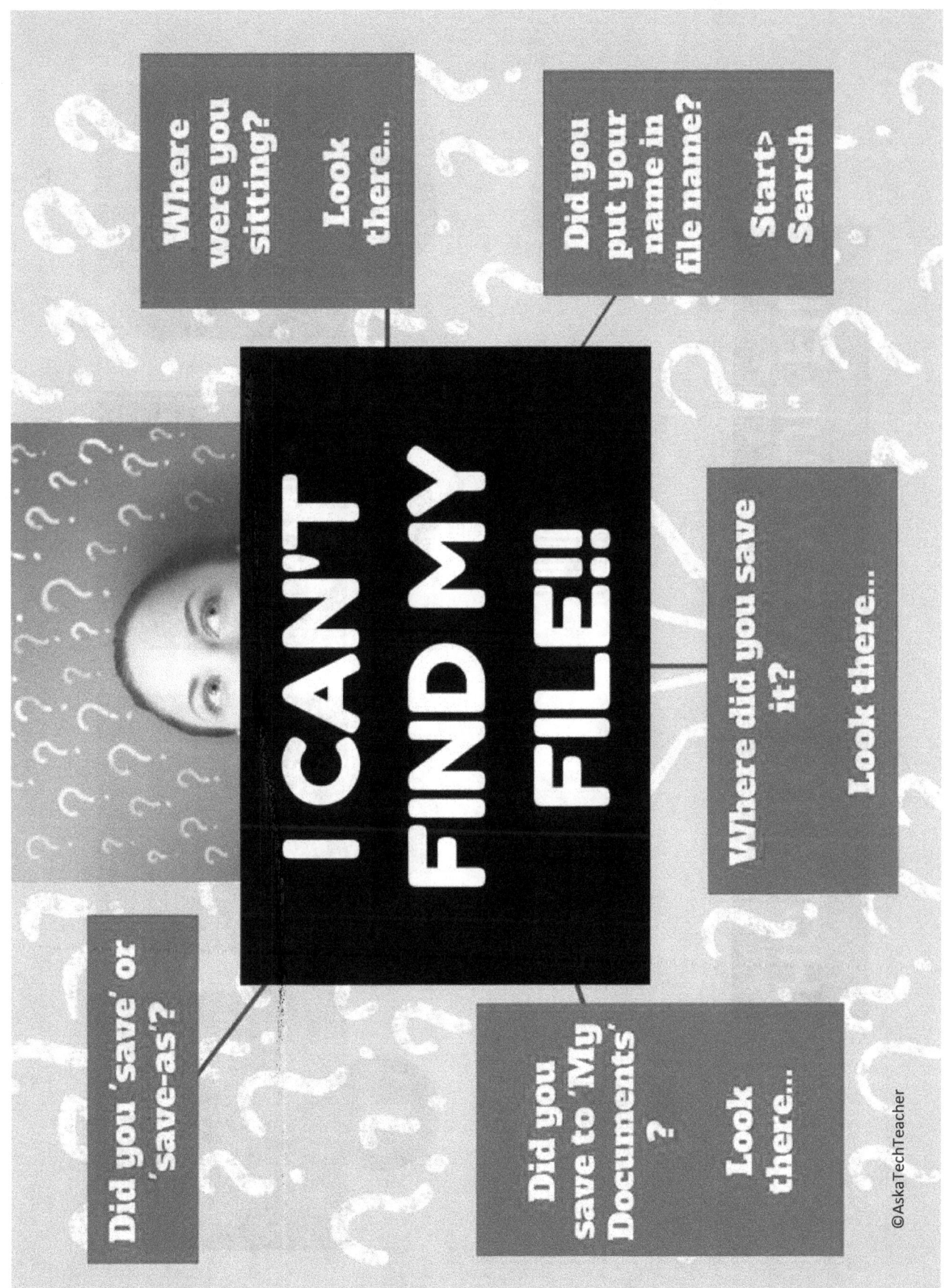

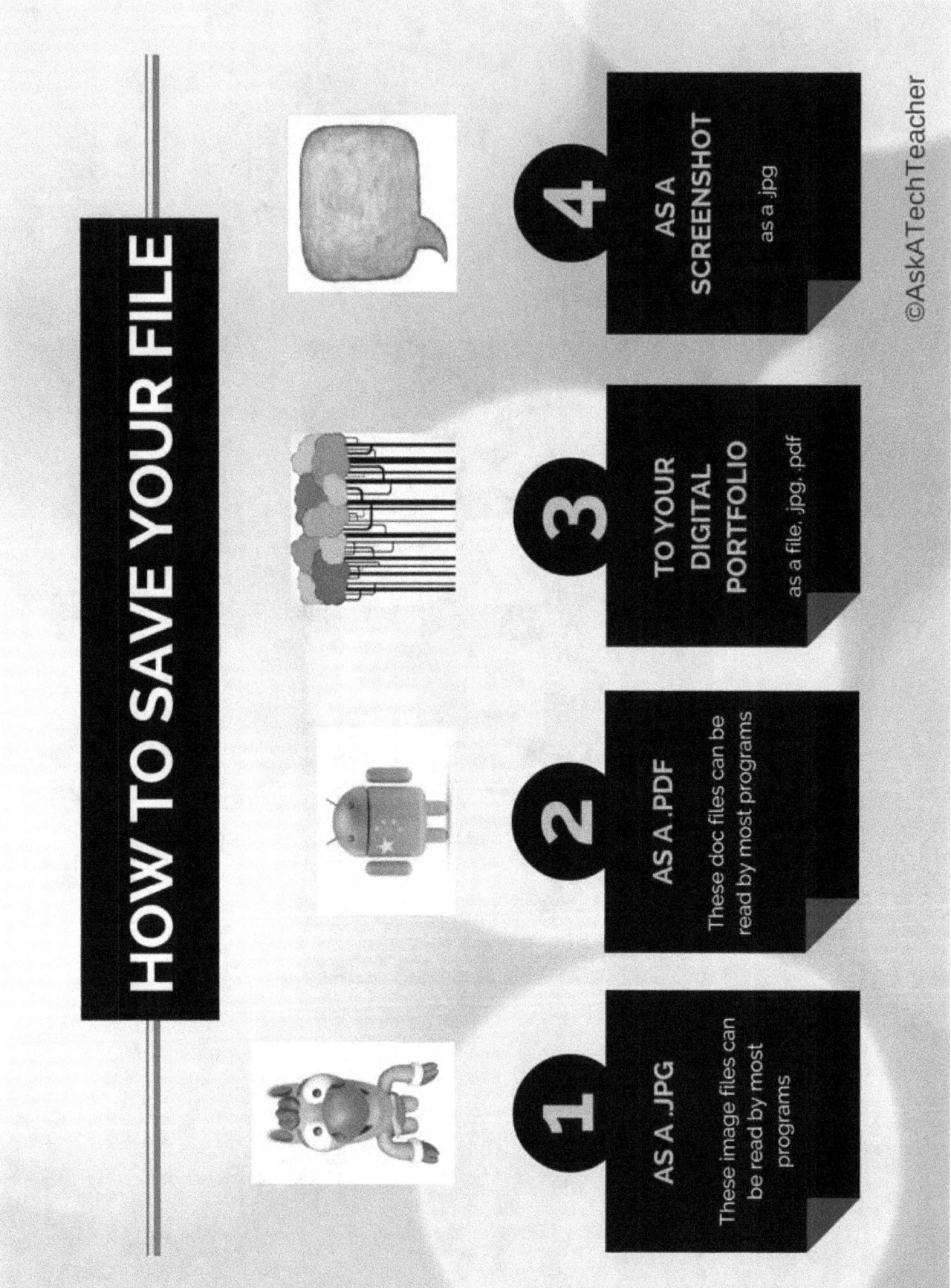

STEPS FOR INTERNET RESEARCH

- **Know Key Words**
- **General understanding of topic**
- **Reliable site extensions**
- **Read sidebars, headings, hyperlinks**
- **Read pictures, insets, maps**

GET YOUR DUCKS IN A ROW

©AskATechTeacher

4th Grade Technology Curriculum: Teacher Manual

Homework

Homework may be optional, especially if many of your students don't have digital devices at home. It may also be replaced by authentic use of keyboarding skills and habits during class projects. In this case, students must focus on correct keyboarding habits while typing a class project.

Alternatively, you may offer two-three afternoons a week where students come in to your classroom and do homework at school while siblings are in after-school activities or parents chat with friends.

Submittal of homework:

Last day of the month, via a dropbox or email. Students write 3-5 sentences on the following:

- *Verify they typed 15 minutes 3 times a week (45 minutes a week) every week of month*
- *Share what was easy/difficult*
- *Reflect on how keyboarding affects other classes, homework assignments, life in general*

If students have student workbooks, this is included in their copies.

October

Spend 15 minutes, 3 times a week, on **Popcorn Typer** or another keyboard program that teaches one row at a time—**homerow only**. Repeat the exercise over and over. The goal: memorize key placement. When you can type home row without looking at your fingers, cover keys with a light cloth to hide your hands. For the rest of the month, type with hands covered.

November

Spend 15 minutes, 3 times a week, on **Popcorn Typer** or another keyboard program that teaches one row at a time—**QWERTY row only**. Repeat the exercise over and over. The goal: memorize key placement. When you can type QWERTY row without looking at your fingers, cover keys with a light cloth to hide your hands. For the rest of the month, type with hands covered.

December

Spend 15 minutes, 3 times a week, on **Popcorn Typer** or another keyboard program that teaches one row at a time—**Lower Row only**. Repeat the exercise over and over. The goal: memorize key placement. When you can type the lower row without looking at your fingers, cover keys with a light cloth to hide your hands. For the rest of the month, type with hands covered.

January-May

Spend 15 minutes, 3 times a week, on a keyboard program you use in your school. Try to keep eyes on the screen. The goal: memorize key placement. By mid-month, cover keys with a light cloth to hide your hands. For the rest of the month, type with hands covered.

4th Grade Technology Curriculum: Teacher Manual

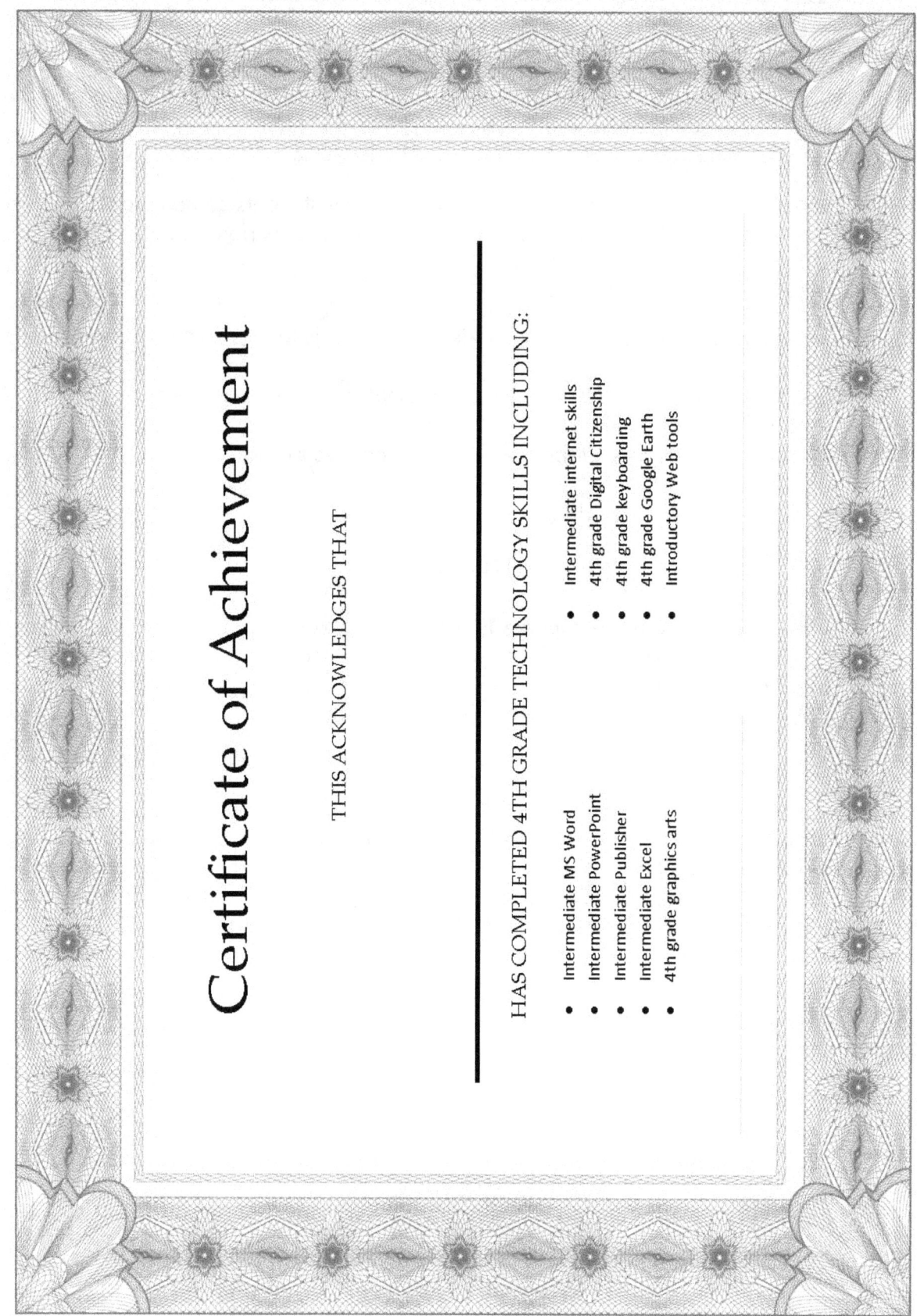

Index

21st Century Lesson Plan 43
About the Author 171
Address 147
Alt Codes 103
Animation 199, 202, 208, 210
annotation tool 12
Appointment Slots 170
Articles 6, 19
ASCII Art 60
Ask a Tech Teacher 17
Assessments 6, 7, 18, 23, 36, 44, 48, 49, 72, 74, 133
avatar 212
benchmark 53
Blogs 10, 66, 69, 95
BrainPOP 110
Brainstorm 49, 178, 179, 214
Brochure 147
calendar 69, 70, 71, 73, 132, 170, 212
Canva 138
Cells 64, 97, 124
Certificate of Completion 6, 18, 205
checklist 114, 148, 179, 207
Chromebook 15, 36, 37, 73, 75, 84, 85, 100, 105, 212, 213
Class Calendar 69
class internet start page 16, 38, 46, 75, 86, 135, 189, 212
Class warmup 33, 50, 64, 72, 83, 87, 97, 101, 109, 112, 117, 124, 127, 131, 136, 143, 147, 153, 158, 165, 169, 174, 178, 181, 187, 192, 199, 201, 204, 208, 210, 211, 214
clipboard 129
Cloud 70
Code 19, 101, 103, 107
Coding 10, 12, 18, 101, 102, 105, 107, 212
Collaboration 7, 10
Columns 124
Common Core 5, 7, 8, 17, 45, 59, 70, 75, 76, 78, 81, 82, 102, 105, 107, 124, 133, 149, 160, 161, 163, 166
Common Core State Standards 8

common tech problems 73, 74
Compare/contrast 35, 71, 79, 137, 214
computer problems 74
Content Standards 169
Copyright 17, 119, 123, 127, 140, 160, 204, 229
cover 35, 137, 140, 166, 167, 176, 177, 185, 193, 194, 195, 197
CPU 36
Crop 127
Ctr+P 53, 136, 148
Ctr+S 142, 146
Ctr+Z 124
curriculum map 10
Cursor 117
Cyberbullying 88, 90
Dance Mat Typing 72, 83
desktop publishing 137, 143, 147
Diagram 112, 157
Differentiation 7, 13, 44
Digital citizenship 33, 44, 64, 87, 88, 109, 112, 117, 124, 127, 143, 147, 158, 169, 178, 181
Digital communications 88
Digital Devices 7, 15, 19
Digital footprint 88
Digital law 88
digital lockers 70
digital neighborhood 44, 109, 112, 113, 212
Digital Portfolios 70
Digital privacy 88
Digital rights 88
digital rights and responsibilities 90
Digital search and research 88
Digital storytelling 165, 169, 174, 178
Digital Student 34
domain-specific tech vocabulary 50, 83, 97, 109, 112, 117, 127, 131, 136, 153, 158
Dropbox 70
DTP 11, 18, 136, 137, 138, 143, 144, 147, 149, 150, 165, 169, 171, 172, 174, 178, 182, 212, 214
Email 6, 64, 66, 67, 215
Embed 33, 123, 158
End of Year Team Challenge 212

4th Grade Technology Curriculum: Teacher Manual

evaluating websites 114
event sequences 149
Evidence Board 33, 35, 64, 72, 73, 83, 87, 101, 131, 153, 165
Evidence of Learning 73, 147
Excel 18, 144, 149, 181, 186
Exit Ticket 7, 12, 16, 71
Fair use 89, 91, 128, 140, 215
Find My File 215
Flier 18, 136
Font 117, 136
footer 121
Format 127
F-row 36
Games 10, 18, 60, 181
Genius Hour 182
GIF 201
Gmail 67
Goodreader 12
Google Apps 70
Google Calendar 69, 170
Google Docs 70, 118, 120, 123, 126, 150, 159, 160, 162, 187
Google Earth 6, 10, 11, 18, 73, 97, 98, 99, 100, 169, 170, 173, 174, 178, 181, 187, 192, 199, 201, 202, 204, 208
Google Earth presentations 202
Google forms 111
grammar 93, 120, 126, 131, 135, 158, 162, 163, 166, 175, 196, 199, 202, 214
graph 213, 214
Graphic 143
graphic organizer 153, 155, 156, 157
Graphic Organizers 18, 153
Graphics 10, 11, 193, 213
Greeting cards 136, 141
Habits of Mind 7, 14, 45, 76
Haiku Deck 192
Handles 147, 169
Hardware 10, 33, 37, 39, 50, 72, 84
hardware problems 73, 76
higher order thinking 7
Homework 18, 35, 88, 112, 137, 153, 236
Hour of Code 101, 102, 104
image copyrights 89, 91
images 140

important keys 52
inquiry 8, 12, 15, 16, 127
internet 199
Internet privacy 11
Internet Research 18, 109, 112, 187
Internet safety 89, 189
Invention Convention 182, 183, 188, 189, 195
iOS 159
iPads 36, 44, 46, 53, 80, 108, 118, 120, 148, 159, 163, 167, 192
ISTE 8
Jeopardy 211
Keyboard assessment 52, 53
Keyboarding 6, 7, 11, 16, 18, 19, 35, 44, 50, 51, 52, 55, 59, 64, 72, 83, 84, 87, 97, 109, 112, 117, 124, 127, 131, 136, 143, 147, 148, 153, 158, 165, 169, 174, 178, 181, 186, 187, 192, 199, 201, 204, 208, 210, 211, 213, 215
keyboarding hints 231
keyboarding technique 52, 147
laptop 15, 95
Logins 64, 65
Mac 84, 97, 100, 105, 118, 213
MacBook 15
Macro 101, 122
mindmapping 12
Minecraft 79, 104
monitor 33
mouse 36, 37, 50, 213, 214
Mouse Skills 10
Mulligan Rule 34, 72, 83, 84, 97, 121, 130, 180
National Educational Technology Standards ... 5
Netiquette 64, 87, 89, 90, 109, 112, 214, 215
Netiquette Rules 215
Notable 12
Office 365 .... 70, 73, 118, 120, 132, 170
Online presence 88
Online research 187
Open Office 150
Outline 18, 83, 85, 86
Padlet 46, 47, 69, 72, 73, 111, 115, 132, 157, 170
Parts of a website 110
passwords 89, 90, 109
PC 15, 33, 36, 72, 84, 214
PDF 151
Photoshop 6

237

Photoshopped 214
pictures 178
Placeholder 136
Plagiarism..89, 91
Posters 13, 19, 215
posture 72, 83, 212, 213
PowerPoint........ 187, 192, 193, 194, 205, 206, 208
Presentation Boards..73
Presentation Tools 213
Presentations............11, 18, 59, 194, 197, 208, 210
print border.................................146, 174, 175, 176
Print preview 178, 180
Problem solving 9, 11, 18, 33, 44, 50, 64, 72, 73, 74, 76, 77, 83, 87, 97, 101, 109, 112, 117, 124, 127, 131, 136, 143, 147, 153, 158, 165, 169, 174, 178, 181, 187, 192, 199, 201, 204, 208, 210, 211
Problem Solving Board 131
Programming......................10, 102, 103, 104, 212
Public domain 89, 91, 140
Publisher.............. 69, 138, 140, 144, 149, 167, 174
Question Board 143
quotes 76, 110
QWERTY.......................35, 97, 109, 112, 136, 236
Research................................11, 114, 116, 123, 215
Research skills 169, 181
Resize 171
Right-click 33, 109
risk takers..13
Rows 124
rubric 74, 87, 119, 120, 132, 136, 146, 151, 152, 153, 158, 169, 174, 178, 180, 187, 197, 198, 206, 209
rules 33, 34, 49, 90, 93, 100, 113, 122, 169, 210, 212
SafeSearch 129
save your file..86
scholarly research.....................128, 140, 160, 229
Science 104
Scope and Sequence 6
Scratch 44, 104
sharing...7, 70
Shortkeys 50, 103, 104, 213
SignUp Genius 73, 132, 170
Skills 64

Slideshow 187, 192, 197, 198, 199, 201, 204, 208, 209, 210
smartphone 13, 78
Social media 89
software 7, 8, 15
Speak Like a Geek 33, 50, 64, 72, 73, 83, 86, 87, 97, 101, 109, 112, 117, 124, 127, 131, 132, 133, 135, 136, 143, 147, 149, 153, 158, 165
speed and accuracy quiz....................................52
speed quiz 53, 148, 202
Spell-check...53, 148, 152
spreadsheet 6, 43, 125, 144, 149, 167, 181, 182, 183, 184, 186, 213, 214
Standards for Mathematical Practice 78, 105
storyboard 188, 189, 190, 193, 194, 195, 196, 197, 200
Storybook.....18, 165, 169, 174, 176, 177, 178, 180
Stranger Danger 89
Student digital portfolios....................................70
Student workbooks..........................7, 11, 16, 236
Surface tablet 100, 105
Symbaloo..46, 47
Tab..124
table 37, 88, 124, 125, 126, 127, 128, 129, 130, 139, 142, 144, 146, 155
Taskbar..112, 165
tech lab 15
Tech Rules..212
Technology...2
Technology Fails..77, 80
Texting 66, 94
Timeline 18, 143, 144, 146, 147, 149, 150, 152
Toggle 112, 165
Transition 201, 208, 210
trifold 139, 143, 144, 145, 146, 147, 152
tri-fold brochure 150
TuxPaint..166
Twitter..66, 92
Typing 64
UN and PWs..38
Virtual Wall...49
Visual learning 11
Vocabulary 9, 10, 11, 19, 33, 44, 50, 64, 71, 72, 83, 86, 87, 97, 101, 109, 112, 117, 124, 127, 131, 136, 143, 147, 153, 158, 161, 162, 165,

169, 174, 178, 181, 187, 192, 199, 201, 204, 208, 210, 211, 214
VoiceThread 196
warm-up 7, 12, 16
Watermark 121, 152, 174
website address 110
Weebly 69
Windows 7, 39, 100, 105
WinXP 97
Wix 69
Word 6, 85, 118, 120, 122, 123, 155
Word cloud 158, 159, 160, 161
word processing 43, 60, 83, 85, 87, 117, 118, 120, 121, 124, 126, 127, 131, 133, 134, 136, 139, 140, 144, 150, 165, 167, 174, 180, 182, 188, 193, 214
Wordle 71
Wordpress 69
Wrap 127, 192
writing skills 92, 94, 120, 134, 165, 174

Which book	Price (print/digital/Combo)
K-8th Tech Textbook (each)	$25.99 + p&h
K-8 Combo (all 9 textbooks)	$248-450
K-8 Student workbooks (per grade)	$199/640/1900 (room/school/district)
35 K-6 Inquiry-based Projects	25.99 + p&h
55 Tech Projects—Vol I,II, Combo	$18.99 /$35.38–digital only (free shipping)
K-8 Keyboard Curriculum—3 options	$20 and up + p&h
K-8 Digital Citizenship Curriculum	$19.95/25.99/50.38 + p&h
CCSS—Math, Language, Reading, Writing	$26.99 ea/80 for 4–digital only (free s&h)
K-5 Common Core Projects	$29.95/23.99/48.55 + p&h
Themed webinars	$8-30
Summer PD classes (online—for groups)	$795
Summer tech camp for kids	$179 + p&h
College credit classes (online)	$497 and up
Digital Citizenship certificate class	Starts at $29.99
Classroom tech poster bundles	Start at $9.99
PBL lessons--singles	$.99 and up
Bundles of lesson plans	$4.99 and up (digital only)
Tech Ed Scope and Sequence	$9.99 and up (digital only)
New Teacher Survival Kit	$285-620+ p&h
Homeschool Tech Survival Kit	$99 + p&h
Mentoring (30 min. at a time)	$50/session
169 Tech Tips From Classroom	$9.99 (digital only)
Consulting/seminars/webinars	Call or email for prices

Free sample? Visit Structured Learning LLC
Prices subject to change
Email Zeke.rowe@structuredlearning.net
Pay via PayPal, Credit Card, Amazon, TPT, pre-approved school district PO

www.ingramcontent.com/pod-product-compliance
Lightning Source LLC
Chambersburg PA
CBHW080224170426
43192CB00015B/2740